D0919685

The Grotesque Depiction of War and the Military in Eighteenth-Century English Fiction

FOUGHT ALL HIS BATTLES O'ER AGAIN
AND THRICE HE SLEW THE SLAIN —

Publish'd   1st Jan.y 1782.

Courtesy of The Huntington Library

The Grotesque Depiction of War and the Military in Eighteenth-Century English Fiction

David McNeil

DELAWARE

Newark: University of Delaware Press
London and Toronto: Associated University Presses

Associated University Presses
440 Forsgate Drive
Cranbury, NJ 08512

Associated University Presses
25 Sicilian Avenue
London WC1A 2QH, England

Associated University Presses
P.O. Box 488, Port Credit
Mississauga, Ontario
Canada L5G 4M2

The paper used in this publication meets the requirements
of the American National Standard for Permanence of Paper
for Printed Library Materials Z39.48-1984.

Library of Congress Cataloging-in-Publication Data

McNeil, David, 1955–
   The grotesque depiction of war and the military in eighteenth-
century English fiction / David McNeil.
    p.   cm.
   Includes bibliographical references.
   ISBN 0-87413-369-6 (alk. paper)
   1. English fiction—18th century—History and criticism. 2. War
stories, English—History and criticism.   3. Military art and
science in literature. 4. Grotesque in literature. 5. Soldiers in
literature. 6. War in literature. I. Title.
PR858.W37M35   1990
823′.509358—dc20   88-40584
                                                     CIP

To Kathleen

Vasco. We swaddled your Duke home; he and the rest
   Of your bruis'd countrymen have wondrous need
   of capon's grease.
Leonell. Strange giddiness of war; some men must groan
   To further others mirth.

—D'Avenant, *Love and Honour* (1649)

All to the feast, the Feast of Blood! repair.
The high, the low, old men and prattling babes,
Young men and maidens, all to grace the feast,
Light-footed trip,—the feast, the Feast of Blood!

—Joseph Fawcett, *Civilized War* (1798)

Contents

Illustrations

Preface

THE BEGINNING OF my interest in the subject of war as a cultural spectacle can be traced to a visit I made with my grade-six class to the Musée du Fort in Quebec City. With wide-eyed wonder, my classmates and I watched a brilliant mechanical reproduction, done with miniatures and moving pieces, of the battle of the Plains of Abraham. The use of lighting, smoke, and sound effects brought to life Wolfe's sneaky dash up the cliff and Montcalm's gallant stand. When our teacher emphasized the seriousness of the show by pointing out that we were witnessing one of the most important battles in British colonial history—an event that would set the bells ringing throughout England and decide the future of Canada—all we could do was giggle with delight. Years later I became increasingly interested in war as literary spectacle and cultural fascination. At Concordia and McMaster, there were people who kept me intrigued with the subject and with the age that is known as the Enlightenment but that saw almost constant war among European nations: David Taylor, David Blewett, Douglas Duncan, Joseph Sigman, Michael Bishop, and Graham Roebuck. A number of friends then and later were also helpful, particularly Joe Gibson and Deborah Laycock.

At Dalhousie I must thank James Gray, who fed me much I did not know about the military, and who listened patiently to what I did. A number of my students have shared my Shandy-enthusiasm and offered their insights: David Stewart, Anne Johnson, and Leigh Bateman. I would also like to thank the Clark Library in Los Angeles for its generous fellowship and the opportunity to participate in the seminar, "War and Society: 1660–1800," directed by Stephen Baxter. A debt is owed Professor Baxter and the members of that seminar, especially Christopher Brooks and Lt. Col. Terence Freeman. My appreciation also goes to the staff of the Clark Library, the Killam Library, the Huntington Library, and the Mills Memorial Library, and to the editors at the University of Delaware Press and Associated University Presses. Help with the illustrations was kindly given by Susan Naulty of the Huntington, Martha Katz-Hyman of Colonial Williamsburg, and

11

Duncan Smith of the British Museum. Dalhousie University also provided a research grant to help complete this project, and Pamela Perkins suggested many improvements to the final draft. Finally, I would like to thank Erin, my wife, who has supported me through many difficult campaigns not the least of which has been this book.

Part of chapter 2 has appeared in the *Dalhousie Review* (67, 2/3). An earlier version of chapter 5 was published in *Studies on Voltaire and the Eighteenth Century*. I thank both journals for permission to reproduce these sections here. I would also like to thank the following university presses for permission to cite from their texts: Nebraska, Florida, Wesleyan, California, Yale, Oxford, and Cambridge. The Editorial Committee of the Yale Editions of the Private Papers of James Boswell has graciously allowed me to cite from *Boswell on the Grand Tour: Germany and Switzerland*, reprinted by permission of McGraw-Hill. The following publishers have also kindly given their permission for quoted material: Basil Blackwell; J. M. Dent; Holmes & Meier; Methuen; Harcourt Brace Jovanovich; Heinemann; and Macmillan (London). I hereby acknowledge permission to quote from *Eighteenth-Century English Literature* by Geoffrey Tillotson, copyright © 1969 by Harcourt Brace Jovanovich Inc., reprinted by permission of the publisher, and to quote material reprinted from *The History of Tom Jones, A Foundling* by permission of Wesleyan University Press, copyright © 1975 by Martin C. Battestin & Fredson Bowers. The illustrations are reproduced with the permission of The British Museum, The Huntington Library, Plas Newydd, and the Colonial Williamsburg Foundation. The Laguerre print was provided by the Courtauld Institute of Art.

Textual Note

SPELLING AND CAPITALIZATION have been retained for the seventeenth- and eighteenth-century texts cited. However, the long *s* has been modernized.

The Grotesque
Depiction of War
and the Military
in Eighteenth-Century
English Fiction

Introduction: Fontenoy and Theory

The Battle of Fontenoy, the Grotesque, and Homo Ludens

THE BATTLE OF Fontenoy (1745) has become famous for a bizarre incident that for many epitomizes the absurd gallantry commonly associated with the professional militarism of the age. Sixteen thousand scarlet-clad British infantry began their notoriously slow yet steady march to meet the enemy. These red lines of men were accompanied by the always ominous and hypnotic drumbeat. Having reached the crest of a hill, the British suddenly found themselves only thirty paces from the French army. After a terrible silent pause, it is said, Lord Charles Hay of the First Guards stepped forward, doffed his hat, pulled out a pocket-flask and drank to the health of the French: "We are the English Guards, and we hope you will stand till we come up to you, and not swim the Scheldt as you did the Main at Dettingen!"[1] It was a taunting reference to the inglorious and disastrous French retreat two years earlier. Cheers and laughter rippled through the English lines. The insult, however, was apparently lost on the French officers who politely returned the greeting of their English counterparts. According to Voltaire, Hay then invited the French to fire first: "Gentlemen of the French Guards, fire!"[2] The comte d'Auteroche responded: "Gentlemen, we never fire first; fire yourselves."[3] An English guardsman, looking down the barrels of the French muskets a few yards away, was heard to remark in a cavalier fashion: "For what we are about to receive may the Lord make us truly thankful."[4] J. W. Fortescue writes that the French had fired before the English "had done laughing."[5] Voltaire suggests that the British accepted the French counteroffer. Regardless of who fired first, the legend of the Fontenoy parley reflects the natural association between war and the grotesque.

The aim of this study is to explore the appropriateness of the grotesque mode for addressing the specific subjects of war and militarism. By considering a selection of eighteenth-century prose fiction that deals with these subjects, I hope to demonstrate how the genre critic might move beyond purely descriptive

17

analyses to a fruitful recognition of the organic relationship between form and content. This direction is implied by Jeffrey
Beusse, who recalls Benedetto Croce's attack on "artificial distinctions" in literature, and the answer by Wellek and Warren to
that attack—that the locating of a "common denominator" in
descriptive mode study was a useful exercise while a judgmental
evaluation of those modes was not. Beusse goes on to outline the
shortcomings of purely descriptive mode studies that do not
connect "generic form" and "contents."[6] More recently, Alastair
Fowler has admitted that it is "a half-truth that literature has been
liberated from decorum of subject" and "that no kind is indifferent to its subject."[7] It is not merely coincidental that a grim,
sarcastic humor in literary treatments of war and militarism
occurs in various texts at least as far back as the comedy of
Aristophanes. War focuses attention on human folly and base-
ness—so much uncontrolled passion (aggression, revenge, fear),
so many killed before their time; hence, it always serves as ready
fuel to fire the satiric imagination. For the satirists of the eighteenth century, there was enough fuel of this kind to keep the
grotesque vision ablaze, for, according to Quincy Wright, England or Great Britain was at war for 86 of the 140 years from
1660 to 1800 and participated in twenty-three different conflicts
including seven major European wars.[8]

My first task is to define the "grotesque" as a literary mode and
point out why it may best capture or express what is a common
reader response to facetious descriptions of battle or the military.
During the last twenty years, there has been a boom in critical
theory about the literary grotesque.[9] Wolfgang Kayser's *The Grotesque in Art and Literature* (originally published in German in
1957) was a major force in popularizing and sanctioning the
mode. Kayser described many of the characteristics that he felt
were intrinsic to the grotesque, such as its connections to the
irrational, the bestial, and the mechanical. For some Kayser's all-
inclusive approach threatened the utility of the term, and there
has been a movement away from strict applications of the modern theory to a rediscovery of the relevance of former meanings of
the term, as in the "*grottesca*" or grotto-like art of Renaissance
literature.[10] Willard Farnham locates the idea of strife in the
decorative grotesque of the early middle ages and then analyzes
this grotesque element in Shakespeare.[11] Mikhail Bakhtin traces
the evolution of carnival laughter in the grotesque humour of
Western literature and claims that this saturnalian or festive
spirit, which he also calls the "carnivalesque," peaked in

Rabelais.[12] Bakhtin contends that Rabelais's Picrocholine War
transcends travesty and the mock-heroic and is a comic celebration of the "historic process."[13] Not surprisingly, Neil Rhodes in
his book *Elizabethan Grotesque* points to the similarities between Rabelais and Thomas Nashe.[14] As far as the eighteenth
century is concerned, there is Arthur Clayborough's *The Grotesque in English Literature*, yet his Jungian approach has limita-
tions despite some insightful comments on Swift.[15] Tony
Tanner's article on the *Dunciad* and the grotesque is noteworthy
for how cleverly Tanner makes his readers see that often the only
authentic distortion in Augustan satire is the implied rational
norm—that reality, when scrutinized, *is* wildly irrational and
ugly.[16]

The modern theory of the grotesque has tended to coalesce
around John Ruskin's identification of two features: one, the
ambivalence of the ludicrous and the fearful, and two, the element of play.[17] One might even conceptualize the grotesque as a
spectrum that would have examples that are predominantly ludicrous, or "sportive" to use Ruskin's term, at one end and fearful
or "terrible" at the other.[18] Likewise, it may be said that the
grotesque does range from expressions of "noble" sophistication
and awareness to "ignoble" engagement and ignorance.[19] Yet
while Ruskin's terms are useful in locating opposite poles, works
of art often contain combinations of these opposites in complex
ways; hence we should be cautious about easy and judgmental
distinctions. Who would not agree that Sterne possesses both the
noble and ignoble? As readers, we feel elevated when we are in
the realm of the noble and uncomfortably low when we encounter the ignoble, but this difference should not lead us to denigrate
the latter, which can often be understood according to the festive
saturnalia or Bakhtin's idea of carnival laughter.

While generally endorsing Ruskin's ludicrous-fearful duality,
modern critics have quibbled with his claim that either one or
the other dominates and have argued instead for the perfect
ambiguity between these two elements.[20] But Ruskin's theory
may be more applicable to an actual reading experience. We tend
to regard a grotesque passage as predominantly fearful or ludicrous rather than as absolutely equal in both respects, even
though there is always some degree of ambivalence involved.
Kayser clearly outlines the usefulness of the grotesque, in terms
that are equivalent to discourse theory, when he claims that it
"applies to three different realms—the creative process, the work
of art itself, and its reception."[21] And Clayborough is the only

critic of the grotesque who points out that there may be different reactions to the grotesque according to the different personality dynamics of the reader or spectator.[22] Reader A might find Gulliver's description of human warfare to his Houyhnhnm master more ludicrous or fearful than Reader B. Furthermore, if what we call "personality" is kinetic or if any given reader's frame of mind can differ from one reading of a particular passage to another, then one might find Gulliver's description to be more ludicrous than fearful one time and the reverse on a second perusal. The discourse of the grotesque depends upon a number of variables.[23]

Modern critics have also made meaningful studies of how the fearful and ludicrous elements interact, and these studies have helped to explain how the grotesque operates. According to Lee Byron Jennings, the ludicrous element acts as a defense mechanism against the threat posed by the fearful.[24] By laughing at the absurdities of war, for instance, we protect ourselves psychologically against war's frightening aspects. In other words, our anxieties find an unconscious outlet in laughter. Yet this is only one possible effect. Laughter—when raised by a horrible subject like war—contains a facetiousness that may also be disturbing. Hence, as the basic elements of the grotesque are paradoxical, so may be the reader's reaction.[25] War is horrible; laughing at war can alleviate the horror, but it can also produce guilt. How could you laugh? How beastly! This relaxation-tension paradox is what makes the grotesque such an intense aesthetic experience. Morse Peckham's idea of art as constituting "cognitive tension" between "formal expectancies" and the "violations" of these expectancies serves as a general model for the dynamism of the grotesque.[26] To disturb is to move.

The implied cruelty in laughing at some deformed person or state of misery, such as war, leads us to another aspect of the grotesque—its primitiveness. In his history of the mode, Thomas Wright traces the grotesque to "a feeling deeply implanted in human nature" and manifested at the dawn of man's satiric animosity:

> When, before people cultivated either literature or art, the chieftain sat in his rude hall surrounded by his warriors, they amused themselves by turning their enemies and opponents into mockery, by laughing at their weaknesses, joking on their defects, whether physical or mental, and giving them nicknames in accordance therewith,—in fact, caricaturing them in words, or by telling stories which were calculated to excite laughter.[27]

This fantastic portrait brings together two Hobbesian ideas: (1) that the natural state of man is one of warfare and (2) that laughter is a feeling of "sudden glory" caused by the "apprehension of some deformed thing in another."[28] Wright's portrait merges these ideas by depicting the spirit of battle completely in terms of play or the witty jest. Satire naturally has a militant side, and conversely physical combatants are often depicted (from Homer onwards) engaging in verbal duels of boasting and ridicule, rodomontade, and scurrilous abuse. One again thinks of Hay's insult in the infamous Fontenoy parley. It is not surprising, therefore, that Ruskin identifies "play" as an integral part of the grotesque.[29] Play is present in both the fantasy component and in the attitude of the artist. For one to have this attitude, a certain distance from the subject must exist.

These comments also point to the closeness and interrelation of the grotesque and satire. When scholars refer to a work as satiric, they usually mean that in some way that work ridicules an identifiable human folly or vice with the intent to reform. Northrop Frye's description of how satire presents this ridicule suggests that the grotesque mode is itself a fundamental part of satire: ". . . a moral norm is inherent in satire: satire presents something as grotesque: the grotesque is by definition a deviant from a norm: the norm makes the satire satiric."[30] In turn the grotesque often contains a satiric element, but the target of this satiric element is incorrigible human folly, and so the object of ridicule or the attack is either punitive or purely instructional. Hence the grotesque tends to emphasize the fallen nature of the human world with tones that range from caustic sarcasm, as in Swift, to comedic celebration or at least stoicism, as in Sterne.

The attack of ridicule is not the only organic link between the grotesque and war. In his famous sociological study, *Homo Ludens: The Play-Element in Culture*, J. Huizinga includes a chapter entitled "Play and War."[31] Huizinga associates play with the "irrational" and emphasizes its pervasiveness both in sport and drama (which he also calls ritual). From a distance, or I might say the sidelines, war resembles a game with its teams, strategies, rules, and—most important—winners and losers. A war normally polarizes allied forces. Battle tactics are elaborately researched, practised, and executed. This latter feature became prominent with the rise of standing professional armies in the latter half of the seventeenth century: "The English army held regular peacetime manoeuvres from 1685."[32] Elaborate maneuvers involving artillery and dragoons were held in Hyde Park in

1716 and 1723 for, in the words of David Chandler, "the delectations of the citizens of London."[33] Wars are formally declared, conducted according to certain conventions (this was especially true with respect to the so-called limited wars of the eighteenth century),[34] and concluded by official treaties. All games involve ritualized behavior, but military organizations bask in ritual. There are uniforms (some of which were ridiculously ostentatious in the eighteenth century), ranks, drills, parades, ceremonies, and all kinds of structures that impose an artificial order.[35] Two of Roger Caillois's four categories of play are immediately recognizable here: the *agon* or competition factor, and the mimicry or simulation factor. However, Caillois's other two categories, *alea* and vertigo, are also present insofar as war involves a certain exultation having to do with chance and danger respectively.[36]

Because armies can be ungovernable monsters, so to speak, they require an unnaturally extreme discipline to operate effectively. The life of the common foot soldier was so harsh in the eighteenth century that only the destitute tended to enlist and largely did so against their will.[37] Recruiting irregularities, such as the king's shilling, were frequent. Although the British army never had a draft that was equivalent to naval impressment, the Recruiting Acts in the Spanish Succession War forced many vagabonds and criminals to enlist, swelling Marlborough's ranks with what Fortescue refers to as the "scum of the nation."[38] Needless to say, only strict discipline could keep these soldiers within the accepted standards of pillage and unruliness. It could even be argued that the military commitment to force, so basic to the military's *raison d'être*, naturally carries over in individual behavior; hence rape and plunder can become natural to a man of arms for whom unrestrained violence and ruthlessness are the norm. Grotius makes this point in *The Law of War and Peace*: "when arms have once been taken up there is no longer any respect for law, divine or human; it is as if, in accordance with a general decree, frenzy had openly been let loose for the committing of all crimes."[39] Furthermore, domestic military violence was essentially what Swift feared about standing armies and what Fielding, to a lesser degree, was reacting to in *Tom Jones*.

Then there is the play community that continues after the game. Regardless of side, soldiers are bound by their profession, their common sense of special duty and power. Here one thinks of Captain Blunt and his comrades in Shadwell's *The Volunteers* (1693) or the friendship between uncle Toby and Corporal Trim.

But in the eighteenth century, the services of military commanders with less national allegiance than uncle Toby could be bought, and in a sense their careers resembled that of the modern professional athlete.[40] The officer ranks of most armies involved their own mercenary feature—the purchased commission. Those who were not so inclined to play at war on the field could buy themselves the opportunity to parade about as an officer decked out in his regimentals to impress the likes of a Lydia Bennet.

In an age of "genteel" decorum, the formalities of war take on a heightened sense of absurdity. Take the story of Lord Ligonier, a Hugenot refugee who was captured at the battle of Laffeldt (1747). Instead of being executed (as were the Scots who fell into English hands), he was, in his own words, received most cordially by the French king: "Well, General, we will have the pleasure of your company at supper tonight."[41] Smollett seemed to see this martial gentility as a perverse French affectation. In his play *The Reprisal*, an English sailor refers to the polite manners of his French captors as "nothing but sneaking fear and henheartedness . . . a kind of poverty of spirit, or want of sincerity."[42] The French type is epitomized by Marquis Bertran, a character in D'Urfey's *The Campaigners* (1698) who insists—in the most courteous language and despite an admission to the contrary by his former foes—that the English were the true victors at Landen.[43] However, the sense of war's incongruous politesse can be illustrated with an English example such as Marlborough's scribbled note to Sarah after Tallard's surrender at Blenheim: ". . . beg you will give my duty to the queen, and let her know her army has had a glorious victory, Monsr. Tallard and two other generals are in my coach and I am following the rest."[44] But the image that usually comes to mind when one thinks of the gentlemanly sportsmanship of eighteenth-century military command is again that of the English and French officers at the battle of Fontenoy each politely inviting the other side to fire first. As a historian, Voltaire followed the convention of fictionalizing many such speeches, and the image itself is misleading insofar as getting the other side to fire first was a perceived strategic advantage rather than a cavalier gesture.

Moreover, it might be said that this very strategy of advancing yet waiting for the enemy to open fire, born as it was out of the modern military science that marked the late seventeenth and early eighteenth centuries,[45] required an unnatural, grotesque discipline on the part of the infantry. The strategy was based on the assumption that after receiving the enemy's fire, the advanc-

ing yet-to-shoot lines could not fail to panic their foes into fearful
flight. The gaps left in the line by those who fell with the enemy's
opening shot were quickly filled by those in the second line.
Sufficient numbers and an overall resolve fixed to the beat of a
drum were what counted. This kind of enlightened warfare effectively reduced the individual soldier to nothing more than a toy-
piece or puppet, which according to Kayser is another feature of
the grotesque.[46] The play element involved on the part of those
who direct battles from a safe distance has been popularly expressed by the image of the mad officer moving his little miniatures on a grand tablemap. It comes as no surprise that toy
soldiers, which were being mass-produced in Nuremberg by the
time Sterne created the character of uncle Toby, were the favorite
playthings of monarchs like Louis XIV and were intended to
cultivate an enthusiasm for military stratagem.[47] The enlightened
or professional warfare of this general period was marked by
Vauban's highly elaborate and complex designs of siegecraft and
fortification, designs that appear in ichnography as delightful
geometric shapes. This new military science spawned diction-
aries of military terms, one of which contained the suggestion
that war was so prevalent that European news would not be
"intelligible to Persons unskill'd in Military Affairs."[48] Naturally
enough, military science was to be one of the satiric targets of
The Memoirs of Martin Scriblerus.[49]

Finally, the game or play feature of war that was particularly
relevant at this time was the spectator factor. Actual sieges and
battles were witnessed firsthand by the French court. War has
always held a popular vicarious attraction evinced by the numerous pictorial or narrative battle representations of any age, representations that vary from straightforward histories to artistic
interpretations. One thinks not so much of the daily reports in
the *London Gazette,* the official government paper, but of the
ostentatious glorification of war in the decorative tapestries of
Marlborough's Blenheim Palace or LeBrun's paintings in the *salon de la guerre* and the *Grande Galerie des Glaces* at Versailles.
Perhaps the best indication of war's popular appeal is the inclu-
sion of Captain Sentry in "The Spectator Club," because the
"military Part of his Life has furnish'd him with many Adventures, in the Relation of which he is very agreeable to the Company . . ."[50] It is clear that humankind possesses a morbid
curiosity about death and violence, especially when it is perpe-
trated on a grand scale.

There is a rich oral tradition of the military narrative or story in which soldiers, both as *raconteurs* and listeners, indulge. Nestor, for instance, entertains the younger soldiers with a description of the mythic battle between the Lapithae and the Centaurs in *The Metamorphoses* (bk. 12). Similarly, Captain Blunt's old Cavalier comrades get drunk and relive all their old battles from Edgehill to Brentford. Then, of course, there is uncle Toby all-too-ready to entertain anybody who will listen, and even those who do not, with his account of King William's wars. The military seems to feed on its own glorious history, and this necessity to fictionalize ultimate life-death experiences seems more natural than the perverse spectator delight of the nonparticipating curious.

Distance is the key factor in maintaining a grotesque perspective on war. For those who are not on the sidelines but in the thick of battle, war is certainly not a game. There was nothing playful in how the advanced infantry at Fontenoy withstood an intense and continual barrage of "round shot," which they had to watch as it bounced toward them on the hard ground "and bowled over files of men."[51] Nor was there anything playful in how grapeshot decimated ranks at close range. War is by nature fraught with the fearful. As a political armed conflict, it is certainly born of fear, fear of a perceived enemy—its intentions and motives always viewed suspiciously and cynically. As far as individual battles are concerned, the advantage in the eighteenth century was believed to go to the side that could best maintain discipline and control fear. One contemporary military handbook even mentions the use of verbal deception in the heat of battle to exacerbate and manipulate the natural fears of the enemy: ". . . sometimes after the first Charge, an Army hath cryed out, *Look how they run in the Rear.* Such Words, and false Reports have disordered and defeated the best and most resolute Armies: for the least fear discourages Soldiers in such a critical time."[52] Language can always prove to be an excellent weapon, and the legends of such battle tricks become popular entertainments in military folklore.

To see the ludicrous side of war requires detachment. Louis XV and his entourage, who watched the battle of Fontenoy from a nearby hill, were not detached enough to see anything ludicrous in the slaughter and maiming of 15,000 men a few hundred yards away. Perhaps one has to be as distanced as Voltaire's Mecromegas, inhabitant of Sirius (*Mecromegas* chap. 7), or Chaucer's Troilus, who laughs at the Trojan War from the eighth sphere (*Troilus and Criseyde* 5.1809–25). From a distance one sees only the numbers, and mass numbers by themselves tend to take on a meaninglessness that prevents normal rational and emotional responses. How incredibly absurd and wasteful are wars when viewed as petty squabbles blown out of all reasonable proportion!

There are two Renaissance theories of war that encouraged its treatment in the grotesque mode, and both of these appear in modified forms in the eighteenth century. The first held that war was a divine scourge meant to punish man for his sins; the second saw war as part of an inexorable cycle in the affairs of men: peace led to plenty, plenty to pride and envy, pride and envy to war, war to poverty, and poverty back to peace again. Paul Jorgensen calls the first "Christian" and the second "Classical."[53] However, there is a version of the so-called Christian view in antiquity, as references to Bellona's whip seem to be common in Roman epics.[54] St. Augustine cites the scourge view at the beginning of The City of God when he attributes the barbarian invasion of the Roman empire "to that divine providence which is wont to employ wars for the castigation or humiliation of morally corrupt characters, as well as to provide a trial by such affliction for righteous and praiseworthy men."[55] As a stock sermon it was certainly repeated throughout the eighteenth century by writers such as Jean Delmé who published A Spiritual Warning for Times of War in London in 1701. Satire has also traditionally been seen as a scourge, and as decorous or well-performed satiric performances can become entertaining spectacles for third parties (we are amused at seeing others punished or punishing themselves) so it is precisely in this function that war attracts such historical curiosity. Humankind tends to gawk at its own recorded barbarism.

The cyclical view of war, exactly as it is sketched out above, has been traced back to the fifteenth century, but it almost certainly derives from the Roman historians.[56] Dryden seems to draw upon it at the end of "Absalom and Achitophel" (1027–30). Although one might be inclined to think of it as classical, the Old Testament contains a similar idea: "To every thing there is a season, and a time to every purpose under the heaven. . . . A time to love, and a time to hate; a time of war, and a time of peace" (Ecclesiastes 3:1–8). In fact, war is a dominant theme throughout the Old Testament, and perhaps the most explicit expression of the scourge theory is Isaiah 10:24–26 in which the Lord outlines how the Assyrians are to be used as a "rod" or "scourge" against Israel.[57] Historians and theologians could easily endorse some combination of these theories, as did Justus Lipsius who uses phrases such as "Every Ebb and Flow . . . of human affairs" and the "Rise and Sett of Kingdomes" in his outline of the scourge theory in *War and Peace Reconciled,* translated into English in 1672.[58] The sense of mechanical inevitability attached to the cyclical view encourages amusement and hence the ludicrous, but the ominous prospect of any war will usually occasion fear on the part of those involved. In the following study, I argue that the ludicrous-fearful duality, the sense of mechanical inevitability, the playful attitude, the morbid curiosity and delight in spectacles of violence are all best understood according to the theory of the grotesque.

As one would expect, the cyclical and scourge theories were modified and absorbed into the "enlightened" thought of the period 1660 to 1800. The opening of Clarendon's *The History of the Civil Wars* is noteworthy for how the inevitable sense of the first is blended with the chastisement factor in the second, and the result couched in the language of scientific observation:

> . . . I say, though the immediate finger and wrath of God must be acknowledged in these perplexities and distractions, yet he who shall diligently observe the distempers and conjectures of time, the ambition, pride, and folly of persons, and the sudden growth of wickedness, from want of care and circumspection in the first impressions, will find all this bulk of misery to have proceeded, and to have been brought upon us, from the same natural causes and means which have usually attended kingdoms swoln with long plenty, pride and excess, towards some signal mortification, and castigation of Heaven.[59]

In the words of Sir George Clark, "Seventeenth-century writers . . . took a rationalist view of war."[60] A rationalist approach could recognize how economic growth is generated by the existence of war or human vice. Mandeville in *Fable of the Bees* singles out "Soldiers" for their notorious vices and defends luxury for creating military employment rather than leading a nation to decay.[61] However, enlightened skepticism is not far beyond this kind of economic rationalization, and certainly the English civil war fed the skepticism that colors much Restoration satire. Hobbes's famous statement, "that during the time men live without a common power to keep them all in awe, they are in that condition which is called war,"[62] must have seemed at the time more like a glib comment on the previous ten years in England than a philosophical abstraction. Like Clarendon, Voltaire merged the concepts of inevitability and chastisement when he called war "le partage affreux de l'homme" [the dreadful lot of man] and "un fléau inévitable" [an inevitable scourge].[63]

Goldsmith outlines a rationalist view of war that might be described as a modification of the cyclical theory. According to Goldsmith, a developed and populous nation will begin to contend for territories claimed by others since conquest is the only way for it to expand: "Among polite nations, whatever may be the pretext for war, if it be examined to the bottom, it will be found to proceed from a nation, by long peace becoming too numerous, and consequently desirous of occupying those regions possessed by another."[64] This model resembles the prosperity-envy-war part of the cyclical view. Part of Goldsmith's argument, perhaps the weakest part, is that relatively less developed nations—with fewer inhabitants—live more harmoniously with their neighbors because they are more concerned with meeting their natural needs in their immediate environments. In simple terms, war is nature's way of controlling the population. This argument, repeated by Malthus in *Of Population* (1798), leads Goldsmith to conclude, "War, therefore, unceasing war, is the consequence of refined society: it is a natural evil, which arises from the nature of an happy society."[65] Despite the flaws, his rationale possesses a seductiveness that can disturb one's conscience. Surely the monstrous violence of war cannot be part of a natural process?

But even the old body politic philosophy could be used to support the idea that war was a natural means of restoring proper equilibrium. If a nation did not blow off a little steam by taking on its neighbors, then it could count on the "humours" of fragmentation to bring on the fever of a civil war. Plato was careful to distinguish a civil faction from a foreign war and argue that the former bled a nation while the latter was often essential for national security.[66] Theories on civil and foreign conflicts and how the two are related remained important to eighteenth-century writers. A letter of opposition to *The Jacobite's Journal* expresses Fielding's condemnation of the Pretender's cause as an insurrection that plays into the hands of the French: "Shall we quarrel among ourselves, when the common Enemy of us all is at our Doors?"[67] A civil war encourages a nation to develop a sense of collective shame, and England after Cromwell may have actually felt an affinity with both France and the German states insofar as the latter two had both suffered through civil wars that were fomented by religious zeal.[68] One might well cite Pope as a spokesman for the Augustan conscience: "A dreadful Series of Intestine Wars, / Inglorious Triumphs, and dishonest Scars."[69]

This study is arbitrarily restricted to prose fiction. My generic approach falls into the category of "modes of perception," to use Schiller's terminology, as opposed to "genres of composition,"[70] so certain poetic and dramatic selections could have been included. Chapter 1 surveys some of these selections as well as classical and Renaissance antecedents so that the rich tradition and eighteenth-century pervasiveness of the grotesque-war association can be documented. First the subject of perspective is used as a means of drawing together a number of texts that reveal why war lends itself to the grotesque. Then the subjects of conflict in language and conflict as language are considered to highlight how fundamental the ludicrous-fearful incongruities can be when a writer describes war or engages in satiric exchanges about war. Chapter 2 is devoted to Swift, primarily *Gulliver's Travels*; here Swift demonstrates his uncanny ability to expose the horrible escalations of modern, professional warfare and the spectacle of war. Various Renaissance and classical theories of war also find their way into Swift's writing. In chapter 3, Smollett's *Roderick Random* is examined within the context of the picaresque hero and his military career. Military enlistment and the colonial expedition to Cartagena are both treated in a grotesque mode. Domestic military subjects, such as troop unruliness and purchased commissions, are the targets of Fielding's satiric indignation in *Tom Jones* and *Amelia*. These are discussed in chapter 4 along with Fielding's concept of military grandeur. Like Fielding, Sterne came from a military family, and this fact seems to explain the sympathy with which both regarded those who had served in the army. Moreover, this sympathy invites one to use the grotesque rather than satire as a generic approach. The military veteran and "humour" are the focal points for such a discussion of *Tristram Shandy* in the last chapter.

1

Tradition and Proliferation

War as Grotesque: The Importance of Perspective

THE WAR IN HEAVEN in *Paradise Lost,* which has fascinated critics with its humorous exaggeration, might well be associated with the grotesque. It is generally agreed that the comic element derives from the movement to an objective perspective, namely that of God. On the first day of the battle there are a number of single combats, and these are said to represent the futility of ancient warfare.[1] During the second day the rebels attempt to advance with their "devilish enginry" (bk. 6, line 553), a symbol of man's perverse science of artillery or destruction. Then the battle escalates into something resembling a mythic snowball fight with mountains being hurled back and forth. Following Hesiod (see *Theogony* 664–819), Milton finally has God intervene to bring the conflict to an end.

Satan's engine is representative of mankind's science of artillery, or more generally of modern warfare, which, like the ancient, fails to resolve the conflict.[2] Michael Lieb argues that Milton's progression from a closely focused picture (i.e., the single combats) on the first day to the more distanced view the second and finally to the omniscient position of God produces the sense of "mockery" that characterizes the passage.[3] As I have demonstrated, this detached perspective is a standard feature of the grotesque view of war. Ultimately, the passage gives the impression of a kind of metaphysical farce with God pulling all the strings. This sort of divine intervention is, of course, not very different from the Homeric tradition except that, as Matthew Prior observes, Homer's gods often act in the manner of lowly mortals.[4]

This distanced perspective is necessary to the writer whose purpose is to highlight the universal. Another way to get a distanced perspective or a sense of universal objectivity about war and military ambition is to imitate a classical satire on the sub-

ject. Johnson repeats and effectively updates Juvenal's diatribe against conquerors and conquests by arms in "The Vanity of Human Wishes" (1749). The universality of the satire is contained in the idea of war as the manifestation of a single man's pride, an idea that is easily connected to the *maxima e minimis* doctrine (great consequences follow from small events). Two individual sketches of modern military conquerors, Charles XII of Sweden and the Elector of Bavaria, frame that of the ancient Xerxes; they also recall Juvenal's Alexander and Hannibal and thereby associate the notion of individual pride leading to monstrous wars with a parallel view of history.

Of course denunciations of military leaders are frequently found in writers who attempt to take a larger view of history and political events. Robert Burton, for instance, echoes Seneca's comment on Alexander the Great:

> Alexander was sorry because there were no more worlds for him to conquer; he is admired by some for it, *animosa vox videtur, et regia,* 'twas spoken like a prince; but as wise Seneca censures him, 'twas *vox inquissima [sic] et stultissima,* 'twas spoken like a bedlam fool; and that sentence which the same Seneca appropriates to his father Philip and him, I apply to them all.[5]

Swift and Fielding also attack the idea of military greatness in conquest, but the room for interpretation here is wide as indicated by the fact that Swift lashes out against Marlborough while Fielding defends him.

Johnson bears a close resemblance to Sterne in being able to deride the grotesque aspects of war while defending the individual soldier.[6] The masculinity of war is suggested by Johnson's famous declaration that any real man would rather follow Charles XII into battle than Socrates to hear a philosophical lecture.[7] Johnson himself apparently served with the militia, but Boswell—who saw a musket, sword, and belt in the doctor's closet for militia duty—found the prospect of his eminent friend as a soldier "laughable."[8] (Perhaps Johnson would have made a rather ludicrous Falstaffian figure, yet the image of Boswell obsequiously pursuing a commission in the English Foot Guards is equally laughable.) One may also cite the "Bravery of the English Common Soldiers," an essay in which Johnson perspicaciously argues that the courage of the English soldier was not due to strict, Prussian-like discipline and training but stubborn English pride and the desire for independence.

On the other hand, there is the suppressed *Idler* No. 22, which depicts two vultures staring down hungrily and appreciatively at a corpse-strewn battlefield. The paper resembles a beast fable and concludes with the observation that humankind is "a friend to vultures" because man's frequent and fierce battles provide them with savory feasts. The older vulture refers to a battlefield as one might describe a simmering stew: ". . . the ground smoking with blood and covered with carcasses, of which many are dismembered and mangled for the convenience of the vulture."[9] The misanthropic and sarcastic tone of the piece reminds one immediately of Swift, and this also helps explain why Johnson later excluded it. The same vulture image is used in his pamphlet on the Falkland Islands crisis to describe the battle-eager who would involve so many in the usual miseries of war for the sake of "a bleak and gloomy solitude, an island thrown aside from human use."[10]

To minimize a territorial dispute as being disproportionate to the sacrifice of human life is, of course, a traditional argument. One thinks of Martin the Manichean in *Candide* who remarks on the prize for which England and France are locked in the Seven Years' War, ". . . ces deux nations sont en guerre pour quelques arpents de neige vers le Canada [these nations are at war for a few acres of snow in Canada].[11] Goldsmith repeats Voltaire's sentiments by having Altangi attribute the war to the conflicting and irrational desire of the English and French for "*fur*" or the unnatural luxuries of "muffs and tippets."[12] Another well-known example is the "How all occasions do inform against me" soliloquy wherein Hamlet observes that Norway and Poland are about to fight for "an eggshell," or "a straw"—"a plot / Whereon the numbers cannot try the cause" (*Ham* 4.4.32–66).

Without a doubt, martial sacrifice has inspired a countless number of stirring lines. Boswell believed that Johnson's description of the miseries of war in the Falkland Islands pamphlet was one of the most eloquent statements on the subject ever penned. The passage on naïveté and perspective serves as a good sample: "It is wonderful with what coolness and indifference the greater part of mankind see war commenced. Those that hear of it at a distance, or read of it in books, but have never presented its evils to their minds, consider it as little more than a splendid game; a proclamation, an army, a battle, and a triumph."[13] With distance, again, comes the view of war as play or a game. Johnson goes on to mock the shallow image of honor as expressed by Addison in "The Campaign." Then he condemns those interests that stand to profit financially by a war effort: "These are the men who, without virtue, labour, or hazard, are growing rich as their country is impoverished; they rejoice when obstinacy or ambition adds another year to slaughter and devastation; and laugh from their desks at bravery and science, while they are adding figure to figure, and cipher to cipher, hoping for a new contract from a new armament, and computing the profits of a siege or tempest."[14] The sharpness of this indignation against military profiteering makes one see just how close Johnson could come to the sardonic Swift.

The scavenger motif appears in various forms in grotesque descriptions of war. First, there is the sense of terrible human waste and loss as in the *Iliad* when the "peerless charioteers" are pictured "lying upon the ground dearer far to the vultures than to their wives."[15] Then there is the festive tone of Thomas Nashe's Jack Wilton, a mercenary soldier, who quickly moves from one battle to the next "like a Crowe that still followes aloofe where there is carrion."[16] The festive or Rabelaisian nature of this cyclical materiality is, according to Rhodes, a dominant feature of the Elizabethan grotesque of which Nashe is the best exemplar: ". . . both Nashe and Rabelais use grotesque food imagery to remind us of the essential similarity between our own flesh and the flesh we feed it with."[17] In his book on Rabelais, Bakhtin reminds us just how extensive culinary imagery is when it comes to the description of war. Dismemberment, death, and decay may all be celebrated if one takes a cosmic view of the physical world.[18] But this is the realm of saturnalia as opposed to the satiric, and the latter characterizes how the scavenger motif appears for the most part in the late seventeenth and eighteenth centuries. Examples may be found in Samuel Butler, who in a prose character of a soldier refers to war as "a Monster in a Labyrinth that feeds upon mans flesh, For when it is once engaged it is a matter of exceeding difficulty to get out of agen."[19] The idea of war as consumption is also expressed in Arbuthnot's *History of John Bull*: "*Law* [allegorically meaning war] *is a Bottomless-Pit, it is a Cormorant, a Harpy, that devours every thing*."[20] Similarly, when Swift, Smollett, and Johnson use the scavenger motif, it is strongly satiric.

At this point we might return to Johnson's "Vanity of Human Wishes" wherein the pageantry and prospect of public glory are seen as universal seductions of the military:

> The festal blazes, the triumphal show,
> The ravish'd standard, and the captive foe,

> The senate's thanks, the gazette's pompous tale,
> With force resistless o'er the brave prevail.[21]

To become celebrated heroes in recorded history is enticement enough. But Johnson counters these strong attractions, which he understood so well, by alluding to the financial costs of war, "Where wasted nations . . . / [are] age to age in everlasting debt."[22] This comment reflects the contemporary updating that goes along with classical imitations. The Tory suspicion that the "moneyed interest" played a role in perpetuating hostilities to generate greater profits was prevalent at the close of the Spanish Succession War during which Marlborough amassed a fortune. Johnson seems to have been one of those rare individuals who could see the absurd nature of military pageantry and, at the same time, enjoy it as much as the average person. He is reputed to have liked fireworks and yet wrote a scathing attack on the expense of the spectacular 1749 pyrotechnical display in Green Park, which was held to celebrate the Peace of Aix-la-Chapelle and which inspired Handel's famous *Musick for the Royal Fireworks*. Surely people could, according to Johnson, divert themselves with more civil and responsible forms of entertainment: ". . . how many widows and orphans, whom the war has ruined, might be relieved, by the expence which is now about to evaporate in smoke, and to be scattered in rockets . . . [?][23] True human amusement, however, depends much more on sheer spectacle rather than responsible action.

In "On Public Rejoicings for Victory" (1759), Goldsmith draws a full picture of English citizens intoxicated with jubilation after the news of Wolfe's victory at Quebec reached London. Particularly interesting is how Goldsmith outlines a parallel between the war itself and the rituals of celebration:

> If triumphs are gained abroad, we shout for the victory at home; if they illuminated a city that soon must fall with infernal fire of bombs and hand-granades, we illuminated our streets not less with faggots and candles; if their artillery thunders destruction in the ears of the enemy, we eccho them with squibs and crackers at home, no less terrifying to a female ear; if some bravely fighting for their country lose their lives and fall dead on the field of battle in its defence; we have our bouts as well as they, and can produce our hundreds who have upon this occasion bravely become votaries for their country, and with true patriotism not disdained to fall dead—drunk in every house.[24]

The narrator then describes a tour of the city that first leads him to a punch-house where prospects for taking Paris and "*Lewis the Small* by the beard" are heard with delight.[25] After encounters with a quarreling couple, shouting mobs and all kinds of firing rockets (one of which singes his wig), the narrator takes refuge in another coffeehouse where satires on the French bring forth "loud fits of laughter."[26] This is followed by two more club stops before the narrator gives his own views on war—views that contain the spectacle idea and connect it to the theory that sees war as part of a natural cycle:

> A COUNTRY at war resembles a flambeaux, the brighter it burns, the sooner it is often wasted. The exercise of war for a short time may be useful to society, which grows putrid by a long stagnation. Vices spring up in a long continued peace from too great an admiration for commerce, and too great a contempt for arms; war corrects these abuses, if of but a short continuance. But when prolonged beyond that useful period, it is apt to involve society in every distress.[27]

It is obvious that Goldsmith was not against all wars, and that he possessed a keen eye and curious mind for irrational behavior. The colorful "flambeaux" analogy, along with the extended war and celebration parallel, recognizes the festive spirit of military nationalism.

Some sense of military pageantry was easy to create in the smaller towns and villages for recruiting purposes. To draw men into the military one must represent it as a desirable alternative to the drudgery of common life. Sergeant Kite performs this duty admirably in Farquhar's comedy *The Recruiting Officer* (1707) by referring to the military as "relief and entertainment" from domestic frustration:

> If any gentlemen soldiers or others have a mind to serve her Majesty and pull down the French King, if any 'prentices have severe masters, any children have undutiful parents, if any servants have too little wages, or any husband too much wife, let them repair to the noble Sergeant Kite at the Sign of the Raven in this good town of Shrewsbury and they shall receive present relief and entertainment.[28]

Kite proceeds to get a few of the town simpletons drunk and declares, "Thus we soldiers live, drink, dance, play . . ." (*RO* 2.2.11). Farquhar himself had served as a recruiting officer in Shrewsbury during the winter of 1705–6, and his experience is

comically dramatized in the character of Captain Plume whose
song can be called something of a *danse macabre:*

> Over the hills, and o'er the main,
> To Flanders, Portugal, or Spain;
> The Queen commands, and we'll obey,
> Over the hills and far away.

(RO 2.3.47–50)

This celebratory spirit is easily connected to the saturnalia or to
Bakhtin's notion of the carnivalesque, and its association with
military characters and events is common—Burn's "The Jolly
Beggars" comes to mind, featuring, as it does, the drinking songs
of the "SODGER LADDIE" and his "doxy."[29] Then there are those
who only wish to use the external glitter of military uniform to
show themselves off to advantage, like Shadwell's fops Sir Nicholas Dainty and Sir Timothy Kastril in *The Volunteers.*

It might be noted that Farquhar was certainly not the only
officer to write a humorous stage comedy drawn from his own
military experience. Charles Shadwell, an officer who served in
Portugal during the Spanish Succession War, had a pair of military comedies produced at the Theatre-Royal. *The Fair Quaker of
Deal, or The Humours of the Navy* (1710) features the hilarious
contrast between the gruff old commodore Flip and the gentleman Captain Mizen. The former curses and laughs at the "Sea-
Fops," while the latter orders perfume, muslin curtains, and
sweet-powder on board, then attempts to get everybody in a
white shirt and declares Tuesday visiting day to show off himself
and his "new" navy.[30] *The Humours of the Army* (1713) appeared three years later with another strong cast of stock characters—such as Brigadier *Bloodmore,* the boisterous officer; Captain *Mattematicks,* the French engineer; and "Bisket," a sutler—
all of whom help create a full comic picture of campaign life.[31]
Types like these set the pattern that would be followed by later
novelists such as Smollett, whose Captain Whiffle in *Roderick
Random* resembles Mizen and whose Trunnion in *Peregrine
Pickle* may be based on Mizen's counterpart Flip.

Farquhar's Sergeant Kite and Captain Plume are, of course,
variations on the Falstaff prototype. Falstaff embodies the features of the grotesque military man, and his corrupt recruiting
practices are necessary to satisfy his appetite for the physical—
drink, food, and love. Identifying the medieval and Renaissance

grotesque as representing a conflict between the high and low, or the conflict that resides in nature itself, William Farnham calls Falstaff the "'monstrous body' in the tradition of grotesque animal and man-animal figures" that symbolize a world at war with itself.[32] Falstaff's famous soliloquy on honor (*I Hen. IV* 5.1.127–41) may be interpreted as a manifestation of this conflict, for from one perspective honor is nothing more than just a word and yet from another this kind of rationalization is nothing more than cowardice.

Stated another way, the conflict is between personal or selfish motives and a commitment to the greater political cause. The grotesque depiction of enlistment involves both. First, there are the mercenary motivations of a soldier like Jack Wilton, who campaigns solely for personal gain, or a recruiting officer like Plume, who induces recruits with a promise of plunder: "What think you now of a purse full of French gold out of a / monsieur's pocket, after you have dashed out his brains / with the butt of your firelock, eh?" (*RO* 2.3.154–56). In the tradition of the picaresque, however, the hero is usually drawn into the military out of utter desperation or by coercive violence as opposed to any conscious mercenary motive. Such at least seems to be the fate of Smollett's Roderick Random and Voltaire's Candide or earlier picaresque heroes like Grimmelshausen's Simplicissimus and Estebanillo González. When all else fails, one can always become a soldier, or the nadir of a young man's misfortune may well be military conscription. Even Farquhar's Sergeant Kite admits that he himself was induced by "Hunger and ambition": "The fears of starving and hopes of a truncheon" (*RO* 3.1.125–26). Those who denounce war are by implication challenging the trade of the soldier. Erasmus does exactly this is his dialogue featuring Hanno and the soldier Thrasymachus, who declares, "I heard from professors that everyone has a right to live by his trade." Hanno replies: "A splendid trade—burning houses, looting churches, violating nuns, robbing poor people, murdering harmless ones!"[33] Second, there is the naive youth whose heart beats to the beat of the drum and who falls victim to Johnson's "triumphal show." One also thinks of Burton's tirade against the idea of war as an honorable activity. To fight for empire, or worse still for religious conviction, is what Erasmus attempts to explode in *Dulce Bellum Inexpertis* (war is sweet to those who know it not) and *Querela Pacis* (*The Complaint of Peace*), but his humanitarian ideal cannot be reconciled with the practical reality of a world so fraught with fear and mutual suspicion. As long as men distrust one another the profession of carrying arms will continue.

Moreover, the whole question of consumption and perspective is also related to the idea of war as spectacle. In an aside on battles, Robert Burton offers a variation of the food-chain idea that passes beyond the physical to the spiritual sphere: ". . . [minerals are food for plants, plants for animals, animals for men; men will also be food for other creatures, but not for gods, for their nature is far removed from ours; it must therefore be for devils]; and so, belike, that we have so many battles fought in all ages, countries, is to make them [devils] a feast, and their sole delight" (*AM* 1:187). Human conflict has also been portrayed as something to amuse the gods. Augustine employs the demon-as-scavenger motif in connection with war and joins it to the idea of play: "[t]he great abundance of dying men that enriched the gods of the lower world put them too in the mood to enjoy sport, though to be sure, the venomous wars and blood-stained quarrels, accompanied by deadly victories, now on one side, now the other, themselves provided great sport for demons and rich banquets for the nether gods."[34] The concept that runs through much of the foregoing discussion is that of grotesque consumption: either of men by war and military profiteers or of war by those who are in a position to be amused by it. In a human world of intrinsic conflict, it is simply a matter of consume or be consumed; distanced from this world, one can enjoy the conflict as sport or spectacle.

Somewhere in the middle is the perspective of the nation as a whole or the body politic. In the Renaissance, a foreign war was popularly believed to be a necessary purge for "humours" and military spirits that would otherwise erupt in civil conflicts. Francis Bacon expresses the idea in "Of the True Greatnesse of Kingdomes and Estates": "No Body can be healthful without *Exercise*, neither Naturall Body, nor Politique: And certainly, to a Kingdome or Estate, a Just or Honourable Warre, is the true *Exercise*. A Civill Warre, indeed, is like the Heat of a Feaver; But a Forraine Warre, is like the Heat of *Exercise*, and serveth to keepe the Body in Health: For in a Slothfull Peace, both Courages will effeminate, and Manners Corrupt."[35] The theory feeds into the grotesque view of war in the later seventeenth and eighteenth centuries. Dryden seems to draw upon it in one of the tirades he wrote for the character of Thersites—that physically deformed, scurrilous abuser of the Greeks. The speech, not in Shakespeare's

Troilus and Cressida, plays on how war has the advantage over other calamities in disposing of a nation's fools:

> What shoales of fools one battle sweeps away! How it purges families of younger Brothers, Highways of Robbers, and Cities of Cuckold-makers! There's nothing like a pitch'd Battle, for these brisk Addle-heads! Your Physitian is a pretty fellow, but his fees make him tedious; he rids not fast enough; the fools grow upon him, and their horse bodies are poyson proof. Your Pestilence is a quicker Remedy, but it has not the grace to make distinction; it huddles up honest men and Rogues together. But your battle has discretion; it picks out all the forward fools, and sowses 'em together into Immortality.[36]

In *Encomium Moriae*, Erasmus has Folly boast about the fact that she is responsible for the bravery of soldiers. If one regards self-sacrifice for a greater ideal folly, then the boast is certainly legitimate. It all depends on one's perspective.

As we shall see, understanding the paradox between the honorable ends of war, a love of country and God, and its horrific means, mass slaughter, is central to understanding Sterne's uncle Toby. Furthermore, the subject of love, like war, is commonly featured in either its high or low forms, and both can be directly related to war. As far as the low form is concerned, there is the intricate and farcical connection between love and war in Aristophanes's *Lysistrata*, or the mythic lust of Paris giving rise to the Trojan War. The satirical indictment of war as arising from such a base passion is epitomized in the character of Thersites. In the *Iliad*, Thersites denounces the childish dispute between Agamemnon and Achilles over concubines and questions their manhood, "ye women of Achea" (*Iliad* 2.235–36). Such Mars-Venus associations are frequent. When Paris returns from his combat with Menelaus, he immediately leads Helen to bed and says, "for never yet hath desire so encompassed my soul" (*Iliad* 3.442). Thersites, himself, is depicted as a source of more internal squabbling among the Greeks, who fall into a dispute after Achilles kills Thersites for "reviling him for his supposed love for Penthesileia" (see Hesiod, *The Aethiopis* 1). Shakespeare casts Thersites into the role of the malcontent who associates lust with venereal disease and pronounces judgment on the entire conflict: "All the argument is a whore and a / cuckold, a good quarrel to draw emulous factions and / bleed to death upon. [Now the dry suppeago on the / subject, and war and lechery confound all!]" (*Tro* 2.3.72–75). Dryden retains this essential malcontent nature and in rewriting the same lines connects the pestilence that has stricken the Greek camp to the disease of love: "Now the Plague on the whole Camp, or / rather the Pox: for that's a curse dependent on those that fight as / we do for a Cuckolds queen" (*T&C* 3.1.5–7). Soldiers have always been depicted as rollicking love 'em and leave 'em men; Captain Plume's comment on recruiting officers makes this point rather succinctly: "I thought 'twas a maxim among them to leave as many / recruits in the country as they carried out" (*RO* 1.1.219–20). Then there are the Ovidian war metaphors that are frequently applied to the game of love; they pervade Restoration and eighteenth-century comedies and the novels of Fielding and Sterne.

Robert Burton effectively connects the low and high notions of love and relates both to war in the Third Partition of his *Anatomy*. All human love can have either "*Profitable, Pleasant,* [or] *Honest*" objects, and when an honest object—such as virtue or wisdom—is lacking, love is doomed to break out "into enmity" and "open war" (*AM* 3:18, 29). To die for one's country may be spoken of as most honest: "Dulce et decorum pro patria mori ['tis sweet and honorable to die for one's country]," but it is of "little worth" if it "proceed not from a true Christian illuminated soul" (*AM* 3:31, 32). According to Burton, "religious melancholy" is a subspecies of "love melancholy," and "melancholy" here may be understood as disease. Furthermore, love of the deity is at the root of more physical violence than the love between the sexes, and Burton is not sure of how to respond to this Venus-Mars madness, "a stupend, vast, infinite ocean of incredible madness and folly . . . such comedies and tragedies" (*AM* 3:313; see also 3:348, 372–73).

In the heroic tragedy of the Restoration, love and war were linked in a formulaic manner, and the extremities of this formula lent themselves to ridicule. Buckingham's *The Rehearsal* provides us with a good example of how the grotesque mode can be an inspired parody of the heroic. The heroic tragedies themselves are referred to by the character Johnson as "such hideous, monstrous things," that intend to "elevate and surprise" by a chaotic succession of "Fighting, Loving, Sleeping, Rhyming, Dying, Dancing, Singing, Crying; and every thing, but thinking and Sence."[37] Especially hilarious as far as the love-war dichotomy is concerned is the scene in which Volscius, with one boot off to make love to Parthenope, cannot decide between honor (putting the boot back on to answer the call to battle) or love (taking the other boot off to complete his amorous design) and so he limps off with a single shod foot (*Rehearsal* 3.5). Certainly, the frequent vacillations between amorous and pugnacious passion render the dilemma of Dryden's Almanzor or even his Antony vulnerable to parody.

Perspective, of course, is shaped by immediate political and personal circumstances. After the Glorious Revolution (or glorious farce as some like to call it), Dryden took solace in the prospect of at least maintaining English liberty and enjoying a good laugh at human folly, as he remarks in the preface to *Amphitryon*: "The Merry Philosopher, is more to my Humour than the Melancholick; and I find no disposition in my self to Cry, while the mad World is daily supplying me with such Occasions of Laughter."[38] However, perspective may also be a state of mind; Dryden did write *Troilus and Cressida*, which contains a rather universal commentary on war, at the height of the Popish Plot hysteria. One aspect of Thersites's grotesque nature in the play is that as much as the scurrilous abuser enjoys deriding the Trojan War and the Greeks, he also enjoys watching a good battle: "Now these Rival-rogues will clapperclaw one another, and I shall have the sport on't" (*T&C* 5.2.135–36). The inherent paradox here is not an unusual one. Despite Burton's tirade against war in his "Satyricall Preface," the idea of viewing a battle as recreational sport comes up in the Second Partition of the *Anatomy* when Burton outlines possible remedies for melancholy (*AM* 2:76–77). This is the notion of war as grotesque spectacle, which we located in the perspective of the gods and which Swift, Smollett, Fielding, and Sterne all address.

The Grotesque as War: Language in Conflict

We have seen how war may be viewed as grotesque; it is now time to shift our discussion to the conflict in the language of the grotesque. First, we shall consider the language that is in conflict with itself. Then we will consider literature or language as assault. The idea of the language of war as in conflict with itself stems from the preceding discussion of war as spectacle or attraction. Few of us and few writers on war have ever actually witnessed a battle. Battle descriptions in all ages, especially the neoclassical period, tend to be formulaic; moreover, standard motifs and their variations are easily recognizable. When felicitous rhetorical or figurative language is used to describe war, we find ourselves caught in a discourse that is both appealing and repulsive; the form pleases, yet the subject remains horrible. This paradoxical situation can be said to explain why Johnson would

supposedly tell Mrs. Thrale that one of the most visually grotesque couplets in "The Vanity of Human Wishes" was in fact his
favorite: "Th' incumber'd oar scarce leaves the dreaded coast /
Through purple billows and a floating host."[39] Aphra Behn's
Oroonoko provides us with many gruesome images of mutilation, typical of sensational travel writing, yet they lack a self-
conscious decorative sense and are perhaps representative of the
extreme "terrible" end of the grotesque spectrum.

Renaissance literature is certainly rich with decorative descriptions of death and war. Nashe's Jack Wilton, for instance,
recounts the battle of Marignano in a sharp and facetious manner: "the sprightly *French* sprawling and turning on the stained
grasse, like a Roach new taken out of the streame."[40] This kind of
simile, while very graphic, somehow strikes the reader as a
product of disrespectful witticism. Rhodes may again be cited:
"the stylistic feature which best epitomizes the grotesque in
Renaissance literature is the 'base comparison'."[41] The twitching
fish simile puts one in mind of Sidney's Aristotelian notion that
"those things which in themselves are horrible, as cruel battailes,
unnatural monsters, are made in poeticall imitation, de-
lightfull."[42] One may always derive an aesthetic pleasure from
the form even when the subject is horrible; in fact, the grotesque
may be considered a self-conscious mode in that the artist or
writer, in an intentional and playful way, reminds us that the
representation is not real.

Sidney's own battle descriptions in the *Arcadia* can be said to
involve delightful imitation insofar as the wit in the euphemism
draws attention away from the content of the description. For
instance, Sidney uses a life-in-death image similar to the fish-
out-of-water French with the limb that continues to twitch after
being dismembered: "There lay armes, whose fingers yet
mooved, as if they woulde feele for him that made them feele"
(*PWPS* 1:388). Classical and euphemistic styles combine in his
description of the first major engagement between Cecropia's and
Basilius's forces. After "the terrible salutation of warlike noyse,"
the sides meet lance against lance, some of which "did staine
themselves in bloud; some flew up in pieces, as if they would
threaten heaven, because they fayled on earth" (*PWPS* 1:387).
This kind of reversal or inverted order is expressed repeatedly, as
is the unnaturalness of the slaughter:

> The earth it selfe (woont to be a buriall of men) was nowe (as it were)
> buried with men: so was the face thereof hidden with deade bodies,

to whome Death had come masked in diverse manners. In one place lay disinherited heades, dispossessed of their naturall seignories: in an other, whole bodies to see to, but that their harts wont to be bound all over so close, were nowe with deadly violence opened: in others, fowler deaths had ouglily displayed their trayling guttes.

(*PWPS* 1:388)

Similarly, there are the dead horses who "lay uppon their Lordes . . . and in death had the honour to be borne by them, whō in life they had borne" (*PWPS* 1:388). For all the euphemistic balance and order, chaos prevails and the madness of mankind infects the natural world, including the horses: "Some having lost their commaunding burthens, ranne scattered about the field, abashed with the madnesse of mankinde" (*PWPS* 1:388). There is a cosmic quality about the description that reverberates with epic grandeur, for the action is anything but trivial—in other words, language must be extended into similes or catalogues to capture a sense of the whole battle.[43]

What is interesting about this description in terms of Sidney's idea of *"Poesie"* as "an Art of *Imitation*" or a "speaking *Picture*" (*PWPS* 3:9) is that it bears a resemblance to Paolo Uccello's painting "The Rout of San Romano," which Sidney may have seen in Florence in 1574.[44] The painting actually consists of three panels, and the striking similarity with Sidney's description is in the second panel with its emphasis on horses, depicted in utterly wild motion and dead heaps. Broken lances and other arms are also scattered about. Pope-Hennessy's remark on Uccello's mode may even be transposed to Sidney: "Again and again, the artist's will to realism is mitigated by his all-pervading decorative sense."[45] The grotesque transforms the ugly into spectacle. (On the subject of imitation, it is worth noting that Grimmelshausen based his own battle description in chapter 27 of *Simplicissimus* [1668] on this one in Sidney's *Arcadia*, which was translated into German in 1629.[46] The other possibility is that both Sidney and Grimmelshausen were imitating an earlier third text.)

Sidney, in another part of the same battle passage, concentrates on sound images in what truly becomes a spectacular "speaking picture" of ugliness: "The clashing of armour, and crushing of staves; the justling of bodies, the resounding of blowes, was the first part of that ill-agreeing musicke, which was beautified with the griselinesse of wounds, the rising of dust, the hideous falles, and grones of the dying" (*PWPS* 1:388). The phrase "ill-agreeing musicke" may contain an irony that would be lost on the modern reader who does not know that music references were conventional in Renaissance battle descriptions.[47] Of course, the euphemisms here are all part of Sidney's attempt to approach the epic or heroic. Clearly more facetious is the humor in how Sidney describes the slaughter of the rebels.

This description, which in style is modeled on the mythic battle between the Lapithae and the Centaurs as presented in Ovid's *Metamorphoses*, actually consists of two episodes. The first relates the circumstances leading to the rebellion and the successful defence of Basilius and his family by the two princes, Musidorus and Pyrocles. I will borrow a phrase from the chapter title and dub this episode, added in the *New Arcadia*, "five memorable strokes." The second depicts Musidorus, sometime later, suddenly meeting with the "scummy remnant" of the rebellion, who fled when it was first suppressed. This episode is part of the *Old Arcadia*. (Sidney's revision did not get this far.) Hence, although the revised *New Arcadia* generally reflects a movement from the pastoral to the epic, this Ovidian mode of grotesque slaughter can actually be said to have been one element that was present in the *Old Arcadia* and expanded in the revised text. The general interpretation of these episodes is that Sidney's humor may be deemed appropriate according to Elizabethan attitudes on peasant insurrections.[48]

The facetious humor is justified because the mob is considered to be a deformity. According to the Renaissance theory as developed from classical sources by Madius (*De Ridiculis* 1550), the combination of deformity or *turpitudo* and surprise or *admiratio* was considered to be the true source of the risible.[49] L. P. Wilkinson essentially sees Ovid's Lapithae-Centaur battle in *The Metamorphoses*, where "grotesqueness merges into humor," the same way insofar as the form is "charming . . . an element of neatness and grace [is] involved," which the Greeks would call χάρις.[50] John Dryden describes the same effect in his famous analogy for the finest of raillery: ". . . there is still a vast difference betwixt the slovenly butchering of a man, and the fineness of a stroke that separates the head from the body, and leaves it standing in its place."[51] And so when the princes cut the rebels to pieces in *Arcadia*, they do so with a flair that is matched only by Sidney's own euphemism.

In the first episode, for instance, a "half dronke" miller is neatly dispatched as Musidorus "thrust his sword quite through, from one eare to the other; which toke it very unkindlie, to feele such newes before they heard of them, in stead of hearing, to be put to such feeling" (*PWPS* 1:312–13). This kind of symmetrical slaughter as in ear-to-ear neck slashing or temple-to-temple skull skewering occurs in the *Iliad* (4.501–4, 20.472–74), the *Aeneid* (9.418–19), and the *Metamorphoses* (12.335).[52] In the scummy remnant episode we find a life-in-death image that is more comic than the twitching limbs referred to in the general battle description. Musidorus begins to chase one of the rebels: ". . . the first he overtook as he ran away, carrying his head as far before him as those manner of runnings are wont to do, with one blow strake it so clean off that, it falling betwixt the hands, and the body falling upon it, it made a show as though the fellow had had great haste to gather up his head again."[53] The description recalls Archelochus's death in the *Iliad*: ". . . far sooner did his head and mouth and nose reach the earth as he fell, than his legs and knees" (14.465–68, see also *Iliad* 10.455–56). In fact, many of the memorable strokes are patterned on anatomical details in Homer or Virgil, and it is worth noting that Pope commended Homer's diversity in such anatomical detail as the source of "Surprize and Applause"—successive slaughters must be made spectacular to hold reader attention.[54]

Although Sidney's style has that self-conscious Ovidian humor, Sidney never does imitate Ovid's commonest motif of one limb being pinned to another or to some object. In the *Metamorphoses* for example, Petraeus gets "pinned" to a tree; Dorylas's hand is likewise fixed to his forehead; and Hodites's tongue is joined to "his chin and his chin to his throat" (see 12.331, 12.387, and 12.458). Of course, there is a long tradition of Homeric battle parody beginning with Hesiod's "The Battle of the Frogs and Mice," which was translated by Samuel Parker in 1700 and Thomas Parnell in 1717. Parker, who adopts the title "Homer in a Nutshell," appears to take the allegorical aspect of the poem—the mechanical, fatalistic process of history—very seriously but illustrates his point with a mock-heroic simile that suggests possible irony: ". . . Superiority and Dominion are the most slippery Things in the World, and have their Vicissitudes of Rising and Sinking as necessarily as two Buckets in a Well."[55] Another variation on the Homeric parody is represented by *War, an Epic-Satyr* (1747), apparently written by Stephen Barrett, which uses epic devices somewhat facetiously to satirize French motivations in the War of the Austrian Succession.

The last three "memorable strokes" in Sidney's first episode constitute one graceful flow of action that can be described as a ballet of slaughter. Immediately after stabbing the miller, Dorus slices a braggart in half, and this act sets up the final stroke, which is an interesting comment on the grotesque itself. The last victim is a "poore painter" who is present to obtain some first-hand experience for his picture of the battle "betwene the *Centaures* and *Lapithae*" and therefore "very desirous to see some notable wounds, to be able the more lively to express them" (*PWPS* 1:313).[56] Witnessing death and mutilation feeds his imagination: ". . . the foolish fellow was even delighted to see the effects of blowes" (*PWPS* 1:313). Perhaps the painter's holding of a "pike" makes him fair game, but twice we are told that he is standing still—amazed at the stroke which cuts the braggart in two—when Musidorus "(with a turne of his sword) strake of both his hands" (*PWPS* 1:313). Hence, "the painter returned, well skilled in wounds, but with never a hand to performe his skill" (*PWPS* 1:313). This coup de grace reads like wanton cruelty, and yet there is a graceful harmony about its spontaneity—it just feels like the thing to do! Ultimately, Sidney makes an effective comment not just on the perverse human attraction to bloodshed but on the perverse demands and momentum of artistic form.

How should a battle be reproduced in art? The question, of course, must distinguish between literary, dramatic, and artistic media, yet it nonetheless poses a dilemma similar in all of them—how to manage the conflict between form and content. One of the most humorous parts of *The Rehearsal* occurs when Bayes outlines his solution to this problem. In a conscious effort to avoid, on the one hand, gory action as unfitting for ladies and, on the other, the "dull prolixity" of "a long relation of Squadrons here and Squadrons there" (5.1.176, 174–75), Bayes represents the battle in *recitativo* with only two actors—one singing, the other "in a warlike posture" (5.1.200–201) to satisfy both the ear and eye.[57] The battle as *recitativo* of course parodies *The Siege of Rhodes*. Dryden's own method of having several messengers update a battle is also parodied by Buckingham. As Shakespeare well knew and as Johnson expresses it in *The Rehearsal*, people do like "a little fighting" (5.1.206–7). After all, it isn't real and it entertains, but Bayes's conscious imitation (i.e., the hobbyhorses on stage or the dead actors simply getting up and walking off stage at the end of the scene) renders all ridiculous. So do Pope's form-as-content metaphors when he contrasts Homer's style of battle description to that of Virgil by alluding to their respective heroes: "When we behold their Battels, methinks the two Poets resemble the Heroes they celebrate: *Homer*, boundless and irresistible as *Achilles*, bears all before him, and shines more and more as the Tumult increases; *Virgil* calmly daring like *Aeneas*, appears undisturb'd in the midst of the Action, disposes all about him, and conquers with Tranquillity."[58] Lastly, the importance of the epic trope in Augustan thinking on felicitous description is humorously expressed in Martinus Scriblerus's recipe for an epic poem: "For a *Battle*. Pick a large Quantity of Images and Descriptions from *Homer's* Iliads, with a Spice or two of *Virgil*, and if there remain any Overplus, you may lay them by for a *Skirmish*. Season it well with *Similes*, and it will make an *Excellent Battle*."[59] Stylized language aims to please the literary palate.

We have seen how Sidney uses language that is in conflict with itself—the horrible battle delightfully imitated in words. We have also seen how he uses language as conflict—the facetiously described slaughter of the peasant rebels. The final aspect of the grotesque and war that requires attention derives from this idea and can be expressed as the literature or language that serves as a tool of conflict. The word as weapon.

Satire, in its varying forms, is one of the most obvious of these weapons. That England was at war for much of the period between 1660 and 1800 partially accounts for why this was also a golden age for political and national satire. The first truly memorable satire of this kind is probably Samuel Butler's *Hudibras*, which of course looks back to the civil war and is an attack on the Puritans. What is especially artful about *Hudibras* is that, although Butler specifically ridicules the Presbyterian and Independent causes with Sir Hudibras and Ralpho respectively, the whole civil conflict is itself satirized as seen in the opening lines:

> When *civil* Fury first grew high
> And men fell out they knew not why;
> When hard words, *Jealousies* and *Fears*,
> Set Folks together by the ears,
> And made them fight, like mad or drunk,
> For Dame *Religion* as for Punk.[60]

Moreover, in Book 3 Butler derides the Puritans by emphasizing their own propensity for inner dissension; hence, the insidious nature of civil faction is common to both the Puritan satire and the grotesque view of universal human conflict:

> For now the War is not between
> The Brethren, and the Men of sin:

But Saint and Saint, to spill the Blood,
Of one another's Brotherhood.[61]

As a quixotic simpleton, Sir Hudibras is a mock-heroic knight of
chivalry, but as an allegorical representative of the Presbyterians,
he and his misadventures constitute a travesty of the civil war. In
this sense, Butler's poem resembles the Picrocholine War in
Rabelais's *Gargantua and Pantagruel,* which, according to
Bakhtin, both mocks the military aggression of Charles VI and
represents mock-heroically a lawsuit that was pending in
Rabelais's Loire community. Both Rabelais and Butler also
indulge in verbal exuberance. In fact, the conflict between
Rabelais's King Picrochole and Grandgousier arises when the
cake bakers of Lerné answer a request to sell some of their wares
to the shepherds of Seuilly with a barrage of abusive epithets.
Language is the weapon that draws the first hot blood, so to
speak.

A less memorable yet remarkable satire is Matthew Prior's
burlesque ballad, "On the Taking of Namur by the King of Great
Britain, 1695." Prior composed the poem to commemorate the
English recapture of that town and to retaliate for Boileau's "Ode
Sur la Prise de Namur, 1692," written on the occasion of Louis
XIV's conquest. Sir William Trumball's response to Prior's wish
for anonymity wonderfully expresses the link between satire and
war: "I see no reason why the author should be ashamed of
battering B[oileau]'s poem, and reducing it, any more than we the
Castle, since it is our honor that everything that concerns Namur
be on our side."[62] Congreve and Pittis also wrote odes on the
taking of Namur,[63] and this trend prompted an anonymous reviewer to ask the question, *"Whether the late Siege and Taking of*
Namur *deserves the Great and Extraordinary Applause some*
People are pleased to bestow upon it?"[64] The reviewer singles
out a particularly bad piece by a Mr. Denn and observes that
"NAMUR might still have been in the Possession of the *French,*
had his Hero (my Lord *Cuts* [sic]) fought no better than he [Denn]
writes."[65] Prior continued his Boileau and French bashing into
the War of the Spanish Succession. In his 1704 satirical poem "A
Letter to Monsieur Boileau Despreaux; Occasion'd by the Victory
at Blenheim" (1704), he humorously remarks that " 'Tis mighty
hard" to express the battle's events in verse and concludes "Nor
ever shall BRITANNIA's Sons refuse / To answer to thy Master, or
thy Muse."[66] A glance at Thomas D'Urfey's song collection *Wit*

and Mirth: Or Pills to Purge Melancholy clearly demonstrates that Louis le Grand and the French remained popular targets of ridicule. This popular cultural phenomenon can also be seen in Swift, Smollett, and to a lesser degree, Sterne. Swift's fellow Scriblerian, John Arbuthnot, lampooned *le Roi Soleil* as "Lewis Baboon" in *The History of John Bull*. Tom Brown had a go at the French king in an interesting epistle–adaptation of the dialogue form; dead figures send letters to the living, and the one Scarron sends to old Lewis is an ironic and scathing indictment of that monarch's "greatness."[67] Much of Swift's and Smollett's satiric artillery was directed at domestic targets (e.g., Marlborough, Pitt, the Whigs). However, even when satire transcends the immediate political and social sphere and attempts to strike at universals, or when it may more accurately be called the grotesque, it nonetheless seeks to conquer reader opinion.

In reviewing a history of Italy by Francesco Guicciardini, Goldsmith links the debunking mentality or perspective of the historian to the opportunity for risible delight on the part of the reader. He accuses Guicciardini of debasing the subjects of his study: "The persons who figure in his drama are almost all knaves or fools, polite betrayers, or blustering ideots. In short, the history before us may be stiled a truly misanthropical performance. To a person inclined to hate the species, what ample matter will it not afford, both for ridicule and for reproof."[68] Goldsmith then gives us a grotesque description of Charles VIII of France (via Guicciardini) who "resolved to play the conqueror": "a body as deformed as his intellects were contemptible, of a very short stature, bandy-legged, of a puny constitution. . . . who can forbear smiling at an account like this . . . such a diminutive ideot!"[69] And so the grotesque element in satiric engagement is a prime source of humor for a third party.

A plethora of battle poems marks the eighteenth century. One immediately thinks of Addison's famous ode "The Campaign," which commemorates Marlborough's triumph at Blenheim. (I might again mention Prior, who wrote a similar piece on the Ramillies victory.) Here, too, a polemic can be identified. John Philips answered the heroic abstractions of Addison's "Campaign" with concrete images and epic gruesomeness in a poem entitled "Blenheim." The following is a description of chain-shot that was normally used in naval battles to bring down an opposing ship's rigging but occasionally made an appearance on the battlefield:

Large globous Irons fly, of dreadful Hiss,
Singeing the Air, and from long Distance bring
Surprizing Slaughter; on each side they fly
By Chains connext, and with destructive Sweep
Behead whole Troops at once; the hairy Scalps
Are whirl'd aloof, while numerous Trunks bestrow
Th' ensanguined Field. . . .[70]

Whether such graphic language blows away Addison's
"wond'rous tale" is debatable,[71] but at least the dedication to
Harley makes clear what Philips's political agendum was. The
straightforward odes bask in patriotism and do not contain the
sense of satirical play that marks Prior's Namur poem, but hundreds of less distinguished "Campaign" imitations appeared
regularly in the monthly magazines. Perhaps the most elegant
ode on a military event is the subtle piece by Collins, "Ode
Written at the End of 1746," which exquisitely captures a somber
sense of loss by avoiding narrative spectacle and emotional indulgence. The more successful emotional poems tend to focus on
maimed veterans and their poverty-stricken families.

At the other end of the scale from the eulogistic language of the
ode is the bloodthirsty rhetoric that figures prominently in literary dialogues depicting military personages in some kind of
verbal dispute. For example, in Lucian's *Dialogues of the Dead*,
No. 12, Alexander and Hannibal bicker like children over the
claim to the greater military accomplishment. Hannibal boasts
that he "slew such numbers on one day that [he] measured off
their rings by bushels, and bridged . . . rivers with the dead."[72]
Often the rhetorical duel will be between a military figure and a
nonmilitary one. Prior's dialogues are especially interesting for
this very reason. One features Charles the Emperor in a squabble
with Clenard the Grammarian over the relative importance of the
profession of arms, which plays such a key role in history, and
that of the academic, who is responsible for recording history.
When Charles's argument that "you live upon us" is convincingly
refuted, the military man, in the spirit of his profession, draws
his "main Argument"—a "great Battering Piece . . . [to] Strike
[Clenard] Dead at once."[73] A second depicts Cromwell in a dispute with his mad porter, a Bedlamite who obviously gains the
upper hand with the following comment: ". . . there is indeed
one Difference between you Public Madmen, and we Sedentary
Gentlemen if We happen to be a little Crazed about Love, Learning or Religion while you are ravaging Nations, and setting the

world on fire."[74] As we shall discover, Fielding made his own contribution to the dialogue genre.

Plautus's *Miles Gloriosus* seems to have set the standard for the military braggart, whose language often reaches the height of grotesque metaphor and hyperbole. One is reminded of the scene in *Tamburlaine the Great* Part 2 in which Tamburlaine attempts to kindle a lust for conquest and war in his sons by telling them that his "royal chair of state" shall be advanced on a field "sprinkled with the brains of slaughtered men."[75] The rhetoric then becomes more ludicrously excessive as Celebinus responds with, "For, if his chair were in a sea of blood, / I would prepare a ship and sail to it"; and Amyras is hard pressed to sound even more enthusiastic:

> And I would strive to swim through pools of blood,
> Or make a bridge of murdered carcasses,
> Whose arches should be fram'd with bones of Turks,
> Ere I would lose the title of a king.[76]

Bloodthirsty rhetoric is meant to impress in lieu of bloodthirsty action.

Nothing is more common in the *Iliad* and the *Aeneid* than taunts and goading words before actual combat, unless it be the spurning speeches of the victors that follow. Epic warriors themselves continually remind each other that war is physical combat and not just rhetorical repartee, as Menoetius reprimands the boastful Meriones: ". . . it beseemth not in any wise to multiply words, but to fight" (*Iliad* 16.631). Likewise, Aeneas concludes his long answer to Achilles by comparing the two of them to "women, that when they have waxed wroth in soul-devouring strife go forth into the midst of the street and wrangle one against the other with words true and false" (*Iliad* 20.251–55). It is safer to vaunt after the enemy has been dispatched to avoid inspiring him unnecessarily. Patrocles, for example, mocks Cebriones's diving form after smashing his head with a stone and flipping him out of a chariot: "Hah, look you; verily nimble is the man; how lightly he diveth! In sooth if he were on the teeming deep, this man would satisfy many by seeking for oysters, leaping from his ship were the sea never so stormy, seeing that now on the plain he diveth lightly from his car. Verily among the Trojans too there be men that dive" (*Iliad* 16.744–50). But with the enemy dead, one loses the satisfaction of seeing one's insult strike home. Furthermore, even if one boasts over a fallen foe, one still risks incurring the wrath of a comrade-in-arms, which is what happens to Patrocles. At any rate the boaster usually ends up like Pharus in the *Aeneid*—with a spear in the mouth: "Lo! as Pharus flings forth idle words, he [Aeneas] launches his javelin and plants it in his bawling mouth" (*Aeneid* 10.322–23), or like the butcher-rebel in Sidney's *Arcadia* who calls Pyrocles "vile names" only to have the lower part of his jaw hacked off, "where the tongue still wagged, as willing to say more" (*PWPS* 1:312). Gibes are a literary commonplace in military history as far back as Herodotus who records that a Babylonian rebel "mocked" Darius and his besieging army "with gesture and word": "You will take our city when mules bear offspring."[77]

This soldier-as-rhetorician motif brings us back to the legendary parley at Fontenoy. Who fired first? Although English historians have generally agreed that it was the French, the incident must ultimately remain one of history's "Paper Imbroglios" as Carlyle called it.[78] Lord Charles Hay's saucy insult—requesting that the French not flee across the river to the rear—if it in fact was made, epitomizes the graceful charm of poised wit in extraordinary circumstances. It may also be called the first shot. Historians will never know if it was felt by any of the French, but Hay certainly felt the piece of lead that brought him down almost as soon as he finished his verbal act (he was mistakenly reported to have been killed).[79] Despite any cavalier demonstration of bravado, most of the men lined up on that hill must have been shaking with fear. After the opening volleys, the English infantry column managed to advance to a position almost abreast the French artillery. If terror had not already seized the English, it must have done so here. The French command (consisting of the Maréchal de Saxe, who had been moved about the field in a wicker chair because of his dropsy; the Duc de Richelieu; and his Royal Highness) managed to quell the panic in their troops and decided to rake the enemy with a cannonade. The English held their position as best they could, but with grapeshot tearing gaps in their lines and cannonballs bounding over the hard ground towards them, it was only a matter of time before the day was lost.

The battle of Fontenoy is notable for a number of reasons. The Duc de Gramont, who was largely responsible for the French disaster at Dettingen, fell propitiously at the first artillery discharge. Army surgeon La Mettrie, who would one day draw upon his military experience to write *l'Homme machine*, worked furiously and was heard to say, "English and French all one to you, nay, if anything, the English better!" An English camp sutler was said to be cutting the lace from a dead officer when a ball shore off her head—a sister plunderer merely picked up her scissors and continued the job. Perhaps Voltaire is right in calling the English a "deliberate gloomy people."[80] As for the French, they celebrated in grand style, and victory on the field soon passed into literary form—Voltaire's eulogy apparently sold 21,000 copies in a day. Lastly, it is also to Voltaire that readers owe the proverbial account of the Fontenoy parley which rates as one of the most civilized spectacles or fictions in the annals of military history.

2

Swift: War and History, the Rhetoric of the Grotesque

Swift and War before *Gulliver's Travels*

FOR MUCH OF Swift's adult life to 1713, England was embroiled in war—specifically King William's War (1688–97) and the War of the Spanish Succession (1701–13). Although Swift could follow the Jacobite Rebellion of 1715 and the 1718–20 war with Spain from Dublin, these were relatively minor actions compared to the grand continental campaigns. The exile to Ireland, hence, provided Swift with the distance required to achieve a more detached and objective view of human warfare when he came to write *Gulliver's Travels* in the early 1720s than that which he had had when he was trying to topple Marlborough with *The Examiner* and *The Conduct of the Allies* in 1710 and 1711. However, as his objectivity in the *Travels* is by no means perfect, so it might also be said that many of the ideas underlying the portrayal of war and the military in the *Travels* can be elucidated by examining a selection of Swift's earlier works. Robert C. Gordon has identified the salient features of Swift's attack on the emerging modern science of warfare and the connection of this attack to the contemporary debate over standing armies.[1] In this chapter, I shall suggest that the grotesque provides a useful theoretical framework for explicating the spectacle of war and its connection to historical discourse in *Gulliver's Travels*.

To date, Swift's identification with the grotesque has been characterized by attempts to focus on the complex contradictions and energies of his personality. Arthur Clayborough accounts for the imaginative intensity of Swift's satire by applying a theory of the grotesque based on a conceptualized matrix of Jungian psychology that involves the progressive (direct thinking or logic) and regressive (the unconscious dream or fantasy) forces of the mind.[2] As social criticism, Swift's satire reflects his "progressive aspect," but as an indulgence in expressive fantasy it conveys his

exuberant entertainment of the unconscious. Peter Steele applies
a looser theory of the grotesque to Swift and his writings by
examining how Swift handles "disease, madness, filth, and violent stress as some of the mortal modes of man."[3] Patrick
Gleeson's dissertation, *"Gulliver's Travels* as a Version of the
Grotesque" (1964), also identifies more general characteristics of
the grotesque mode: "deliberate contradiction, surprise, ambivalent attack, narrative discontinuity and distortion."[4] Gleeson
puts forth a good case for the presence of these characteristics in
the *Travels* but does not treat the subject of war or any of the
passages dealing with military affairs in any depth. Although
Carole Fabricant does not draw upon the theory of the grotesque
in *Swift's Landscape,* she does focus on the subject of perception
and claims that "Swift's characteristic mode of observation . . .
can produce grotesque distortions."[5] I would like to draw more
extensively from the work of Ruskin, Kayser and Bakhtin, and
refocus the discussion on Swift's texts as opposed to his personality.

A review of how Swift treats the subject of war or uses war
motifs in his earlier writings will contribute to a study of the
Travels. One of the games of literary history is to celebrate or
degrade according to political allegiance. While Swift mastered
this craft in his attack on Marlborough, he had begun to exercise
it in his early odes. His "Ode to the King, On his Irish Expedition, and The Success of His Arms in general" (1691) eulogizes
King William as a great monarch simply by repeating the banally
expressed virtue of *"Doing good."*[6] The poem stands out for the
last two stanzas, which actually consist of a fierce denunciation
of Louis XIV, who has lately "grown so impudently Great"
(*Poems* 1:10, line 120).[7] In the final image, which anticipates *A
Tale of a Tub,* Louis is said to have a venereal disease and to have
fallen "sick in the *Posteriors* of the World" (*Poems* 1:10, line
146). The denunciation overshadows any sustained praise for
William whose merit is unsuccessfully measured by its opposite,
the gross and perverted *"Tyrant"* Louis (*Poems* 1:10, line 119).[8]

This ridicule of Louis XIV, of course, prefigures the digression
on madness in *A Tale of a Tub* wherein the narrator identifies
"The Establishment of New Empires by Conquest" as one of the
"greatest Actions that have been performed in the World, under
the Influence of Single Men."[9] Two examples follow. The first is
"Harry *the great of* France" who suddenly amasses "a mighty
Army" (G&S, 163):

It was afterwards discovered, that the Movement of this whole Machine had been directed by an absent *Female*, whose Eyes had raised a Protuberancy, and before Emission, she was removed into an Enemy's Country. . . . HAVING to no purpose used all peaceable Endeavours, the collected part of the *Semen*, raised and enflamed, became adust, converted to Choler, turned head upon the spinal Duct, and ascended to the Brain. The very same Principle that influences a *Bully* to break the Windows of a Whore, who has jilted him, naturally stirs up a Great Prince to raise mighty Armies, and dream of nothing but Sieges, Battles, and Victories.

(G&S, 164–65)

This absurd, physical explanation of the mechanical *"Vapour"* (G&S, 164) is easily connected to the paradoxical love-war relationship discussed earlier, and W. A. Speck argues that Swift himself held such a view.[10]

The second example is the *"Present French King,"* Louis XIV who "amused himself to take and lose Towns; beat Armies, and be beaten; drive Princes out of their Dominions; fright Children from their Bread and Butter; burn, lay waste, plunder, dragoon, massacre Subject and Stranger, Friend and Foe, Male and Female" (G&S, 165). The King's amusement in winning and losing suggests the playful or sportive attitude toward war, and war's indiscriminate destruction is also emphasized. The perverse pleasure of the warmonger comes from scaring the helpless and wreaking havoc in an absurdly random way, on "Subject and Stranger" or "Friend and Foe." All this because of a vapor that concentrates in his *"Anus"* and concludes in a *"Fistula"* (G&S, 166). In these *"Teterrima belli / Causa"* portraits (G&S, 165), Swift ridicules the mechanistic science but also presents examples of the *maxima e minimis* doctrine that he himself seems to have imbibed from Sir William Temple.[11] What is particularly relevant about this section of *A Tale*, however, is its connection to the low bodily imagery that Bakhtin singles out as a feature of the grotesque.[12] It is precisely in the materiality of his existence that man may recognize and celebrate his fallen nature, and Swift clearly celebrates the ludicrous aspect of the *maxima e minimis* doctrine.

Swift's grotesque view of military achievement and the language used to express that achievement may also be seen in his 1705 mock encomium on Baron John Cutts who was given the nickname *"Salamander"* due to his intrepidity in the face of fire (*Poems* 1:83, line 22). The poem begins with a summary of bestial similes routinely found in epic literature to capture intense moments of combat:

> As we say, *Monsieur*, to an *Ape*
> Without offence to Human Shape:
> So men have got from Bird and Brute
> Names that would best their Natures suit:
> The *Lyon*, *Eagle*, *Fox* and *Bear*
> Were Hero's Titles heretofore.
>
> (*Poems* 1:83, lines 5–10)

Humorously rejecting "Bucket" or "Pump" (*Poems* 1:83, line 20) as suitable metaphors, Swift cites Pliny's legendary comment on the salamander's coldness as being sufficient to extinguish fire and concludes that the reptile would then be an apt emblem for Cutts's courage. Kayser has mentioned a number of animal images that are associated with the grotesque, and the salamander can easily be grouped with those "creeping animals which inhabit realms apart from and inaccessible to man."[13] The beast simile itself suggests that abstract language is somehow inadequate to capture concrete reality. The essence of the simile acts as a kind of burlesque or metaphysical conceit and evokes the traditional comic-satiric celebration of military courage as foolishness—as in Falstaff's soliloquy on honor or in Folly's boasting about being responsible for war in *Encomium Moriae*. Hence Swift's Bedlamites may have what it takes to lead a regiment: "IS any Student tearing his Straw in piece-meal, Swearing and Blaspheming, biting his Grate, foaming at the Mouth, and emptying his Pispot in the Spectator's Faces? Let the Right Worshipful, the *Commissioners of Inspection*, give him a Regiment of Dragoons, and send him into *Flanders* among the *Rest*" (G&S, 176). By assuming the norm of a greater perspective and denying the view of individual commitment and bravery, Swift highlights the madness that is part of military valor.

The irony contained by the idea of military greatness (e.g., Alexander the Great) is dealt with further in one of the "Additions to The Tale of A Tub," contained in *Miscellaneous Works*, 1720 (G&S, 305–6). Here the narrator first endorses Hobbes by generalizing about human conflict: "The State of War [is] natural to all Creatures" (G&S, 305).[14] War is then simply defined as "an attempt to take by violence from others a part of what they have & we want"; and it is then in accordance with this definition that greatness can be measured:

The higher one raises his pretensions this way, the more bustle he makes about them, & the more success he has, the greater Hero. Thus greater Souls in proportion to their superior merit claim a greater right to take every thing from meaner folks. This [is] the true foundation of Grandeur & Heroism, & of the distinction of degrees among men. . . . The greatest part of Mankind loves War more than peace: They are but few & mean spirited that live in peace with all men.

(G&S, 305)

This passage also signals Swift's familiarity with the theory, popular during the Renaissance, that a foreign war is the best prevention against a civil one: "War therfor [is] necessary . . . to purge Bodys politick of gross humours. Wise Princes find it necessary to have wars abroad to keep peace at home" (G&S, 305). Swift sarcastically implies that the modernist thinker is attracted to this kind of theoretical rationalization.

One of the traditional arguments against the superiority of humankind over animals is the observation that animals do not normally fight with members of their own species. Nor are animals capable of exercising an art of warfare: "Brutes having but narrow appetites are incapable of carrying on or perpetuating war against their own species, or of being led out in troops & multitudes to destroy one another" (G&S, 306). These ideas anticipate many of the issues raised in Part 4 of *Gulliver's Travels*. Does humankind possess reason or a grotesque faculty that only serves to increase natural vices?

War is the central metaphor for the polemical dispute mock-heroically portrayed in *The Battle of the Books*. The popularity of the mock-epic battle simile in the eighteenth century can be associated with a playful view of the world as Hobbesian or the world as fraught with contention. Mock-heroic language itself is a game of association that pokes fun at both petty action and high discourse; hence, it is no surprise that Bakhtin identifies the parodic as part of the carnival laughter of the grotesque.[15] In the mock-heroic or mock-epic, contention is made ludicrous through inflated style. Unlike travesty (the low burlesque), the mock-heroic or high burlesque does not usually strike a disturbing chord because of the trivial subject matter. The playing out of the ombre hand between Belinda and the Baron in Pope's "Rape" is an example of the perfectly ludicrous. But Swift's *Battle of the Books* seems somewhat of an exception by virtue of its gruesome language. For example, Homer is portrayed as enacting one of his most common and grotesque anatomical motifs, ("ἐγκέφαλος δὲ ἔνδον," *Iliad* 11.97–98, 12.185–86, and 20.399–400) when he slams together the heads of two moderns: "He took *Perrault* by mighty Force out of his Saddle, then hurl'd him at *Fontenelle*, with the same Blow dashing out both their Brains" (G&S, 246). There is no physical substance to this slaughter other than a linguistic one; nevertheless, language has a substance of its own.

Swift begins the work with a mocking reference to Mary Clark's almanac sheet as a source for the cyclical theory of war: "Riches produceth Pride; Pride is War's Ground, &c." (G&S, 217). In their note, Guthkelch and Smith reproduce the inscription of the theory in full which appeared in the upper left-hand corner of the almanac sheet next to a figure showing the signs of the Zodiac:

> War begets Poverty,
>   Poverty Peace:
> Peace maketh Riches flow,
>   (Fate ne'er doth cease:)
> Riches produceth Pride,
>   Pride is War's ground,
> War begets Poverty, &c.
> (The World) goes round.
>
> (G&S, 217, n. 1)

As I have said, this cyclical theory is actually classical in origin, and Swift's readers may well have been expected to recognize it as such. Temple's influence is also clear.[16] Swift alters the usual version of the theory by going on to argue that poverty, rather than pride, has a tendency to invade prosperity inasmuch as a needy country will try to steal from an affluent one. However, the notion of poverty leading to aggression against prosperity also has a classical antecedent, as in Lucan's *The Civil War*: "For when Rome had conquered the world and Fortune showered excess of wealth upon her[,] virtue was dethroned by prosperity . . . poverty, the mother of manhood, became a bug-bear; and from all the earth was brought the special bane of each nation."[17] In any case, suggesting that the Moderns are poor plunderers of the rich Ancients is a statement that smacks of classical theory and hence is indirect support for the Ancients.

The Battle of the Books does reveal something of what Swift thought about the modern science of warfare. The Moderns are said to rely more on the "greatness of their Number" and "continual Recruits" than the Ancients who carry on the war with "Resolution" and "Courage" (G&S, 221). It should come as no surprise that the first Recruiting Act, which was required to meet Marlborough's demand for more men, was passed in 1703, the year before *The Battle* was published.[18] The narrator also mentions the propaganda war (which of course is what *The Battle*, being a literary one, is really all about) that takes the form of "both sides hang[ing] out their Trophies": "These Trophies have largely inscribed on them the Merits of the Cause; a full impartial Account of such a Battel, and how the Victory fell clearly to the Party that set them up" (G&S, 221). Guthkelch and Smith note that this may be a reference to the "Catholic celebrations on the supposed victory at the Boyne" (G&S, 221, n. 2). However, the writing of an "impartial Account" to claim victory is probably more of a general statement on the growing tendency for countries to print records of glorious actions to gain popular support. Swift realized long before his own personal war against Marlborough that the pen could serve as well as the sword. The Spider's web or "Castle [is] guarded with Turn-pikes, and Palissadoes, all after the *Modern* way of Fortification" (G&S, 229), and the Spider boasts about his "*Improvements in the Mathematics*" (G&S, 231)—all of which puts one in mind of Vauban's elaborately geometric fortification designs. Lastly, the army of the Moderns includes some rather inglorious components: "several Bodies of *heavy-armed Foot*, all *Mercenaries*" (G&S, 236), "a confused Multitude" (G&S, 237), "infinite Swarms of *Calones*," and "Rogues and Raggamuffins, that follow the Camp for nothing but the Plunder" (G&S, 238). Throngs of camp sutlers and followers were a notorious part of the armies in the late seventeenth and eighteenth centuries, since the armies needed stores of provisions and since battles generally did not threaten civilians as much as they left corpse-strewn fields ripe for plunder.[19]

As Philip Pinkus has argued, Swift both defends his patron Temple and satirizes the whole polemical dispute.[20] In fact, although there is no doubt about Swift being an Ancient, the mock-epic style of the narrative and the frequent references to Homer as a model are ambiguous endorsements. Swift recognized comic potential in the Homeric simile, especially the low domestic ones. Boyle's attempt to chase Bentley and Wotton at the same time is compared to a spinning woman chasing her geese over the common (*Iliad* 12.433–36).[21] Then there is the climactic slaying of the twain when Boyle fires his lance—a witty combination of the Ovidian skewer motif and the low simile:

> B——ntl——y saw his Fate approach, and flanking down his Arms, close to his Ribs, hoping to save his Body; in went the Point, passing through Arm and Side, nor Stopt, or spent its Force, till it had also pierc'd the valiant W——tt——n, who going to sustain his dying

Friend, shared his Fate. As, when a skilful Cook has truss'd a Brace of *Woodcocks*, He, with Iron Skewer, pierces the tender Sides of both, their Legs and Wings close pinion'd to their Ribs; So was this pair of Friends transfix'd, till down they fell, joyn'd in their Lives, joyn'd in their Deaths; so closely joyn'd that *Charon* would mistake them both for one, and waft them over *Styx* for half his Fare.

(G&S, 258)

The ludicrous effect is achieved through an incongruity or conflict between language and substance.

Incongruous language distinguishes Homer's deformed character of Thersites (*Iliad* 2.211–75), the character on whom Swift models Bentley.[22] Like Thersites, Bentley is said to be ugly and deformed; furthermore, Bentley's abusive language and scurrilous demeanor is characteristic of what has come to be known as Thersitical satire. The difference between the two is that Bentley is a major figure in the action of *The Battle*, whereas Thersites appears in only one scene of the *Iliad*. (Of course in *Troilus and Cressida* Dryden follows Shakespeare in expanding Thersites's role.) Furthermore, Homer's Thersites seems to be little more than a camp follower; Bentley, on the other hand, fancies himself as the superior Modern. In the *Iliad*, Odysseus scolds Thersites for his presumption in rebuking Agamemnon and instead of answering Thersites's criticisms, he deals the deformed jester a blow that makes him cry. Swift bases Scaliger's response to Bentley on Odysseus's, but no blow is struck. One might contend that Thersites embodies man's cruder pugnacious spirit; his abrasiveness is the "slovenly butchering," as opposed to the fine stroke, to use Dryden's terms.

The truly deformed creature in *The Battle* is "a malignant Deity, call'd *Criticism*":

The Goddess herself had Claws like a Cat: Her Head, and Ears, and Voice, resembled those of an *Ass*; Her Teeth fallen out before; Her Eyes turned inward, as if she lookt only upon herself: Her Diet was the overflowing of her own *Gall*: Her *Spleen* was so large, as to stand prominent like a Dug of the first Rate, nor wanted Excrescencies in form of Teats, at which a Crew of ugly Monsters were greedily sucking; and, what is wonderful to conceive, the bulk of Spleen encreased faster than the Sucking could diminish it.

(G&S, 240)

She attempts to rally the idle Moderns and, beginning with Wotton, takes "the ugliest of her Monsters, full glutted from her Spleen, and flung it invisibly into his Mouth; which flying strait up into his Head, squeez'd out his Eye-Balls, gave him a distorted Look, and half-turned his Brain" (G&S, 243). The negative call to arms takes the form of a critical rebuke, whereas its positive counterpart aims to inspire with love of an ideal such as defence of country or freedom, or the "honey" of the Ancients.

Even if Swift's style resembles that of Ovid, the details of *The Battle* derive for the most part from Homer. Bentley's nighttime raid is loosely based on the one carried out by Odysseus and Diomedes (*Iliad* 10.465–539). Boyle recognizes the stolen armor in the hands of Bentley just as Achilles does his own on Hector (*Iliad* 22.331–36). Wotton prays for success against Temple, and the reader is told that the prayer is partially granted and denied as was Achilles's prayer for Patrocles (*Iliad* 16.249–52). As for Wotton's cowardly attack itself, it may have a Homeric source in Euphorbus's stabbing of the blind Patrocles (*Iliad* 16.805–17) or it may show the influence of Shakespeare who has Achilles slay an unarmed Hector (see *Tro.* 5.8). So much for epic heroism. Boyle appears in armor "*given him by all the Gods*" (G&S, 256) as Achilles receives replacement armor forged by Hephaestus (*Iliad* 19.8–13).

There are other Homeric motifs that are pregnant with the ridiculous. Swift has Dryden trade armor with Virgil (much to Dryden's favor), as Hector exchanges gifts with Ajax after their evenly fought contest (*Iliad* 5.301–5). That the latter two part as friends is not exactly a statement on the ridiculousness of war, but it does hint that there is no real conflict between Greek and Trojan with the obvious exception of Menelaus and Paris. Shakespeare follows up his own Hector-Ajax contest with a joint feast of Trojans and Greeks, which accentuates the same idea (*Tro.* 4.4–5.2). How could men get along so wonderfully if they are at war? Another Homeric motif, which Swift uses grotesquely, concerns fate that deals out death in a way that mocks the intentions of the participants. Aristotle fires an arrow at Bacon; it misses Bacon but strikes "*Des-Cartes*" (G&S, 244) in the eye. Similarly in the *Iliad*, Aias throws a spear at Polydamas, "And Polydamas himself escaped black fate, springing to one side; but Archelochus, son of Antenor, received the spear; for to him the gods purposed death" (*Iliad* 14.462–64). All human action takes on an insignificance in face of destiny or divine control. *The Battle* ultimately demonstrates that Swift was not just given to exposing the human fascination for violent spectacle; he was also sensitive to the role of language in this fascination and to the ludicrous nature of the conventional discourses for expressing violent spectacle.

Naturally, any discussion of war and Swift must eventually involve the Duke of Marlborough. Much has already been written on how Swift attacks what he portrays as Marlborough's avarice in *The Examiner* (especially No. 16) and elsewhere.[23] The political struggle has been analyzed in detail by critics like Foot and Ehrenpreis.[24] Some particular notice might here be made of *The Conduct of the Allies* (1711) since although it is a wholly political piece, it does contain a depiction of the grotesque in how the nation itself has been drawn into a protracted and self-destructive war. Swift's purpose was not to condemn war in the abstract but to show how an immediate peace would benefit Britain. He goes to great length in arguing that Britain's allies have not lived up to their obligations, and that therefore Britain has carried more than her fair share of the burden. The discrediting of Marlborough is chiefly on the grounds that those who wish to prolong the war, the whiggish *"Monied Men"* (*PW*, 6:41), only do so for their own financial advantage. Although the tone of *The Conduct* remains eminently serious throughout, Swift occasionally employs a witty understatement or rhetorical climax to clarify the issues. For one thing, Marlborough's image as a great conqueror had to be put in perspective: "Getting into the Enemy's Lines, passing Rivers, and taking Towns, may be Actions attended with many glorious Circumstances: But when all this brings no real solid Advantage to us, when it hath no other End than to enlarge the Territories of the *Dutch*, and encrease the Fame and Wealth of our *General*, I conclude, however it comes about, that Things are not as they should be . . ." (*PW*, 6:20). Having thus disarmed the other side, Swift quickly goes for the kill by expressing the ever-increasing debt in extreme terms: "But the Case is still much harder, We are destroying many thousand Lives, exhausting all our Substance, not for our own Interest, which would be but common Prudence; not for a Thing indifferent, which would be sufficient Folly, but perhaps to our own Destruction, which is perfect Madness" (*PW*, 6:20). Political bias aside, Swift definitely has a special gift for highlighting what he perceives—rightly or wrongly—as the absurdity of human action. Furthermore, he expresses the absurdity with what appears to be just plain old, but badly needed, clear thinking.[25]

To clinch his point about ending the war, Swift merely reminds the reader of England's remote interest in it: "What Arts have been used to posssess the People with a *strong Delusion*, that *Britain* must infallibly be ruined, without the Recovery of *Spain* to the House of *Austria*?" (*PW*, 6:58). Reflective questions like this could almost be said to raise Swift's argument above the dust of Tory-Whig infighting, but we know better. There is a satiric element in the question that indicts both those in power for misleading the masses and the masses for being stupid enough to follow. Treaty obligations and the specter of Catholic dominance are forgotten; hence the reasons for Britain's involvement in the war seem ridiculously petty.

The manipulation of perspective in *The Conduct* is perhaps what does look forward to the grotesque portrayal of war in *Gulliver's Travels* (1726). Swift manages at times in the former to give the impression that he has some distance from the immediate political situation. He sarcastically implies that the continental war is the sport of Marlborough (*PW*, 6:22–23). In one of his early "Thoughts on Various Subjects," Swift elucidates the distancing "time" factor that naturally blurs one's perception of the importance of causal detail in past wars: "REFLECT on Things past, as Wars, Negotiations, Factions; and the like; we enter so little into those Interests, that we wonder how Men could possibly be so busy, and concerned for Things so transitory: Look on the present Times, we find the same Humour, yet wonder not at all" (*PW*, 1:241). Minute exigencies normally blind men to the ridiculous nature of immediate conflicts and their escalation. At one point in *The Conduct*, Swift actually invites his reader to imagine what value the captured French standards will have for future generations: "IT will, no doubt, be a mighty Comfort to our Grandchildren, when they see a few Rags hang up in *Westminster-Hall*, which cost an hundred Millions, whereof they are paying the Arrears, and boasting, as Beggars do, that their Grandfathers were Rich and Great" (*PW*, 6:55–56).[26] This imaginative exercise allows Swift to single out the ephemerality of military glory and conquest against the more lasting reality of debt-financing.

The universal aspect of Swift's personal attack on Marlborough is succinctly expressed in the closing lines of "A Satirical Elegy" (1722), written on the occasion of the Duke's death and while Swift was also writing the *Travels*: "From all his ill-got honours flung, / Turn'd to that dirt from whence he sprung" (*Poems* 1:297, lines 31–32). The affinities between this statement and the conventional satiric attacks on military conquerors in the tradition of Juvenal's "Satire 10" are obvious. One of course thinks of Johnson's "The Vanity of Human Wishes," which ridicules the ambition of Charles XII and the Elector of Bavaria (lines 191–254). Unlike Johnson, however, Swift did not have any distance from his subject; neither did Fielding when he wrote "Of True

Greatness," which also mocks military conquerors but ironically defends Marlborough. As always, the enduring human conception of merit or infamy in physical conquest remains a product of faith and literary discourse.

Gulliver's Travels: History, Spectacle and Rhetoric

My use of the term "grotesque" to describe Swift's treatment of military issues in the *Travels* is supported by Ehrenpreis's theory that Swift, feeling the heat of possible persecution for his economic pamphlets as early as 1720, "embarked on *Gulliver's Travels* . . . to convert his repressed impulses [on Irish affairs] into the shape of fantasy": "He would thus generalize his response to the public events he had known and deliver his confirmed views on human nature as it was exhibited in English society, especially in the conduct of government."[27] That Swift returned to viewing war in strictly political terms after the *Travels* is suggested by his remark in a letter to Thomas Sheridan in May 1727 while Swift was still on his London visit: "The Dispute about a War or no War still continues, and the major Part inclines to the latter, although ten Thousand Men are order'd for *Holland*. But this will bring such an Addition to our Debts, that it will give great Advantages against those in Power, in the next Sessions."[28] More detached in Ireland from the Tory-Whig struggle, Swift was able to reverse the emphasis from the political *agon* of satire to a metapolitical statement on the human condition.

Swift addresses the subject of war—its causes, methods and glorifications—in all four Parts of the *Travels*, and in doing so eventually establishes a thematic consistency that serves to unify the work. In almost every instance it is the distortion inherent in human warfare that is emphasized. Distortion is central to the contrasting perspectives of the Lilliputian microcosm of Part 1 and its inversion, the Brobdingnagian macrocosm, in Part 2 insofar as war is made to look petty in both. Part 3 also features a similar view of military suppression and history, and Part 4 contains the most explicit statement on the escalations of war.[29]

The Lilliputians are heavily armed and ready for the worst when Gulliver first awakes. The first Lilliputian whom Gulliver sees has "a Bow and Arrow in his Hands," and when Gulliver attempts to seize one of the little creatures, the Lilliputians fire two volleys of arrows at him as, Gulliver says, "we do Bombs in Europe" (PW, 11:21–22). Although we may recognize universal human fear and suspicion in their military precautions, everything Lilliputian seems somehow ludicrous simply because of its inconsequentiality in relation to Gulliver, with whom we identify. Swift exaggerates this pettiness, in accordance with the basic technique of the grotesque, in various Lilliputian affairs, of which the best example is Reldresal's account of the perennial Big-Endian–Little-Endian dispute. Once again Swift takes aim at one of his favorite satiric targets—religious fanaticism and how trifling differences escalate into monstrous wars. Readers are not so much struck by his statement on religious fanaticism (the so-called wars of religion that marked the seventeenth century were, as all wars tend to be, struggles for political power) as much as they are by how adroitly he exposes the irrational energy, the suspicion and fear, that is self-perpetuating and self-exaggerating. The fear and its escalation are real; the fantasy element of the egg breaking, for example, emphasizes the ridiculousness of the escalation.

In the *Travels* Swift shows a flair for using fantasy to expose the pervasiveness of the irrational, which would otherwise simply blend in with our conception of the natural, and while he does so from a detached objectivity, he maintains an involved subjective position. For example, the historical allegory of Gulliver's capture of the Blefuscudian fleet expresses Swift's endorsement of the Tory view in the War of the Spanish Succession that advocated a shift away from the struggle on the continent to a naval strike against the Spanish and French overseas trade. To the reader, Gulliver's bloodless mission seems like a natural favor that any decent guest would do for a host.

By Part 4 Gulliver himself seems to have attained that distance required to see the depravity and pettiness in human warfare. First there is again and always "the Ambition of Princes," that most horrible *maxima e minimis*; then there is "the Corruption of Ministers, who engage their Master in a War in order to stifle or divert the Clamour of the Subjects against their evil Administration" (PW, 11:245). The sentiments of Swift as a shrewd political analyst, well aware of the strategy of conducting a foreign war to quell domestic unrest, can easily be heard in Gulliver's comments. Exposed to perfect Houyhnhnm reason, Gulliver sees his estimation of humankind plummet. He now regards human warfare as utter madness caused by the most ridiculous, Lilliputian differences:

Difference in Opinions hath cost many Millions of Lives: For Instance, whether *Flesh* be *Bread* or *Bread* be *Flesh*: Whether the Juice of a certain *Berry* be *Blood* or *Wine*: Whether *Whistling* be a Vice or a Virtue: Whether it be better to *kiss a Post*, or throw it into the Fire: What is the best Colour for a *Coat*, whether *Black, White, Red,* or *Grey;* and whether it should be *long* or *short, narrow* or *wide, dirty* or *clean;* with many more. Neither are any Wars so furious and bloody, or of so long Continuance, as those occasioned by Difference in Opinion, especially if it be in things indifferent.

(*PW*, 11:246)

Transubstantiation, the disputable issue between the Catholics and Protestants, is expressed in low-burlesque or travesty terms as an absurd culinary argument, as it is of course in *A Tale*. One cannot help but remember that Rabelais's Picrocholine War commences between the bakers of Lerné and the wine makers of Seuilly, and Bakhtin points to its "travestied allusion to communion" as being part of the greater celebration of human materiality.[30] Although the overall tone of this section in Part 4 is, as I will show, more satiric than saturnalian, the rhetorical effect of the specific passage above with its repetition of "Difference" and the mundane list of items is purely ludicrous, and our laughter arising from the travesty of theological factions is celebratory.

The "indifferent" differences all represent some subject of religious controversy involving Roman Catholicism, the Church of England and Puritanism. Swift's tendency to single out religious wars for special criticism shows that he is continuing the tradition of learned wit that goes back to Burton and Erasmus.[31] To go to war on a spiritual pretense or crusade is a terrible paradox. Religion should cultivate human benevolence not animosity, as it seems to do—to quote Swift, "We have just Religion enough to make us *hate*, but not enough to make us *love* one another" (*PW*, 1:241). Of course, religious differences are often just a means of polarizing the greater struggle for economic and political power. Nevertheless, by reducing the cause of war to some absurdly expressed religious controversy, such as whether bread be flesh or bread, Swift draws attention to how relatively minor disputes can escalate, through passion, into grotesque violence.

The next part of Gulliver's list of casus belli then reads like a casual, yet *ad absurdum*, statement on the natural human propensity for conflict based on inequality: "Sometimes a War is entered upon, because the Enemy is too *strong*, and sometimes because he is too *weak*. Sometimes our Neighbours *want* the Things which we *have*, or *have* the Things which we want. . ." (*PW*, 11:246). The rhetorical balances in this passage emphasize first a kind of absurd reciprocity of contending wills, and second an ironic yet matter-of-fact implication that this contention is perfectly natural. As Guthkelch and Smith suggest, the statement that "Poor Nations are hungry, and rich Nations are proud; and Pride and Hunger will ever be at Variance" (PW, 11:246), is an echo of the cyclical theory of war which gives rise to a resigned cynicism (G&S, 218, n. 1). Finally, the dialectical exuberance of the passage itself, with its contrasts and checks, reenacts the rhythm of exchange that characterizes human conflicts.

Again in the manner of Burton and Erasmus, Swift lashes out at the profession of the soldier: "For these Reasons, the trade of a Soldier is held the most honourable of all others: Because a Soldier is a Yahoo hired to kill in cold Blood as many of his Species, who have never offended him, as possibly he can" (PW, 11:246–47).[32] The direct association of the soldier with the Yahoo points to the animal in man whose fears are still primitive and who acts with instinctive ruthlessness. On the other hand, the phrase "who never offended him" expresses the artificial nature of how wars are fought between beings who have no personal reason to fight but who are acting out—in a grotesquely disproportionate way—the natural animosities of those whom they serve. Hence, it is not inconsistent to see the origin of human warfare as instinctive (a Hobbesian view) and the esca-lated state of war as artificial. Swift then takes the professional element a step further in Gulliver's reference to George I's mer-cenaries: "There is likewise a Kind of beggarly Princes in Europe, not able to make War by themselves, who hire out their Troops to richer Nations for so much a Day to each Man; of which they keep three Fourths to themselves, and it is the best Part of their Maintenance; such are those in many Northern Parts of Europe" (PW, 11:246). The means of escalation is rationalized according to a strictly professional notion of carrying arms. Swift would certainly have objected to any kind of a Mandeville argument that would hold that the military actually provided employment for the lower classes. In "The Answer to the Craftsman," written in 1730, Swift implies that the granting of recruiting privileges to the French army in Ireland would effectively reduce human life to economic produce (PW, 12:173–78), and Louis Landa has noted that this is the same argument Swift uses in "A Modest Proposal."[33] Justifying militarism on the basis of accrued eco-nomic benefits is almost more disturbing than simply reducing human life to cannon fodder, because in the former grotesque barbarism parades in the guise of economic principle.

In Part 2 this theme of escalation or *maxima e minimis* is

developed in relation to the subject of the war engine. In a last desperate attempt to "ingratiate" himself with the king of Brobdingnag who was disgusted with Gulliver's historical account of England, Gulliver offers to reveal the method of producing gunpowder and, with his Brobdingnagian myopia, goes into unnecessary detail about its potential effects: ". . . we often put this Powder into large hollow Balls of Iron, and discharged them by an Engine into some City we were besieging; which would rip up the Pavement, tear the Houses to Pieces, burst and throw Splinters on every Side, dashing out the Brains of all who came near" (PW, 11:134). Even though Gulliver accuses the king of having "*narrow Principles and short Views*" (PW, 11:135) for refusing the offer, the short view really belongs to Gulliver who assumes that everybody is as unscrupulously power-crazy as his fellow Europeans. The king's large view of "those terrible Engines" is idealistic insofar as "he would rather lose Half his Kingdom than be privy to such a Secret" (PW, 11:118, 119). Swift uses these extreme Machiavellian and philanthropic positions, on the part of Gulliver and the king respectively, to highlight the horror of how humankind has collectively and continually searched for leverage in killing power while remaining undeterred by the actual human and physical costs. In Part 1 the situation is reversed. The emperor of Lilliput wants to use Gulliver to reduce "the whole Empire of *Blefuscu* into a Province" (PW, 11:53), and Gulliver rejects the plan on the same humanitarian grounds that the king of Brobdingnag has for refusing to hear how to make gunpowder.

One is tempted to see Swift's denunciation of artillery simply as a reaction to the horrors of modern siegecraft as it was practised by Marlborough and others; however, there is a long tradition of satiric or grotesque denunciations of war engines that preceded Vauban: the description of Satan's cannon in *Paradise Lost* (bk. 6, lines 693–98), which is "dangerous to the Main"; Burton's condemnation of "our gunpowder machinations" in *The Anatomy of Melancholy*; and Erasmus's indignation at the "*Tartareis machinis*" and "*bombardas*" in *Querela Pacis*.[34] In Part 3 of the *Travels* this theme of the grotesque tools of war is expressed in the Laputian loadstone and the suppression of the Lindalino rebellion.[35] The war engine magnifies the killing power of the aggressor and puts a distance between the aggressor and the victim that often allows the former to remain oblivious to the sufferings of the latter. The Laputian technological edge is, in a sense, matched and nullified by the Lindalino use of Adamant towers that render the loadstone mechanism useless. Hence, Swift gives us his own version of how the arms race shifts into higher gear with each new application of science and how the higher gear always means a greater potential for inflicting death and destruction.

The escalating effect of the war engine is reemphasized in Part 4. When his Houyhnhnm master expresses disbelief at an estimate of a million Yahoo casualties in "the long War with *France*," Gulliver smiles at the Houyhnhnm ignorance of the "Art of War" and goes on to give an encyclopedic list of the latest tools of war and the horrid details of battle:

> . . . I gave him a Description of Cannons, Culverins, Muskets, Carabines, Pistols, Bullets, Powder, Swords, Bayonets, Sieges, Retreats, Attacks, Undermines, Countermines, Bombardments, Sea-fights; Ships sunk with a Thousand Men; twenty Thousand killed on each Side; dying Groans, Limbs flying in the Air: Smoak, Noise, Confusion, trampling to Death under Horses Feet: Flight, Pursuit, Victory; Fields strewed with Carcases left for Food to Dogs, and Wolves, and Birds of Prey; Plundering, Stripping, Ravishing, Burning and Destroying.
>
> (PW, 11:247)

This passage immediately follows the absurd casus belli list analyzed above. It poignantly reasserts the fearful or disturbing quality, which is a necessary part of the grotesque, yet is completely lacking in irony that would produce a ludicrous incongruity as in Voltaire's famous battle description in *Candide* (see the opening to chap. 3). Gulliver, of course, is in the middle of his transition from European to Houyhnhnm values. The new weapons and newfangled terms (e.g., "Bayonets" and "Countermines") denote the modern technology and scientific professionalism as they applied to the military.[36] Yet epic motifs, such as "dying Groans" and "Limbs flying in the Air" (see *Aeneid* 11:618–35), give the passage the impression of universal action and literary tradition. (The same two motifs occur in the description of the main meeting between Crecropia's and Basilius's forces in Sidney's *Arcadia*.[37]) Bakhtin locates this weighted sense of the universal or of "historic process" and stylized form with the grotesque.[38] Swift reminds us that the improved tools of destruction only multiply, exponentially, the perennial miseries of armed conflict.

One could call Gulliver's description a vignette of an actual battle and aftermath, moving as it does from the chaos and horror

Battle of Ramillies, Louis Laguerre (1712). *Courtesy of National Trust, marquess of Anglesey, Plas Newydd.* Stripped corpses, flight, pursuit, and plundering are all depicted in this episode of the battle of Ramillies (Marlborough House, staircase). Print provided by Courtauld Institute of Art.

of the battle itself to the slow dying, pillage, rape, and destruction that follow. According to the notion of the *ut pictura poesis*, the vignette can easily be related to contemporary battle scenes as represented in prints and decorative art, and scholars might profitably explore this connection. To be specific, the second part of Gulliver's description ("trampling to Death under Horses Feet") bears a remarkable similarity to Louis Laguerre's episodes of the battle of Ramillies that were commissioned and done for the main staircase in Marlborough House.[39] These scenes feature trampling horses, figures in flight and pursuit, the English victory, and subsequent plundering and stripping of the enemy. Nude carcasses and bodies are also rather prominent. One figure has a haunting expression of terror in his eyes as he runs in vain from the English victors—truly an image to entertain the eye as one saunters upstairs! It is, of course, likely that this latter figure owes something to the attention that Charles LeBrun, the decorative director at Versailles and Laguerre's former instructor, paid to human physiognomy. The irony of Louis Laguerre, godson of Louis XIV, being commissioned to paint a series on the victories of Louis's arch-enemy Marlborough is striking. For unknown reasons, Laguerre left France to pursue a career in England the year that LeBrun finished the ceiling series in the *Grande Galerie des Glaces*, which commemorated the conquests of the Sun King (1684).[40] Modeling much of his work on that of his master and other battle-piece artists, Laguerre had—in addition to his name—the qualifications that would have appealed to a nation that in the words of Farquhar's Archer had occasion to match "Alexander's battles": "We want only a Le Brun . . . to draw greater battles, and a greater general [Marlborough] of our own. The Danube . . . would make a greater figure in a picture than the Granicus; and we have our Ramilies to match their Arbela."[41] "Alexander's battles," of course, refer to those done by LeBrun and displayed in 1673; their popularity is evinced by the fact that official engravings of them were sold in England. Laguerre did the battle episodes that adorn the hall and staircases of Marlborough House in 1713, the year before Swift left for Ireland. When Thornhill was dismissed from Blenheim by the fiery Duchess, Laguerre was an obvious choice for a successor and he completed the murals and ceiling of the Blenheim saloon in 1720.[42]

Laguerre would have been pressured by Marlborough to capture a sense of authentic detail about the battle of Ramillies, and so it is not surprising that the scenes in Marlborough House are based on contemporary prints now in the National Army Museum. Although it is doubtful that Swift saw Laguerre's work in Marlborough House (one can hardly imagine an invitation), the fact that many of the scenes were copied from other sources makes it possible that he had a familiarity with the general genre. That famous battle-pieces were reproduced as popular cultural artifacts is demonstrated by Jacques Casanova's brother, François, who earned a living by copying the battle-pieces of Simonetti.

Laguerre's battle-pieces for Marlborough House emphasize the grisliness and horror of war in a realistic mode and, as such, are certainly less conventional as decorative art than the highly mythical war subjects in LeBrun's work at Versailles, de Vos's sedate and stately scenes in the Blenheim tapestries, or Thornhill's ceiling of the great hall at Blenheim. In the latter, the Duke of Marlborough is depicted presenting—in mythic style—the battle plan for Blenheim to her Majesty, Queen Anne. This allegorical emphasis closely resembles what Norman Bryson sees in the work of LeBrun—the power of text, or discursive history, over image, or figural composition.[43] While recognizing that LeBrun's kind of art exposes a "lack of imagination," Bryson goes on to argue that it shows "a striking symmetry of intellectual design"; he also believes that war, which lends itself to such design or discursive history, is perhaps "the most ancient, and certainly one of the most powerful, of rhetorical *topoi*."[44] It might be noted that Laguerre painted the ceiling of the Blenheim saloon in the classical style of LeBrun. However, in the Marlborough House scenes Laguerre does not mythologize by classical association or historical distance. The realistic horror depicted in these scenes may be more indebted to the style of François van der Meulen and his pupil Jean Baptiste Martin ("Martin des Batailles"), who designed the second set of tapestries for Louis XIV.[45] Other works in which one can recognize the same style of realistic horror include Lemke's series of paintings for Charles XI of Sweden in which, according to Wace, one finds "horsemen in active conflict [and] corpses,"[46] or the set of tapestries that Mitté wove for the Archduke Charles V of Lorraine. The latter includes a piece entitled, "The Battle of Mohacs," which illustrates, again in Wace's words, "little more than a revolting group of headless and naked corpses piled round the edge of a pool."[47] It might be said that both Swift and Laguerre chose to draw attention to the "gawk" factor in how humankind regards military events.

Yet despite the visual impact of Gulliver's imagery, the ultimate effect of the battle description has to do with its language. Accordingly, it could be argued that there is a rhetorical vitality in Gulliver's list that recalls Rabelais's grotesque descriptions of the Picrocholine War in Book 1 of *Gargantua and Pantagruel*. However, the tone is clearly not as festive as it is in Rabelais, a fact that may be cited as evidence for Bakhtin's argument that the grotesque lost its living tie with folk culture after the Renaissance and became clearly more satiric than saturnalian.[48] Claude Rawson perceptively assesses the Rabelaisian exuberance in Swift: "The combination of exuberance and astringency permits some hideous energies to come to life, without letting the exuberance itself turn into a Rabelaisian joy in abundance."[49] The "energies" that Rawson speaks of are explicable according to the ludicrous-fearful interaction of the grotesque. While Swift's subject matter is perfectly disturbing, the cumulative effect of Gulliver's rhetorical momentum and of the battle vignette on the heels of "Whether *Whistling* be a Vice or a Virtue" strikes us as ludicrous. Moreover, Swift's language, resembling what Frye describes as a "verbal tempest" or "verbal exuberance,"[50] is made to imitate the unrestrained violence of war. Form and content truly merge.

After Gulliver's elaborate description, the Houyhnhnm concludes "that instead of Reason" mankind was "only possessed of some Quality fitted to increase [his] natural Vices" (*PW*, 11:248). This kind of rational skepticism can be easily traced to Hobbes and others.[51] As Rochester says so well in his "Satyr Against Reason and Mankind" (1675), man's reason is completely in the service of his fear—a circumstance that gives him all the more reason to fear: "For fear he arms, and is of arms afraid; / By fear to fear successively betrayed."[52] The predicament reflects what is intrinsically grotesque about human conflict.

In contrast to the Houhynhnms, the Brobdingnagians represent a more practical view of conflict and the military in their use of militias rather than standing armies (*PW*, 11:131). The militia option reflects Temple's Tory politics and may itself be termed idealistic insofar as most European countries relied on standing armies to ensure a certain stability at home and a readiness to fight abroad.[53] Ironically, the Tory argument, repeated by Swift, was that standing armies in times of peace threatened domestic stability. Of course, the Tories had a hidden political motive for favoring locally controlled militias; these militias remained in the hands of the Tory landowners as opposed to Parliament. However, the Tory position against standing armies remained weak against the new professionalism and pragmatism of the Whigs and writers like Defoe who saw the necessity of a permanent armed force.[54] Ultimately, one may see Swift's negative comments on the institutionalization of armed force not just as a criticism of the "moneyed interest" who stood to benefit therefrom but also as a more idealistically inspired statement on how naturally humankind capitulates to international fear and suspicion.[55]

Although Gulliver points to pride as the most despicable human passion, fear clearly dominates the action of the *Travels*. We have already seen how natural the Lilliputian fear of Gulliver is. The Brobdingnagian militia is maintained out of a natural fear of civil rebellion. When necessary, the Laputian island is lowered onto rebellious towns "with great Gentleness, out of a Pretence of Tenderness . . . but indeed for fear of breaking the Adamantine Bottom" (*PW*, 11:172). Gulliver is exiled from Houyhnhnmland because "it was to be feared" (*PW*, 11:279) that whatever faculty distinguished Gulliver from the Yahoos could be used to organize the Yahoos into a striking force against Houyhnhnm settlements. These examples all point to the naturalness of fear as a reaction to the unknown. What becomes not so much unnatural behavior as ludicrous distortion is the extreme consequence of this reaction, and it may be said that excessive irrationality marks the last instance of fear in the *Travels*—Gulliver's dread of returning to live among European Yahoos. (In contrast, his efforts to neigh and trot like a horse are perfectly unnatural as well as ludicrous.) After leaving Houyhnhnmland, Gulliver tries to avoid the Portuguese ship and resolves to take his chances on another island inhabited by savages, even after they attack and wound him in the knee with an arrow (*PW*, 11:284). Tracing the depiction of the military and violence in the *Travels* as manifestations of Hobbesian fear is a means of documenting Swift's grotesque view of humankind.

The other human passion that is responsible for war and that Swift depicts as being perfectly natural is the competitive propensity to conquer or to control whatever may be of some use. The subject of colonial conquest arises logically when Gulliver has finished his travels and is asked about his duty to advise the secretary of state on the lands that he, as a British subject, has supposedly claimed for the crown. At first, Gulliver dodges the moral issue. He doubts whether the countries to which he had traveled will be as easy to conquer as the "naked *Americans*" were for "*Ferdinando Cortez*" (*PW*, 11:293). In Gulliver's view, the Lilliputians "are hardly worth the Charge of a Fleet and Army to reduce them" (*PW*, 11:293). He then wonders "whether it might be prudent or safe to attempt the *Brobdingnagians*: Or, whether an *English* Army would be much at their Ease with the Flying Island over their Heads" (*PW*, 11:293). Gulliver, however, must admit that the Houyhnhnms, being rational creatures, are not "so well prepared for War, a Science to which they are perfect Strangers, and especially against missive Weapons" (*PW*, 11:293). But when Gulliver estimates their defense capacity and claims that they are stronger for their "Unacquaintedness with Fear" (*PW*, 11:293), he is forgetting the reason for his own banishment. In any case, Gulliver expresses his own view on how European Yahoos could benefit from the Houyhnhnms: "But instead of Proposals for conquering that magnanimous Nation, I rather wish they were in a Capacity or Disposition to send a sufficient Number of their Inhabitants for civilizing *Europe*" (*PW*, 11:293–94). All this, however, is peripheral to the right of conquest issue.

Gulliver finally admits to having a "few Scruples" about the standard European methods of establishing colonies and empires. What follows is a gruesomely satiric account of the "*modern Colony*":

> A crew of Pyrates are driven by a Storm they know not whither; at length a Boy discovers Land from the Top-mast; they go on Shore to rob and plunder; they see an harmless People, are entertained with Kindness, they give the Country a new Name, they take formal Possession of it for the King, they set up a rotten Plank or a Stone for a Memorial, they murder two or three Dozen of the Natives, bring away a Couple more by Force for a Sample, return home, and get their Pardon. Here commences a new Dominion acquired with a Title by *Divine Right*. Ships are sent with the first Opportunity; the Natives driven out or destroyed, their Princes tortured to discover their Gold; a free Licence given to all Acts of Inhumanity and Lust; the Earth reeking with the Blood of its Inhabitants: And this execrable Crew of Butchers employed in so pious an Expedition, is a *modern Colony* sent to convert and civilize an idolatrous and barbarous people.
>
> (*PW*, 11:294)

Here we have another one of Swift's brilliant vignettes. The references to "Gold" in the quoted passage and "*Ferdinando Cortez*" in the preceding paragraph are enough to satisfy most readers that Spanish colonialism in the Americas is the primary implication. Sharp ironic statements build toward the climax, which resounds with the epic grotesque, "the Earth reeking with the Blood of its Inhabitants."[56] After a sarcastic description of the "Wisdom, Care, and Justice" of the "*British* Nation" in planting colonies, Gulliver simply concludes that "as those Countries which I have described do not appear to have a Desire of being conquered, and enslaved, murdered or driven out by Colonies; nor abound either in Gold, Silver, Sugar or Tobacco; I did humbly conceive they were by no Means proper Objects of our Zeal, our Valour, or our Interest" (*PW*, 11:295). The brutality and greed in the first part of the statement heighten the ironic context of the word "Valour," which otherwise would sit inconspicuously between "Zeal" and "Interest."

Another grotesque distortion is the glorification of war and its corollary, the ambition to attain glory through military conquests. The obvious example is, of course, the emperor of Lilliput, who desires the complete submission of Blefuscu—a wish that leads Gulliver to remark that "unmeasurable is the Ambition of Princes" (*PW*, 11:53). Not only is this passion for military conquest a distortion of true glory, but language is used to distort the truth and create the semblance of glory, as seen in the descriptive title of the Lilliputian emperor as the "Delight and Terror of the Universe" (*PW*, 11:43).[57]

This idea of linguistic distortion is reintroduced in Part 2 as a commentary on historical discourse and the tendency of history to emphasize military events. When Gulliver finishes his account of England to the king of Brobdingnag, he admits to a "laudable Partiality to [his] own Country": "I would hide the Frailties and Deformities of my Political Mother, and place her Virtues and Beauties in the most advantageous Light" (*PW*, 11:133). Ironically, the king first laughs at Gulliver's account of England's "Wars by Sea and Land" just as the reader might laugh at the conflict between Lilliput and Blefuscu (*PW*, 11:106). Gulliver feels insulted initially, but, after adjusting to his miniature status, comes to see the king's response as more natural than contemptuous. The king even tries to give Gulliver a sober second hearing, but the particulars that appear reasonable to Gulliver remain trivial in the king's perspective: "He wondered to hear me talk of such chargeable and extensive Wars; that, certainly we must be a quarrelsome People, or live among very bad Neighbours" (*PW*, 11:131). At least the Brobdingnagian understands what Gulliver is saying, unlike the Houyhnhnms who have no name for "War" nor any concept of its art (*PW*, 11:244).[58] The lack of a Houyhnhnm word for war, a clear indication of war's irrationality, makes European history a difficult matter for Gulliver to communicate to his Houyhnhnm master.

Since the particulars of English politics are beyond Brobdingnagian perception, the king finally pronounces Gulliver's "historical account" as being "only an Heap of Conspiracies, Rebellions, Murders, Massacres" (*PW*, 11:132). His statement constitutes a grotesque commentary on historical discourse and historiography that looks forward to Gibbon's famous declaration that the "materials of history" are "little more than the register of the crimes, follies, and misfortunes of mankind."[59] History, depending primarily on the writer's focus and the reader's impression, often seems like nothing more than an ad infinitum narrative of human war-making, and the resulting rhetorical momentum, like *amplificato,* can produce a ludicrous effect as in Burton's tirade against war in the "Satyricall Preface" of the *Anatomy* (*AM*, 1:55–61). In Bakhtinian terms, history is dialogic—is shaped into spectacle by the reader as well as the writer. The interesting point is that the narrative is often only meant to be accurate and exhaustive, as it is in Temple's own

Introduction to the History of England and "Of Heroic Virtue,"
which seem excessive in their concentration on the matter-of-
factness of war. Temple himself obviously sensed this and concluded "Of Heroic Virtue" with a statement on the greater virtue
of peaceful achievements over military ones, a statement which
appears too contrived and hence falls flat.[60] On the subject of war
and its history or representation, Bryson argues that the enact-
ment of war is equivalent to narrative—put another way, we
understand battles as a series of strategic events. In light of this
sequential emphasis, it may be said that the lowest level of
historiography "consists almost exclusively in a listing of battles" as the "interpretative discipline is at a minimum."[61]
Gulliver's accounts of Europe to the Brobdingnagian king and
later to his Houyhnhnm master amount to burlesques of such
historiography.

Reldresal's explanation of the Big-Endian–Little-Endian conflict implicitly points to how current wars are easily justified by
history's concentration on previous ones: "that our Histories tell
us, there have been six Rebellions raised on that Account" (*PW*,
11:49). Moreover, Gulliver's impression from reading Brobdingnagian histories is that the Brobdingnagians "have been
troubled with the same Disease, to which the whole Race of
Mankind is Subject; the Nobility often contending for Power, the
People for Liberty, and the King for absolute Dominion" (*PW*,
11:138). Swift's own fragmentary history of England, as
Ehrenpreis remarks, shows a concerted effort to focus on consti-
tutional issues as opposed to wars.[62] For Swift, humankind is
responsible not just for creating spectacular violence but for
remembering and recording it spectacularly as well.

The prospect of human history as an endless and hence inevitable series of wars is a fearful one, yet it is precisely this idea of
inexorability that can allow for a ludicrous response. Gulliver
believes that the immortal Struldbruggs must have "the *Pleasure*
of seeing the various Revolutions of States and Empires. . . .
Barbarity overrunning the politest Nations, and the most barbarous becoming civilized" (*PW*, 11:210, my emphasis).[63] Such
"Revolutions" are essentially mechanistic, and the mechanistic,
according to Kayser, characterizes the grotesque.[64] This cyclical
view of history, as we have seen, is traceable to ancient historians
via Temple. Swift, however, usually describes the cycle as going
from the barbarous to the civilized as in the portrait of colonial
aggression; this idea is also a recurrent theme in Temple's gener-
alizations about war.[65] Although Swift's tone is more sarcastic

than that of Rabelais, the belief in a determined course of events essentially constitutes another example of Bakhtin's "merry time" arising from a predictable "historic process."[66]

Swift returns to the subject of military history as fascination and fiction in Gulliver's visit to Glubbdubdrib or the Island of Sorcerers in Part 3. Given the chance to summon anybody he wants from the dead, Gulliver first wishes to see famous military leaders in "Scenes of Pomp and Magnificence": "*Alexander* the Great, at the Head of his Army just after the Battle of *Arbela*," "*Hannibal* passing the *Alps*," and "*Caesar* and *Pompey* at the Head of their Troops just ready to engage" (*PW*, 11:195). These military subjects have been made notorious through the discourse of history, and it is possible that Swift meant to mock the popularity of battle scenes in the decorative painting or historical *tableaux* of artists like LeBrun and Laguerre.[67] As we have seen, Laguerre in the Marlborough House paintings dwells on the spectacle of war's reality, not its myth of glory. Perhaps Laguerre's most provocative decorative art pieces are the murals in the Blenheim saloon. These depict representatives from the four continents (Laguerre himself among the Europeans) all staring forward in homage to the Duke, something like the historic personages coming forward to Gulliver. Moreover, Gulliver, entertained by "Scenes of Pomp and Magnificence" brings to mind de Vos's Blenheim tapestries that replay the Duke's famous victories on the walls of the state rooms for the pleasure of the beholder.

We may digress for a moment on the subject of Blenheim and military glorification. Blenheim Palace is not just adorned by decorative military art, it embodies the very military spirit of the nation as it was blazoned forth by Marlborough. Versailles may have its *salon de la guerre* or even its salon of Mars, but unlike Blenheim it is not in its entirety an architectural monument dedicated to military conquest. Correlli Barnett describes Blenheim as "massive and masculine, it looms across the English countryside like the charge of a victorious army."[68] Another critic writes, "The straight and curving colonnades, projecting and receding masses, and shifting perspectives, recall the manoeuvres of a great military parade, with fanfares of trumpets and drums finding their equivalent in Grinling Gibbons's carved stone grenades, vases, [and] statues . . ."[69] Nor can one forget the thirty-ton bust of the Sun King plundered from Tournai and hoisted above the central portico of the south front, in the words of Jackson-Stops, "like a head upon a pike."[70] One might quote the satirical poem "On Blenheim House" (1714) as a text for a brief guided tour: "There lies the bridge, and here's the clock: / Observe the lion and the cock."[71] Emblems of the English success against the French are everywhere, from the English lion killing the French cock, to the inverted *fleur-de-lis* designs that serve as bases for the numerous grenades and that also appear on Hensington Gate. In a word, Blenheim is the grandiose product of its architects and craftsmen (people like Gibbons and de Vos) who worked as a result of the wave of exuberance that swept through the country after Marlborough's famous victory and subsequent grant of Woodstock by Queen Anne. Vanbrugh himself, the first and chief architect, said that Blenheim was to be "a Royall and a National Monument" and that he viewed it "much more as an intended Monument of the Queens Glory, than a private Habitation for the Duke of Marlborough."[72] This vision, of course, partially accounts for his conflicts with the Duchess, who had more modest designs. It should be noted, however, that these comments were made in letters to Lord Poulet (September 1710), who had just replaced Godolphin as treasurer. Vanbrugh, aware that the ministry was less favorably disposed towards Marlborough, was concerned that the funding of Blenheim would be cut off and hence tried to diminish its function as the Duke's private house while enhancing its public and royal associations.

Swift's disgust at the national expense of Blenheim Palace is well known from his *Examiner*, No. 16. He had mocked Vanbrugh's "deep Rudiments" in architecture and his Blenheim appointment as early as the 1706 poem, "The History of Vanburg's House":

> . . . if his Grace were no more skilld in
> The Art of battring Walls, than building,
> We might expect to find next Year
> A Mousetrap-man chief Engineer.
> (*Poems* 1:87–88, lines 35, 45–48)

But it is not until *Gulliver's Travels* that we find an indictment of military spectacle as decorative art. Evans's lines humorously express the stock deflationary criticism of Blenheim: "'tis very fine, / But where d'ye sleep, or where d'ye dine?" while a canceled Pope couplet states the objection more solemnly: "Alas what *wealth*, which no one act of fame / E'er taught to shine, or sanctified from shame."[73] After a visit to Blenheim, Pope wrote in a letter that it was "the most proud & extravagant Heap of Towers in the nation."[74] As Morris Brownell contends, Blenheim had become notorious for its ostentatious opulence, and Timon's villa in the "Epistle to Burlington" may well represent Pope's criticism of it.[75]

With a typical Swiftian bias, Gulliver claims to be "chiefly disgusted with modern History," which has attributed "the greatest Exploits in War to Cowards" (PW, 11:199). War itself he discovers to be an extremely haphazard affair—a view that may have come to Swift through Polybius.[76] A general renowned for some great victory admits it was ironically owing to his "Cowardice and ill Conduct" (PW, 11:199). Likewise, a misinformed admiral defeats the "Enemy to whom he intended to betray the Fleet" (PW, 11:199).[77] The unjust treatment of another admiral, who sees a youth related to one of the "Emperor's Mistresses" (PW, 11:201) promoted over him, reminds Gulliver that bedroom patronage rather than merit determines military preferment. Starkman claims that the story bears some resemblance to the life of the Duke of Peterborough, Swift's friend.[78] This may be so, but it might be more accurate to say that allegorically speaking the story is, like Part 1 of the *Travels*, a composite of various figures and events related to the subject of bedroom patronage. For instance, the Duchess of Kendal, who was George I's mistress, took a tremendous bribe for getting Wood his coinage patent. It should also be noted that in 1711, Swift himself used his influence to secure Lieutenant Bernage, Esther Johnson's friend, a promotion to captain-lieutenant with a clear path to the captaincy as soon as it became available.[79] Still, in the *Travels* Swift effectively asks how much of military honor is legitimate and why is it that the human imagination needs to fabricate military heroism in the first place. The reference in the following paragraph to "the whole Praise as well as Pillage" being unjustly "engrossed by the chief Commander" (PW, 11:201) is obviously another slur on Marlborough—for Swift, the greatest example of an undeserving military hero.

The literary-historic fascination with recorded battles is only a substitute for live military entertainment. Both the Lilliputians and Brobdingnagians indulge in military exercises and parades, and Swift clearly means to comment on the popularity of such events as public spectacles. The Lilliputian army goes through its drills and mock battles on a stage constructed by Gulliver: ". . . the Emperor was so much delighted, that he ordered this Entertainment to be repeated several Days" (PW, 11:40). Later the emperor of Lilliput gets his army to march between Gulliver's legs—a parade which, considering the poor condition of Gulliver's breeches, "afforded some Opportunities for Laughter and Admiration" (PW, 11:42). Masculinity makes a ludicrous display. From the Lilliputian ridiculous we go to the Brobdingnagian sublime as Gulliver is treated to a sword drill by the Lorbrulgrud militia of giants. It appears "so Grand, so surprising and so astonishing" that it was "as if ten thousand Flashes of Lightning were darting at the same time from every Quarter of the Sky" (PW, 11:138). Earlier Gulliver had termed the "Militia Guard of five hundred Horse . . . the most splendid Sight that could be ever beheld" (PW, 11:115). Part of Gulliver's own act as a miniature creature consists of a pike-drill using "Part of a Straw" (PW, 11:98). While on his third voyage, Gulliver must walk between "two Rows of Guards, armed and dressed after a very antick Manner" on his way into the Glubbdubdrib Palace, and "something in their Countenances" makes his "Flesh creep with . . . Horror" (PW, 11:194). This kind of military play or delightful form appeals to our aesthetic pleasure in grand, artificial enactments of order and precision. Burke's ideas on the artificial infinite as a source of the sublime are applicable here. Burke identifies "infinity" as potentially creating "that sort of delightful horror, which is the most genuine effect, and truest test of the sublime," and he goes on to argue, "Succession and *uniformity* of parts, are what constitute the artificial infinite."[80] Finally, this notion of an artificial infinite or the impression of infinity created by a series of identical members (as in rows of red coats) is structurally close to the concepts of historical recurrence and rhetorical amplification.

Military maneuvers, however, are poor spectacles when compared to the actual battlefield. In Part 4 Gulliver finishes his grotesque description of the "Art of War" with an even more disturbing image of how the morbid human imagination is drawn to such sensational scenes of destruction and death:

> . . . to set forth the Valour of my own dear Countrymen, I assured him, that I had seen them blow up a Hundred Enemies at once in a Siege, and as many in a Ship; and beheld the dead bodies drop down in Pieces from the Clouds, to the great Diversion of all the Spectators.
> (PW, 11:247)

Swift seems to be referring to the popularity of witnessing a siege-bombardment as if it were a fireworks show.[81] In Fortescue's words, the "Court of Versailles was particularly fond of a siege, since it could attend the ceremony in state and take nominal charge of the operations with much glory and little discomfort or danger."[82] The attraction, or "horrifying human need for ugliness" as Graeme Green expresses it, is explained by Clayborough as being the repulsion-fascination paradox that, like the fearful-ludicrous duality, is part of the grotesque's power of ambivalence.[83] It is clear that humankind possesses a morbid curiosity about death and violence. This spectator element, which peaked with the limited warfare of the eighteenth century, brings us back to the idea of war as sport or a game.

Swift was exceptional in his awareness of how fear and mechanical art could distort human conflict, and how history exaggerated the importance, if not the relentlessness, of military events. This distortion naturally gives rise to the spectacle of violence in war and the spectacle of war in history. In other words, Swift reminds us not just of how intrinsically grotesque the modern art of war is but how much of the discourse of war is grotesque as well. Epic gruesomeness is requisite to meet the demand for literary or historical entertainment on the part of the reader. The genesis of some of these concepts—war as a manifestation of the *maxima e minimis* doctrine, for instance—can be located in works prior to the *Travels*, but it is only in the latter that Swift gives them full expression.

3

Smollett: The Grotesque View of Military Service

Military Livelihoods, Mutilation, and the Cartagena Expedition

FEW NOVELS BEGIN with such grotesque action as that of Smollett's *Ferdinand Count Fathom*—the hero's mother covers a battlefield, stabbing wounded soldiers to death and filling her bag with the spoils as methodically and nonchalantly as one might shuck peas.[1] In addition to being a professional plunderer, Ferdinand's mother works as a camp cook and sutler, and these positions confirm her dependence on the military for her livelihood.[2] What is grotesque about the situation is the incongruity of subsisting, or earning one's living, on death and the forces of death (a variation of the scavenger motif). And so like uncle Toby she mourns the peace of Utrecht and prays that "Europe might speedily be involved in a general war, so as that she might have some chance of reinjoying the pleasures and emoluments of a Flanders campaign" (*FCF*, 11). Still this "English Penthesilea" (*FCF*, 14) is more than a ruthless plunderer; she joins Prince Eugene's campaign and is devoutly committed to the cause of Christendom against the Turks. She even tries to encourage the Prince's ranks by boasting that "she had been eye-witness of ten decisive engagements, in all of which her friends had been victorious, and imputing such uncommon good fortune to some supernatural quality inherent in her person" (*FCF*, 14). More importantly, her main concern is to educate her son in the art of warfare by giving him a firsthand view of the campaign. It is also significant that her one act of charity—the saving of Count Melvil—earns her more than killing him would have, for in gratitude the Count adopts Ferdinand and brings him up with the expectation of seeing his preferment in a military career.[3] Despite his martial background and initiation, or perhaps because of it, Ferdinand grows up to resist a military life.

Nevertheless Smollett's novels—especially *Roderick Random*, the central text to be discussed in this chapter—are rife with military characters and hence serve as reminders that soldiers and sailors were a conspicuous part of European society in the eighteenth century. As contentious as the debate sometimes gets over whether or not Smollett is a writer of the picaresque, it can safely be said that from the time of the Thirty Years' War (1618–48), many of the novels commonly associated with the picaresque contain military episodes.[4] The association can be said to begin with the anonymous *Estebanillo González* (1646) and Grimmelshausen's *Simplicissimus* (1668), which portray their heroes' involvements in the bloody Thirty Years' War.[5] However, Nashe's *The Unfortunate Traveller* (1594) predates these and also includes military episodes. In the early eighteenth century, there is Defoe's *Colonel Jack* (1722). The main reason for this association is obvious and does not stretch the case for Roderick's *picaro* nature—the military was often the last resort for those who had no other livelihood. Hence, fictional biographies or autobiographies (the letter pertains to the picaresque—i.e., the *picaro* tells his own story) that contain some vestiges of the low picaresque world can be expected to depict military episodes. An important aspect of the military livelihood is the issue of patronage and preferment that is crucial to the history of a number of Smollett's characters: uncle Bowling, Commodore Trunnion, Godfrey Gauntlet, and Lismahago; their plights and the subject of purchased commissions are addressed in the next chapter, which deals with Fielding's *Amelia*.

The association between war and the picaresque should come as no surprise since the picaresque portrays a violent and corrupt world in which the hero must make his way by either becoming ruthless himself or developing survival tactics. (Whether *Roderick Random* should be called "picaresque" may be debatable, but the novel certainly depicts a world characterized by brutal violence.[6]) The ruthless option seems to best describe Ferdinand Count Fathom, Jack Wilton and Estebanillo Gonzáles; Simplicissimus and Candide represent the opposite insofar as war is the first harsh reality that touches their otherwise perfectly innocent and naive existences. Roderick Random is somewhere in between; he has neither Wilton's mercenary attitude nor the boastfulness of Estebanillo. His naïveté with regard to the military is evident in how he resolves to enlist in the foot guards and dreams of "charging the enemy" at the head of his own regiment.[7] On the other hand, he is not the innocent that Candide and Simplicissimus are, and once pressed on board the Thunder he soon sheds any sense of the "military Don Quixotism" (*PP*, 695) that influences the life of Mr. M—— in *Peregrine Pickle*. Nor does Roderick show the strong interest in military history and affairs that draws Nashe's Jack Wilton and Defoe's Colonel Jack to the battlefield.

It was suggested in the previous chapter that time created a sense of distance between satirists and the objects of their satire and that this distance allowed for the development of a grotesque vision. The theory, at least, could partially account for Swift's travesty of the Spanish Succession War in Part 1 of the *Travels* as opposed to his politically inspired *Conduct of the Allies*. With Smollett and the Cartagena episode of *Roderick Random* (1748), however, the situation is more complex. Two leading scholars on Smollett concur in the belief that the grotesque naval passages of *Roderick Random* were based on a personal diary that Smollett kept on the expedition, which occurred seven years before the novel was published.[8] Conversely, Smollett's more straightforward history and criticism of the expedition came sometime later in "An Account of the Expedition against Carthagene," published anonymously in *The Compendium of Authentic and Entertaining Voyages* (1756). According to Martz, what had seemed "utter folly to the choleric young surgeon's mate became somewhat more understandable upon a mature and calm consideration of objective accounts."[9] Hence, one is tempted to say that time cultivated Swift's grotesque vision but dissolved Smollett's.

Such a conclusion is, however, simplistic. First, even if Smollett did keep a diary, *Roderick Random* was written long after the expedition took place and this probably contributed to its heightened sense of the comic grotesque in comparison to the "Account." In any case, it must be admitted that the "Account" itself contains some grotesque passages that are very similar to those in the novel, so that there is a certain consistency in Smollett's attitude. Unlike Swift, who only knew war in a literary form, Smollett had actually witnessed the spectacular horror of battle and was probably permanently affected by his first impressions. In addition, this discussion ignores the more important issues of literary form and purpose. Both *The Conduct of the Allies* and "An Account of the Expedition against Carthagene" were written in a straightforward manner and meant to convince readers of definite political opinions. *Gulliver's Travels* and *Roderick Random*, on the other hand, are both fictional worlds that exist quite apart from the respective realities that inspired them. Martz recognizes this point in discussing Smollett's novel and perceptively reconciles the fiction to the author's purpose as expressed in the preface: ". . . [Smollett] was justified in warping the facts to achieve his implied purpose in the novel as a whole: to arouse 'that generous indignation which ought to animate the reader, against the sordid and vicious disposition of the world.' "[10]

Roderick's views on the horrors of the Cartagena expedition foreshadow the absurdities that attend his involvement in the battle of Dettingen. The Cartagena expedition was part of the War of Jenkins's Ear (1739–44) which pitted Britain against Spain for control of the Caribbean and which merged with the greater War of the Austrian Succession (1740–48). The War of Jenkins's Ear?! Henry Veits explains how the conflict came to be known by such a ridiculous name:

> Jenkins's brig *Rebecca*, returning from Jamaica to London, was boarded by the [Spanish] guarda-costa off Havana on April 9, 1731. The brig was plundered and one of Jenkins's ears was cut off. This outrage caused considerable stir in London, where Jenkins finally arrived on the Thames, minus his ear. The affair died down, only to be revived in 1738, when Jenkins was examined before a committee of the House of Commons. The story lost nothing in the telling; the ear was even produced for the benefit of the committee. Public indignation was aroused and the "War of Jenkins's Ear" ensued.[11]

The imagination could not conjure up a more ludicrous and fearful pretext for going to war than that of a severed ear! Even though the underlying cause (i.e., control of the lucrative West Indies trade) went well beyond Jenkins's mutilation, there is an irrational morbidity in how wars come by their names.

Roderick first resolves to enlist in the navy because it is the only way he can support himself. He delays doing so until he is absolutely desperate: "I saw no resource but the army or navy, between which I hesitated so long, that I found myself reduced to a starving condition" (*RR*, 139). Similarly, Don Diego in *Ferdinand Count Fathom* must enlist after being "reduced to extreme indigence" (*FCF*, chap. 62). The eighteenth century was no different from many other ages insofar as the military offered a means of employment for those in need, and contemporary fictions reflect this sociological factor. Despite his interest in military affairs, Defoe's Colonel Jack only enlists in Douglas's Regiment because he is destitute and has no other means of survival. Jack's belief that serving in the army was "not unbecoming a Gentleman" is an expression of the positive view of the military career as an honorable profession, a view to which Defoe subscribed.[12] However, this positive view is undermined later in the novel when Colonel Jack, having attained a degree of success in trade, remarks, "I had no dislike to the Business of the Army, but I thought I was a little above it now; and had other things to look to, for that in my Opinion, no Body went into the Field but those that cou'd not live at Home."[13] One might also remember that Tom Jones, having lost his five-hundred-pound note to Black George and without any other prospect in the world, is resolved to go to sea (a seafaring life, like the military, seems to be the other refuge for the indigent) when he meets with the soldiers headed to fight against the Jacobite rebels and joins them as a volunteer.

The beginning of Roderick's military career is actually an interesting combination of personal necessity and coercive violence. On his way to seek a friend's advice about enlisting, Roderick is beaten and pressed aboard the Thunder, a British man-of-war. Boucé points out that Tower Hill, where the abduction takes place, was a favorite spot for the press-gang.[14] This incident is a fitting initiation into the military world. Contemporary prints emphasized the brutality of the press, and violent incidents were frequent.[15] (Playbills would even include notices of a press-gang's willingness to suspend operations the night of a performance.[16]) When Roderick's uncle captains a trading vessel some years later and puts in at Spitheads, thirty members of his crew are pressed (RR, 420).[17] It might be said that the press-gang serves as a symbolic reminder in the novel of how individuals are trapped by the greater sweeps of human conflict.

Although the army never had the equivalent impressment rights, the various Recruiting Acts during the Spanish Succession War were in effect a draft of all unemployed men and some criminals, and would swell Marlborough's ranks with what Fortescue refers to as "the scum of the nation."[18] Similar Recruiting Acts were passed during subsequent wars. Aggressive recruiting practices, such as those used on Voltaire's Candide (see *Candide*, chap. 2), were the norm in times of need. Before Roderick even reaches London, he encounters a recruiting officer who has a nightmare about two recently enlisted "country fellows" who had mutinied and threatened to murder him. The sergeant's nocturnal howl, "Blood and wounds! run the halbert into the guts of him that's next you [presumably his corporal], and I'll blow the other's brains out . . ." (RR, 43) and the nightmare itself reflect the desperate violence that characterized the relationship between the aggressive and deceitful recruiting officer and his target recruit. The corrupt means of enlisting men did create great opportunities for jests. No doubt the popularity of Farquhar's *The Recruiting Officer* depended upon facetious humor like that provided by Sergeant Kite who presses a miner because he "has no visible means of a livelihood, for he works underground" (*RO* 5.5.88–89).

Still, Roderick is never the victim of a wily recruiting officer. After leaving the navy, he decides to leave England, which he calls "the worst country in the universe for a poor honest man to live in" (*RR*, 236), and goes abroad to seek his fortune. Unfortunately for Roderick, men are no less corrupt in France than they are in England, and he is once again reduced to dire straits. At the nadir of his despair, he happens to meet members of the Picardy regiment who are on a picnic with their families. They are actually dancing and singing when Roderick meets them, and he is completely enthralled by their festive and infectious joy. The scene dramatizes the regenerative power of the saturnalia for as the "gaunt" and "ragged" French soldiers, whom Roderick refers to as "a parcel of scare-crows" (*RR*, 244), are animated by the carnival spirit so Roderick himself is transported beyond his depression. Before the festive mood of the scene passes, Roderick has joined. His mercenary status is clear, and he never mentions any scruples about fighting his own countrymen which he goes on to do at the battle of Dettingen (1743). The festive mood, however, soon passes and Roderick's fellow wretches bear up much better than he. The situation of a common sailor was perhaps worse than that of the foot-soldier, much worse according to Johnson. Like Roderick, Lieutenant Bowling only joins the French navy "to prevent himself from starving on shore" (*RR*, 234).

As Roderick is physically coerced to join the navy so he is physically beaten out of it when Crampley, having taken over command of Roderick's vessel, leaves him unconscious on a Sussex beach. Listing as a seaman or soldier was usually for life; specified shorter terms were introduced for the latter towards the end of the Spanish Succession War. Hence, in the second military episode, Roderick must get his discharge from the Picardy regiment through the influence of Strap's patron, a Marquis. Defoe's Colonel Jack departs the Douglas regiment quite abruptly and dishonorably when he deserts to pursue a better opportunity.[19] The penalty for desertion was death, but because of the shortage of manpower the death sentence was often reduced to some kind of brutal corporal punishment. Desertion was a common problem for all eighteenth-century armies, perhaps because of their aggressive recruiting practices, and motivation was, at times, purely mercenary. David Chandler claims that the British army of the early eighteenth century had a significant number of recruits "like Peter Drake" who "were prepared to desert from regiment after regiment, and even drift from army to army, risking dire penalties if apprehended, in search of an easier billet or improved prospects of loot."[20]

The army was a refuge for various criminals like Moll Flanders's Lancashire husband, "Jemy," who at one point is ready to give Moll all his money and join the army. Smollett's Ferdinand resists the military career that lies naturally before him, including the path of preferment offered by Count Melvil, and when forced into battle he quickly deserts the imperial forces only to fall into the clutches of the French army (*FCF*, chap. 19). (Thackeray follows the same pattern in having Barry Lyndon desert the British army only to be forced into the Prussian.) Ruthless reprobates, like Fielding's Northerton, were common in eighteenth-century European armies, since the army tended to attract brutal types who were looking for fast and easy plunder as opposed to a profession or trade.

The grotesque nature of the Cartagena expedition, as Roderick describes it, involves four subject-areas: epidemic disease, mutilation, political satire, and madness (madness really overlaps the other three). The first two subjects arise naturally from Smollett's actual experience as a surgeon's mate, an experience that is fictionalized in Roderick, and Roderick's medical perspective is used to capture the absurdity and horror of the expedition. I will consider epidemic disease first since it really frames the Cartagena expedition. Before the fleet even sets sail it is stricken with a distemper. Roderick's initial description of the Thunder's "sick birth or hospital" sets the grotesque mood for the horrors to follow:

> Here I saw about fifty miserable distempered wretches, suspended in rows, so huddled one upon another, that not more than fourteen inches of space was allotted for each with his bed and bedding; and deprived of the light of the day, as well as of fresh air; breathing nothing but a noisome atmosphere of the morbid steams exhaling from their own excrements and diseased bodies, devoured with vermin hatched in the filth that surrounded them, and destitute of every convenience necessary for people in that helpless condition.
>
> (RR, 149)

A sense of futility pervades the scene. The ship has not even left port and already the medical situation seems hopeless. Rather than provide the infirm with the opportunity to improve, the sick berth ironically contributes to greater infection.

Sick men will only hamper the effectiveness of a military expedition, and hence the only way to deal with epidemics is to proceed as if they did not exist. When Captain Oakhum comes on board, he flies into a rage at the sick list and orders everyone back to his station (RR, 157–59). Several men die and thus relieve the Thunder of having to care for them. The act seems to be a ruthless application of the old military theory, mentioned by Vegetius in *De Re Militari*, that activity is better than medicine to keep military personnel healthy.[21] Medical units actually interfere with military operations by diverting resources away from combat action. The consequences of this standard tradeoff are obvious when the actual attack on Cartagena produces scores of wounded men; the so-called hospital ships have an insufficient number of surgeons and the wounded only deteriorate: "Their wounds and stumps being neglected, contracted filth and putrefaction, and millions of maggots were hatched amid the corruption of their sores" (RR, 187).[22] As an individual member of the medical unit, Roderick simply cannot see that nations go to war to win, not to treat those who fall.

As the expedition is diseased at the outset so it is at the conclusion. A "bilious fever" (RR, 189) breaks out among the fleet and strikes Roderick just after the Thunder sets sail from Bocca Chica. According to John R. McNeill, seventy-seven percent of the "besieging British troops [on the Cartagena expedition] died . . . very few of them in combat."[23] McNeill goes on to conclude, "Without the decisive advantage that yellow fever conferred upon defenders, the French and especially the Spanish would not have been able to hold their Caribbean possessions against Britain."[24] Severe environmental conditions and lack of immunity rendered the British extremely susceptible to yellow fever, and Smollett himself was stricken. The experience is fictionalized in Roderick's own bout with the disease. In the fiction, however, Smollett creates another grotesque incongruity by having Roderick suggest that his recovery is owing to his refusal of "all medicine," which he believes "co-operated with the disease" (RR, 191).[25] The whole naval episode in *Roderick Random* dwells on the theme of human self-destruction. Through his folly and grossly exaggerated animosity, man finds all sorts of unnatural ways of ending his life prematurely. However, a greater

mythic pattern is present here as well insofar as a susceptibility
to disease is generally present whenever military operations are
conducted in a foreign place. The *Iliad* opens with a description
of how the Greek camp is struck with an evil pestilence. As we
have already seen in Swift, the relationship between war and
epidemic disease is symbolic in that both were considered to be
divine scourges. In fact, the pugnacious spirit of humankind is
itself often referred to by satirists like Swift as a diseased manifestation of pride, or a madness, and Roderick, whose perspective is limited to the management of the British force, ultimately
sees the miscarriage of the operation as due to the pride and
dissension among its commanders.

The other subject area of grotesque horror that relates directly
to a surgeon's mate is the human mutilation. (Mutilation and
disease are, of course, connected insofar as the cramming together of amputees increases their infection rates.) Once again
readers may identify the same general policy of individual sacrifice for the greater cause; the limb is cut off so that the body may
live. Grotesque effects are achieved by Roderick's pointing to the
incompetence of people like Mackshane, the head surgeon, who
is as inept as he is ruthless, and who has the reputation of
amputating unnecessarily. When Jack Rattlin suffers a broken leg,
Mackshane quickly decides to cut the limb off (*RR*, 164). Hor-
rified, Roderick and another surgeon's mate take over and set the
leg successfully but at the expense of incurring Mackshane's
bitter wrath. Military surgeons throughout the eighteenth century were generally considered to be little more than butchers
who hacked in haste—granted they did not work in ideal circumstances—and whom men feared almost as much as they did the
enemy.

The most grotesque battle scene occurs before the Thunder
even reaches her destination. Eight French men-of-war are met at
open sea. France is not a declared enemy of Britain at this stage of
the hostilities so an engagement is unnecessary as well as ill-
advised. Nevertheless, Captain Oakhum demands that the
French have someone board the Thunder and this raises the
dispute: ". . . they refused, telling him, if he had any business
with them, to come on board of their ship: He then threatened to
pour in a broad-side upon them, which they promised to return"
(*RR*, 167). Both sides become stubborn victims of their own
threats, and a battle erupts. The incident seems to be Smollett's
comment on the Lilliputian passions that give rise to bloody
wars.

When the engagement begins, Roderick is tied to the deck as a consequence of some drummed up spy charge made by the chief surgeon, Mackshane. Fully exposed to the battle and unable to move, Roderick may be said to be in a gothic-like predicament that plays upon the dread of enchainment.[26] Smollett spares the reader nothing. At first, Roderick is able to contain his agitation but his control soon disappears when, in his own words, "the head of the officer of Marines . . . being shot off, bounced from the deck athwart my face, leaving me well-nigh blinded with brains" (RR, 167–68). Roderick immediately begins to scream with all his strength, and this sudden loss of composure accentuates the overwhelming horror of the scene. But there may be a curious delight for the reader in how well Smollett maximizes the palpability of the trauma. (There is an ironic touch here too— after all, one is inclined to sympathize acutely with poor Roderick, who really is not hurt at all, yet not give another thought to the decapitated officer whose brains have splattered the deck.)

We may digress for a moment on this image since it is one of the commonest and most grotesque epic motifs. Its primitive origin may well be anatomical insofar as the grey matter would stand out against the more familiar color of human mutilation— red. As stated earlier, Swift parodies the motif, which appears thrice in the *Iliad* (see pp. 58–59 above)—as well as three times in the *Aeneid*: 9.753–55, 10.415–16, 20.399–400. The first instance in the *Aeneid* truly approaches the ludicrous as the rampaging Turnus slices Pandarus's skull with classical Grecian symmetry: "he stretches on the ground his fainting limbs and brain-bespattered armour, while, lo! in equal halves his head dangles this way and that from either shoulder." In the second *Aeneid* example, Virgil even mentions that the brains are still warm *("calido")*!

The motif is standard in the classical epic-battle parodies as well. One finds it in Hesiod's "The Battle of the Frogs and Mice" (227–29), and Ovid's *Metamorphoses* contains a wonderful grotesque simile as Phaeocomes levels Tectaphos with a log: "The broad dome of his head was shattered, and through his mouth, through hollow nostrils, eyes, and ears oozed the soft brains, as when curdled milk drips through oaken withes, or a thick liquid mass trickles through a coarse sieve weighted down, and is squeezed out through the crowded apertures" (12.434–38). Golding's translation is even more visually delightful as he uses "roping" for *fluit*.[27] Renaissance examples abound. In Jack Wilton's description of the battle of Marignano, we find the identical torture suffered by Random—human remains suddenly splash on a third party who may be horror-stricken but remains uninjured. Specifically, brains splatter into the face of Francis I like a bowl of porridge in a slapstick comedy: ". . . the French King himselfe in this Conflict was much distressed, the braines of his owne men sprinkled in his face . . . "[28] One is tempted to accuse Nashe of casting Francis I in the Elizabethan equivalent of a vaudeville stooge were it not for the fact that the reference is verbatim from Languet, Nashe's historical source.[29] The popularity of the motif continued long after Elizabethan times as evidenced by Pepys's diary in which one reads the following account of the deaths of the "Earl of Falmouth, Muskery, and Mr. Rd. Boyle" in the battle of Lowestoft: "Their blood and brains flying in the Duke's face—and the head of Mr. Boyle striking down the Duke, as some say."[30] Like Francis I, the Duke of York is splattered with somebody else's brains but then further inconvenienced by being struck down like a pin by an airborne head! The ultimate ludicrous potential of the splattered brains motif was captured in the following couplet on Falmouth's death: "His shattered Head the fearless Duke distains, / And gave the last first proof that he had Brains."[31] One might say that Smollett restores a truly poignant grotesque feeling to what had become a literary commonplace.

Smollett even proceeds further into ghoulish, anatomical details as Roderick proceeds with his narrative: ". . . a drummer coming towards me, asked if I was wounded; and before I could answer, received a great shot in his belly which tore out his intrails, and he fell flat on my breast" (*RR*, 168). Roderick then screams himself into a stupor and stays covered in remains all night. Smollett touches a primitive nerve by bringing together the grotesque horror of human carnage and the more mundane, yet delirious, feeling of not being able to wipe a foul substance from one's face. Angus Ross says that "Roderick is the sufferer by the violence, not a spectator" and concludes that "Smollett's aim is to attack wanton brutality."[32] The incident of course does much more. Roderick's terror stems from being forced to witness and feel, at the closest quarters, the awful bloodshed while not being able to lose himself in "annoying the foe" or in the "society" of his comrades (*RR*, 167). Although it is impossible to determine how far Smollett intended the reader to interpret the scene, Roderick's screams express what every man should feel who does not turn away from the horror of war. It is precisely because soldiers can lose themselves in mechanical functions

and distance themselves from death that so much blood could be
shed. Similarly, it is because writers and readers can focus solely
on the delight of pure language or form that at times they seem
insensitive to substance. To appreciate fully Smollett's art, one
must allow for the connections between form and content; in the
words of Alice Green Fredman, Smollett "has to match violence
with violence in order to behold it; and the affronting grotesquerie that life is forces him to make a crueler grotesque of it
by sort of 'juicing up' the brutality and ferocity."[33] Furthermore,
the notion of "juicing up" does not take away from the authen-
ticity of detail which Boucé and others accord the naval scenes.[34]

Since the engagement with the French men-of-war begins iras-
cibly on a point of honor, it is appropriate that it would have an
equally puerile ending. Captain Oakhum "finding he was like to
gain neither honour nor advantage . . . pretended to be un-
deceived by seeing their colours . . . and went on board of the
French commodore" (RR, 168). Smollett records a similar incident in the "Account."[35] The gory circumstances of Roderick's
predicament are, however, completely fictitious, and this fact
points to Smollett's conscious use of the grotesque mode. The
significance of this episode lies in how senseless the destruction
and death ultimately are and how this waste prefigures the rest of
the expedition. Joanne Lewis Lynn argues that the description of
Roderick's quick recovery from the mess in which he finds himself "is both realistic and a grisly comic symbol of the human
condition in a comic grotesque world": "From such scenes of
horror and bloodshed, Roderick rises again and again, with the
resilience of Punch."[36] Smollett's hero, like Nashe's Jack Wilton,
always rebounds and this pattern is an integral part of the comic
or festive rhythm of the narrative.

The sense of individual madness prevails on board when the
Thunder finds herself in an artillery duel with the fort of Bocca
Chica. Nerves are shattered, and any sense of duty or humanity
disappears when animosity breaks out among the men. A sailor
carries a wounded fellow to the cockpit "where he tossed him
down like a bag of oats" (RR, 181). The man is already dead, and
when the sailor refuses "to heave the body overboard" Morgan,
the first surgeon's mate, gives chase with a knife. The incident is
cut short by the appearance of Jack Rattlin with his hand "shattered to pieces with grape shot" (RR, 182). This time Rattlin's
limb must be amputated, and while Roderick dresses the stump,
Rattlin points to the tactical errors committed by the Thunder
and adds that "there was scarce any body on board, who under-

stood the pointing of a gun" (RR, 182). The madness and panic of battle extends to the medical unit. To strengthen his resolution, the chief surgeon Mackshane "had recourse more than once to a case-bottle of rum" and consequently operates with reckless abandon: ". . . he went to work, and arms and legs were hewed down without mercy" (RR, 183). An inebriated surgeon who amputates unnecessarily at the best of times epitomizes the senseless human mutilation and slaughter. Joanne Lynn is correct in calling this scene "farcical" in that "the comic is . . . firmly in control and serves to heighten, rather than defuse the horror."[37] The parson and purser also indulge in the rum, and the former, whose job it is to calm men in battle, becomes delirious: ". . . he stript himself to the skin, and besmearing his body with blood, could scarce be with-held from running upon deck in that condition" (RR, 183). The madness of this kind of primitive and ritualistic action mirrors the madness of war itself.

The foregoing analysis of the subjects of disease, mutilation and madness shines light on the last category of Roderick's grotesque view of the expedition—the political satire. Here too Roderick speaks very much as the individual who is caught in the action and consequently not entirely objective. Much the same can be said of Smollett, who uses the novel as a means of pointing out how the expedition could have met with more success. First, Roderick calls into question the unnecessary delays of the English fleet. Had the fleet proceeded directly to the target, the Spanish would have been caught unprepared. The tone of Roderick's sarcasm recalls Swift's in *The Conduct of the Allies*: "But if I might be allowed to give my opinion of the matter, I would ascribe this delay to the generosity of our chiefs, who scorned to take any advantage that fortune might give them, even over an enemy" (RR, 179). Next Roderick mocks the site chosen for the camp, "under the walls of an enemy's fortification . . . with a view of accustoming the soldiers to stand fire, who were not as yet much used to discipline, most of them having been taken from the plough-tail a few months before" (RR, 179). This ironic explanation leads to a more explicit criticism of the inexperience of the troops:

> This again has furnished matter for censure against the Ministry, for sending a few raw recruits on such an important enterprize, while so many veteran regiments lay inactive at home: But surely our governours had their reasons for so doing, which possibly may be disclosed with other secrets of the deep. Perhaps they were loth to risk their best troops on such desperate service; or, may be the colonels

and field officers of the old corps, who, generally speaking, enjoyed their commissions as sinecures or pensions, for some domestick services rendered to the court, refused to embark in such a dangerous and precarious undertaking; for which, no doubt, they are to be much commended.

(RR, 179–80)

Wentworth's troops were inexperienced and less than ideal.[38] But part of the answer to Smollett's criticism is found in the parliamentary debates on the expedition and the army. The Duke of Argyll, for instance, in his famous speech in the Lords on the need to promote by merit rather than purchased commissions, referred to the unwillingness of veteran officers to offer themselves in the newly raised regiments because they could not bring themselves to serve undeserving superiors.[39] On the other hand, Smollett may also be using Roderick to make a general statement that transcends political satire. The reluctance of veteran soldiers to join a military operation arises naturally from past experience. There is a slightly different irony about the closing statement, "for which . . . they are to be much commended," insofar as the veterans are wise to stay at home. All military operations depend to a large extent on luring naive recruits into battle.

Smollett then uses Roderick to associate the British force with an absurd chivalry when they fail to press their attack after securing the harbor: "this our Heroes disdained, as a barbarous insult over the enemy's distress" (RR, 185). The high British casualties were not owing to "bad provision and want of water" (RR, 186) but a tactical plan that possessed a complete disregard for human life. A bestial simile is used to convey the inhuman military commitment on the part of the British: "a sufficient number remained to fall before the walls of St. Lazar, where they behaved like their own country mastifs, which shut their eyes, run into the jaws of a bear, and have their heads crushed for their valour" (RR, 186). The sarcasm and wit in the description of the disastrous assault on St. Lazar is reminiscent of Sidney's battle descriptions. Lastly, Roderick's ironical tirade exaggerates not the loss of life (the statistic of 8,000 fit men reduced to 1,500 is correct), but the senseless way in which it was lost.

Through his spokesman Roderick, Smollett offers a more specific reason why the expedition miscarried—a squabble between General Wentworth, commander of the land forces, and Admiral Vernon, commander of the fleet. Herein lies the universal theme of faction. According to Roderick, Wentworth refused to ask

Vernon for the use of some of the fleet's surgeons because "the general was too much of a gentleman to ask a favor of this kind from his fellow-chief"; the Admiral, "on the other hand, would not derogate so far from his own dignity, as to offer such assistance unasked" (RR, 187). These same petty points of honor, which leave the injured in such desperate anguish, also doom the entire expedition. Roderick cites a classical parallel for the discord in Lucan's account of the civil war between Caesar and Pompey: ". . . it might be said of these great men, (I hope they will pardon the comparison) as of Caesar and Pompey, the one could not brook a superior, and the other was impatient of an equal" (RR, 187).[40] The parenthetical request for pardon sharpens the irony. Roderick moves from the profundity of classical allusion to an extremely crude proverb:

> So that between the pride of one, and insolence of another, the enterprize miscarried, according to the proverb, "Between two stools the backside falls to the ground."—Not that I would be thought to liken any publick concern to that opprobrious part of the human body, although I might with truth assert, if I durst use such a vulgar idiom, that the nation did hang an a——se at its disappointment on this occasion . . .
>
> (RR, 187)

Besides serving as an outlet for Smollett's coarse humor, the low bodily image aligns Roderick's analysis with Bakhtin's concept of the grotesque.

Internal dissension is a frequent theme in war literature and goes back to the inglorious opening of the *Iliad*, which features the squabble between Agamemnon and Achilles over concubines. The dispute greatly hampers the Greek war effort, but the more immediate problem for the Greeks is the pestilence, which is determined to be the consequence of the plea made by Chryses, a Trojan priest, to the gods to punish the Greeks for not returning his daughter—Agamemnon's concubine. Agamemnon agrees to return "the fair-cheeked daughter of Chryses" but tells his challenger, Achilles, that he will replace her with the "fair-cheeked Briseïs, that prize of thine; that thou mayest know full well how far mightier am I than thou" (*Iliad* 1.142–44, 184–86). The subject of war in Western literature could hardly commence with a more ignoble instance of dueling male egos. Conflicts involving military characters and delicate points of honor with regard to women are frequent in Smollett. Roderick fights with Captain Odonnell over a liberty the former takes with Miss Lavement. In *Peregrine Pickle*, the hero fights a duel with a captain of a Dutch man-of-war who finds Peregrine dancing with a "lady whom, it seems, he had bespoke for his bedfellow" (*PP*, 350). All these examples are low variations on the Menelaus-Helen-Paris triangle.

The admiral performs one final and mad act of war—the last desperate and unwarranted bombardment of St. Lazar. Various speculative reasons for the order are suggested, one of which was the same cause that "induced Don Quixote to attack the wind-mill" (*RR*, 188). In this scene and the sea battle discussed earlier, Smollett expresses his belief that irrational impetuosity, not calculated strategy, often determines the course of military action.[41] Roderick mentions a few other possible reasons and takes a backhand swipe at the Whig administration back in London: "But all these suggestions surely proceed from ignorance and malevolence, or else the admiral would not have found it such an easy matter, at his return to England, to justify his conduct to a ministry at once so upright and discerning" (*RR*, 188). Unlike Fielding, who defended Vernon, Smollett criticizes the admiral from a conservative Tory position.

Roderick's melancholy grows as the campaign becomes more desperate. In the final section we find the scavenger motif as the human bodies are expeditiously flung overboard, "so that numbers of human carcasses floated in the harbour, until they were devoured by sharks and carrion crows" (*RR*, 189). Out of every death comes a renewed form of life. Out of the expedition comes Roderick's employment and sustenance.

The question that Smollett never does address in the Cartagena episode, or in *Roderick Random* for that matter, is the morality of colonial expansion itself. Granted, the reader is only given Roderick's perspective and Roderick cannot indulge in the luxury of moral philosophy when he is physically destitute,[42] but if we accept the proximity between Smollett as an angry young man and Roderick as narrator, we are struck by how the satire of the novel is wholly directed at the mismanagement of the expedition and not the expedition itself. Later, however, in Matthew Bramble's comments on the commercial activity at Bath, Smollett did express a greater moral view on colonial expansion:

Every upstart of fortune, harnessed in the trappings of the mode, presents himself at Bath, as in the very focus of observation—Clerks and factors from the East Indies, loaded with the spoil of plundered provinces; planters, negro-drivers, and hucksters, from our American plantations, enriched they know not how; agents, commissaries, and contractors, who have fattened, in two successive wars, on the blood of the nation; usurers, brokers, and jobbers of every kind; men of low birth, and no breeding, have found themselves suddenly translated into a state of affluence, unknown to former ages; and no wonder that their brains should be intoxicated with pride, vanity, and presumption.[43]

After the Seven Years' War, Smollett did see how certain commercial enterprises were tied to war activity, its spoils and colonial expansion.[44] One easily recognizes the classical attack on luxury in the above passage, but what is not immediately apparent is the grotesque human costs involved—symbolically represented in the novel by the broken and mutilated veterans who served in the colonial wars: "colonel Cockril, who had lost the use of his limbs in making an American campaign," and of course the memorable Lismahago who was wounded and scalped at Ticonderoga (HC, 55, 189). The grotesque nature of these characters and their histories is summed up by Robert Hopkins:

> Dehumanized by war, Colonel Cockril foreshadows the most grotesque figure in *Humphry Clinker*—Lieutenant Lismahago. Here one must recognize that the atrocities of Indian frontier warfare reported in eighteenth-century British periodicals would have had much the same grim effect on readers as recent atrocities reported in the Congo would have on readers today [1969]. Lismahago's Thurberlike mythic reduction of Indian captivity converts English anxieties about Indian massacres to a ludicrous, demonic myth.[45]

What connects the wise old author of *Humphry Clinker* with the younger man who wrote *Roderick Random* is the tendency to focus on the forms of mutilation and of livelihood with respect to military service. Jenkins's ear, Rattlin's hand, and Lismahago's skull are all reminders of the human barbarism that is suffered by some so that others may control new world opportunity and ostentatious wealth.

The Battle of Dettingen and Military Puffing

As the Cartagena expedition contains more of the terrible as opposed to the sportive grotesque, so it is the reverse in the second military episode in which Roderick joins the Picardy regiment and fights on the French side at the battle of Dettingen.[46] Again he enlists only because he is absolutely destitute.

In Roderick's second military career, Smollett deals more with the behavior of the enlisted men than the tactical skill (or lack thereof) of the commanding officers, as was the case with the Cartagena expedition. My analysis of the grotesque nature of this second military episode focuses on three subjects: the meaning of military service, the escalation to the *argumentum ad baculinum* (argument by the rod), and the practice of rodomontade or military puffing.

The Picardy regiment is soon ordered to Germany, and the physical toil of the march takes its toll on Roderick who is piqued by the fact that his comrades, however ragged and worn in appearance, bear up much better than he. When the men and their wives go dancing off on another picnic, Roderick chooses to remain behind in camp with a fellow soldier. Smollett uses their ensuing conversation to raise various questions having to do with soldier motivation. A veteran in the army, the fellow soldier first tries to bolster Roderick's sagging spirits and in so doing reveals a strong sense of allegiance to his sovereign: "Have courage, therefore, my child (said he) and pray to the good God, that you may be as happy as I am, who have had the honor of serving Lewis the Great, and of receiving many wounds in helping to establish his glory" (*RR*, 245). The veteran is as proud of his wounds as is Sterne's uncle Toby. They are emblematic of his love for his king, who, in his opinion, merits unquestioned devotion by divine right. In other words, the veteran sees no difference between the greater cause and his individual purpose. Roderick, not believing in the absolute power of the monarchy and enlisting out of necessity, looks upon his companion with utter contempt: ". . . I was amazed at the infatuation that possessed him; and could not help expressing my astonishment at the absurdity of a rational being, who thinks himself highly honoured in being permitted to encounter abject poverty, oppression, famine, disease, mutilation, and evident death, merely to gratify the vicious ambition of a prince, by whom his sufferings were disregarded, and his name utterly unknown" (*RR*, 245). Exonerating his own motivation, Roderick goes on to say that one is justified in joining the army if fate can offer nothing better or if it is in defense of one's country. He then launches into a tirade against those who commit "the most flagrant crimes, to sooth the barbarous pride of a fellow-creature" (*RR*, 246). Roderick and the veteran soldier represent the extremes of a familiar debate. The motives of the first are rational yet selfish; those of the second are irrational yet unselfish. The veteran's deep sense of loyalty makes him a better soldier as far as attitude is concerned, but if everyone were to adopt Roderick's view, monstrous and unnecessary wars would not be so likely to occur. It seems that the practical position lies somewhere in between the blind patriotism of the one and the narrow self-interest of the other.

Smollett, it seems, was about as impressed with Louis and his reputation as a grand conqueror as was Swift. In his *Travels* Smollett remarks that "Through all France one meets with statues and triumphal arches erected to Louis XIV in consequence of his victories."[47] Smollett first attributes Louis's victories to his generals and then sarcastically sums up the Sun King's martial achievements:

> He had the humanity to ravage the country, burn the towns, and massacre the people of the Palatinate. He had the patriotism to impoverish and depopulate his own kingdom, in order to prosecute schemes of the most lawless ambition. He had the consolation to beg a peace from those he had provoked to war by the most outrageous insolence. . . . Without all doubt, it was from irony he acquired the title *le Grand*.
>
> (*T,* 104–5)[48]

Aside from the explicitness of the final statement, the passage is Swiftian in its sarcastic tone and diction.

What begins as a friendly conversation between Roderick and his companion soon degenerates into a verbal dispute and then an *argumentum ad baculinum*. The veteran, nettled at how Roderick receives his fatherly advice, quickly associates Roderick's enlightened view with the "notorious" insolence with which the English treat their kings. Recognizing the nationalistic slur as a reference to Cromwell's Roundheads and the Glorious Revolution of 1688, Roderick counters with a plausible vindication of such events based on the principle of reciprocal allegiance between sovereign and subject. Tempers get out of control and Roderick makes a motion to "box" his comrade-turned-adversary on the ear. With his fondness for ceremony, the Frenchman asks for a "parley" to set the terms—in a gentlemanly way—for a duel. The pair duel with swords, chivalric weapons of old, and the veteran gets the better of Roderick. However, when the veteran demands a pardon, Roderick refuses and is disturbed that his opponent "did not bear his success with all the moderation that might have been expected" (*RR,* 247). Moreover, Roderick's refusal to meet the demand is accompanied with a promise that, if his adversary persists, he will respond by asking for satisfaction with the "musket." Thus the new answers the old.

This seemingly mundane confrontation is loaded with implications about human bellicosity. First, there is the simple idea of how quickly friendship can sour and conflict flare up. Second, one sees how strong nationalistic feelings can run, especially when they are piqued. Having just called England "the worst country in the universe," Roderick here is angered by the accusations of the Frenchman into a staunch defense of the English. Third, there is the symbolic conflict between the old, quixotic style of chivalry, and the modern, enlightened kind of political thinking. Zealous patriotism seems to be a chimera, but rational individualism lacks the honorable sense of self-sacrifice. Last of all, the pattern of verbal disagreements escalating into physical altercations is a feature of Smollett's picaresque mode.

Military characters in particular, reflecting the bent of their profession, are often depicted as easily galled and quick to resort to physical action. Of course one immediately thinks of the irascible and opinionated Lieutenant Lismahago and Commodore Trunnion. Several examples may be found in *Peregrine Pickle*. Peregrine himself fights duels with the young soldier Gauntlet and later a French musketeer, both of whom take great offense on a point of honor (*PP*, chaps. 31 and 44). The latter instance recalls Hamlet's "Rightly to be great / Is not to stir without great argument, / But greatly to find quarrel in a straw / When honor's at the stake" (*Ham.* 4.4.53–56). A little later enmity flares up between a pedantic doctor and a Scots officer over the relative merits of ancient versus modern fortifications. The pair threaten each other with swords after the former's ignorance concerning the term "Tortoise" is exposed (*PP*, 270–71). For Smollett, human pride means that to stand corrected is to stand insulted. Then there is the hilarious duel between the two cowards, Pallet and the physician, fought, appropriately enough, on the Antwerp ramparts (*PP*, chap. 68); the episode recalls the duel between Dametas and Clinias in Sidney's *Arcadia* (bk.3, chap. 13). However, the most ridiculous duel in Smollett's fiction is probably the one fought between Captain Minikin and Major Macleavor (see *FCF*, chap. 41). Being in prison, the combatants have no access to the usual weapons and, at Ferdinand's suggestion, agree to blow sulfur smoke at one another to see who will back away first. In *Travels through France and Italy*, Smollett expatiates at length on French punctilio as being responsible for so many men entering into duels in that nation. He even singles out the military as involving men in an absurd dilemma with regard to dueling—the facing of a possible court martial if they fail to meet a challenge, or a possible civil conviction for murder if they kill an adversary (*T*, 135–36). Interesting exceptions to the pattern of physical escalation include the retired general in *Roderick Random* who is remarkable for shamefully walking off the field of battle in a coffeehouse debate when it becomes clear that he does not know what an *"epaulement"* is (*RR*, 263–65). Then there are the pusillanimous braggarts like the lieutenant in the Bath coach who vociferously argues with all only to shy away when physical violence threatens (*RR*, 328–30).

The connection between duelling and war is proverbial. Grotius begins *De Jure Belli* (1.1.2) with a general definition of war as fragmentation and points to the etymological connection between *bellum* and *duellum*. According to Boswell, Johnson, who greatly admired Grotius, once justified "public war" on the basis that honor often necessitated "private war" or duels.[49] Smollett is certainly not the only novelist to portray military characters, like Gauntlet, as being quick to throw down a challenge. For Lieutenant-Colonel Bath (Fielding's man of military "humour"), who fights several duels in *Amelia* including one with Booth, the practice is synonymous with the profession of soldier, as represented by epic tradition:

> What else is all Mr. *Pope's Homer* full of, but Duels? Did not, what's his Name, one of the *Agamemnons* fight with that paultry Rascal *Paris*? and *Diomede* with, what d'ye call him there; and *Hector* with, I forget his Name, he that was *Achilles's* Bosom-friend; and afterwards with *Achilles* himself? Nay, and in *Dryden's Virgil*, is there any Thing almost besides fighting?[50]

Although Colonel Bath has a better handle on his sword than he does Homer, he eventually is killed in a duel by a gentleman with whom he differs in opinion.

Nationalistic prejudices and allegiances play a large role in the disputes that fill Smollett's novels. When Peregrine scores a victory over the musketeer, Pipes refers to "the glory of Old England" (*PP*, 216). Disappointed in his career aspirations, the general in *Roderick Random* is quick to criticize the English in martial affairs while praising the French and Spanish for knowing "how to value generals of merit" (*RR*, 261)—arguments that the French members of the party quickly support. Such rhetoric of frustration and complaint brings a rejoinder from Mr. Medlar, who was not able to "put up with the indignity that was offered to old England" (*RR*, 262). First he reminds the general that as a half-pay officer he had received and was still getting his "bread under the English government"; then he upbraids the Frenchmen present for not showing more respect to the country that serves as their benefactor (*RR*, 262). The disputants reach for swords but are persuaded to continue their argument verbally. In the fictional world of Smollett, conflict is entertainment.

The French army is thrown into the battle of Dettingen (1743) before Roderick and the veteran finally settle their dispute. Here the reader is given another critical analysis of military leadership and strategy. Roderick points to how the French commander, the Duc de Gramont (the same Duc who is brought down by one of the opening artillery shells at Fontenoy), unaccountably left an excellent position of advantage to engage the English on the plain: ". . . providence or destiny acted miracles in their [Allies'] behalf, by disposing the Duc de Gramont to quit his advantageous post" (*RR*, 248). Curiously enough, in his *History* Smollett treats Gramont more harshly by claiming that the French duke was "instigated by the spirit of madness."[51] Perhaps spurred by the remarks of the veteran, Roderick is quick to praise the English for not slaughtering the French after routing them on the plain. Furthermore, Roderick blames the French casualties on their own fear and chaotic retreat: ". . . we turned our backs without ceremony, and fled with such precipitation, that many hundreds perished in the river, through pure fear and confusion; for the enemy was so generous, that they did not pursue us one inch of ground; and if our consternation would have permitted, we might have retreated with great order and deliberation" (*RR*, 248). Hence Lord Charles Hay's famous insult two years later at Fontenoy. The French losses are needless, incurred due to "fear and confusion," and though Roderick may stress this fact only to acquit the English, it certainly adds to the grotesque atmosphere of the scene.

Roderick's eulogistic reference to George II seems somewhat ironic considering his indictment of kings and their vainglory in the previous chapter: "But not withstanding the royal clemency of the king of Great Britain, who headed the allies in person, and no doubt, put a stop to the carnage, our loss amounted to 5,000 men, among whom were many officers of distinction" (*RR*, 248–49). The battle of Dettingen was the last in which the British army was led personally by the monarch. Although Smollett describes the role of George II favorably in *The History of En-*

gland, nowhere does he say that the king was personally responsible for the apparent mercy on the part of the British. In fact, Smollett here blames the British for failing to pursue, which would have resulted in a "total overthrow" of the French; and he continues thus, "Lord Stair proposed that a body of cavalry should be detached on this service; but his advice was overruled."[52] In *Roderick Random*, Smollett uses this claim about Lord Stair being overruled to free the British command of any responsibility in allowing the army to be cornered in the first place. According to Smollett's account in the *History*, it is the Duke of Cumberland who seems to be responsible for getting the allies in this precarious position.[53] Hence Roderick, or Smollett, plays loosely with the facts. The former uses whatever he can to reverse his indignation against the British and champion the cause of English humanitarianism. This complete turnabout is consistent with the picaresque form in which characters and situations are continually being reversed.

As far as the French are concerned, Roderick does say that they "treated the living with humanity" after the English had marched on directly to Hanau leaving their sick and wounded behind (*RR*, 249). In *The History* Smollett is more explicit about the magnanimity of the French: "The Earl of Stair sent a trumpeter to Mareschal de Noailles, recommending to his protection the sick and wounded that were left on the field of battle: and these the French General treated with great care and tenderness. Such generosity softens the rigours of war, and does honour to humanity."[54] To have Roderick deliver such a eulogy would have been incongruous with the nature of the picaresque hero. It would also have been awkward in view of the fact that Roderick then launches into his own satire on how the French boasted about their "victory" after the English departed from the field:

> . . . the genius of the French nation never appeared more conspicuous than now, in the rhodomontades they uttered on the subject of their generosity and courage: Every man, (by his own account) performed feats that would have shamed all the heroes of antiquity.— One compared himself to a lion retiring at leisure from his cowardly pursuers, who keep at a wary distance, and gall him with their darts.—Another likened himself to a bear that retreats with his face to the enemy, who dare not assail him; and a third assumed the character of a desperate stag, that turns upon the hounds and keeps them at bay.—There was not a private soldier engaged, who had not

by the prowess of his single arm, demolished a whole platoon, or put a squadron of horse to flight.

(*RR*, 249)

The bestial similes and boasts of course go back to Homer. A stock character from Roman comedy, the *miles gloriosus*, who uses rhetoric in lieu of real feats in the field, enjoyed great popularity during the Renaissance and afterwards. These traditional structures are given a satiric twist within the context of Smollett's novel for Roderick does not criticize the French braggarts just for hypocritically seeing glory in mass murder, he also mocks them for shamefully having nothing to boast about!

The most memorable *miles gloriosus* in Smollett may well be the lieutenant whom Roderick meets in the Bath coach. After falling to the verbal wit of the Lady next to him, he seizes upon her final comment ("Your bolt is soon shot") and launches into his own hobbyhorsical boast: "You talk of shot, madam, (said he) damme! I have both given and received some shot in my time—I was wounded in the shoulder by a pistol ball at Dettingen, where—I say nothing—but by G——d! if it had not been for me—all's one for that—I despise boasting, G——d d——me!" (*RR*, 324). He then proceeds to describe, with a plethora of the same vulgar epithets, how he bravely retrieved a lost standard from a French musketeer. The next day this "son of Mars," taking offense at a "*Boh!*" from Roderick, stares menacingly back and protests that "he feared no man breathing" (*RR*, 327). He even displays "a pair of pistols," which he claims to have taken "from a horse officer at the battle of Dettingen" (*RR*, 328). Then in a scene that is similar to the one involving the hypocritical gentleman in *Joseph Andrews* (bk. 2, chap. 9) the lieutenant manages to find reason to remain in the coach when it is confronted by a couple of highwaymen (*RR*, 329–30). And so Dettingen becomes the fiction to feed military ego. What really happened at the battle of Dettingen? Smollett, who obviously had an ear for coffeehouse discourse, has Roderick, a veteran of the action, take issue with the partisan view of the retired and frustrated English general:

The discourse was afterwards shifted by an old gentleman of a very martial appearance, to the last campaign, when the battle of Dettingen was fought over again, with so many circumstances to the honour of the French, and disadvantage of the Allies, that I began to entertain some doubts of my having been there in person; and took the liberty to mention some objections to what he advanced.—This introduced a dispute which lasted a good while, to the mortification of all present . . .

(*RR*, 261)

This shift from discourse to dispute is a natural pattern in Smollett's fiction. Men eagerly assert themselves, and contradictory assertions lead them into arguments. Lastly, there is no fitter subject for conflict than a battle, the confusion and detail of which offer ample opportunity for differences.

Who really won the battle of Dettingen was ultimately to be decided by the pen. Various accounts and cases appeared in the *London Magazine,* which actually ran an article entitled "Political and Military Puffing" in July 1743. The author of the article points to both sides as rhetorically trying to win as much ground as possible. In fact, the cited comment by a French correspondent, "Whether it is usual for Generals to leave the Care of their *Wounded* to the *Vanquish'd,*" raises an important question about the supposed English victory at Dettingen.[55] It may well be that Smollett was influenced by this piece when he wrote the French rodomontades quoted above. The article humorously concludes with a reference to the final puffing recipe made by this French correspondent:

> His next Paragraph consists of a ridiculous Proposal for the C——t Cooks, to represent the whole Action in *Puff-Paste,* with a *Sugar-Candy* Trophy in the Middle, guarded with a File of Grenadiers, bearing in a Banner-Roll the following Passage from Sir William D'Avenant:
> *We have had to kill we know not whom, nor why.*
> I repeat these Particulars only to expose them: Some People are never satisfy'd, and when Argument fails, place their last Resource in Buffoonery and Ridicule.[56]

Claiming victory for political propaganda reasons is wittily likened to baking some delicious looking puff-pastry, something that will meet the sweet expectations of an easily fooled public and dazzle with its art of detailed and allegorical reproduction.

Samuel Johnson, with his characteristic acumen, makes a brief but perspicuous analysis in *Idler* No. 20 of slanted histories that emanate naturally from the strength and depth of national identities. In the paper he fictitiously presents opposing English and French accounts of the fall of Louisbourg that speak for themselves. For the historian, and I use "historian" in its broadest sense, there is no getting beyond the heat of conflict since that conflict is a continual polemic involving the universal foibles of humankind: "inveterate prejudice and prevailing passions."[57] This prejudice then expresses itself in a distorted view of military events designed to represent the interested party in the most advantageous light. Johnson continues the analysis in *Idler* No. 30 by suggesting that journalistic partiality owes something to the pressure of public desire (the crucial factor in selling periodicals) and should be understood as a natural manifestation of national interest: "In a time of war the nation is always of one mind, eager to hear something good of themselves and ill of the enemy. At this time the task of news-writers is easy, they have nothing to do but to tell that a battle is expected, and afterwards that a battle has been fought, in which we and our friends, whether conquering or conquered, did all, and our enemies did nothing."[58] Prejudicial appetites demand slanted histories. Grotesque perspectives normally derive from one's having a certain distance from the subject (e.g., Gulliver's view of the Lilliput-Blefuscu war), but the opposite—or not having any distance—is just as likely to produce distortion (e.g., Gulliver's myopic account of English history to the king of Brobdingnag). This postulate suggests that there is an ideal, objective position somewhere in between these extremes, but models such as these are useful only to conceptualize the range of possible perspectives. Distance produces the semblance of objectivity, but distance itself is not necessarily a factor of time or space.

Let us return to the aftermath of Dettingen. Rodomontade renews the animosity between Roderick and the French veteran who "extoled his exploits above those of Hercules or Charlemagne" (*RR*, 249). Roderick deliberately provokes his opponent by countering with an opposite set of exaggerated comparisons: "I magnified the valour of the English with all the hyperboles I could imagine, and decried the pusilanimity of the French in the same stile, comparing them to hares flying before grey-hounds, or mice pursued by cats; and passed an ironical compliment on the speed he exerted in his flight, which, considering his age and infirmities, I said was surprising" (*RR*, 249). These mock-epic similes anticipate the subsequent combat between the two rivals, which is described as a mock-heroic farce. Roderick kicks the veteran "on the breech, which overturned him in an instant" (*RR*, 249). A second duel is fought and Roderick, having since been instructed in swordsmanship, succeeds in disarming his adversary. The physical confrontation, of course, is only a medium for their dueling pride, and so real victory is achieved by humiliating the enemy. When the veteran refuses "to beg his life," Roderick leaves his sword "in something . . . that lay smoking on the plain [presumably dung]" and rejoins the rest of the soldiers "with an air of tranquility and indifference" (*RR*, 250). Joanne Lynn refers to the scene as "a good illustration of the confused and reversed values of a comic grotesque world."[59] Actually, the dispute between Roderick and the Frenchman is an allegorical vignette that demonstrates again how easily differences in opinion can injure pride and lead to physical violence. Their petty dispute can be said to symbolize whatever petty squabble has initiated the War of the Austrian Succession and caught them up in it.

The battle of Dettingen is a focal point in *Roderick Random* for the subjects of military service and fiction. It comes up again when Mrs. Gawky, formerly Miss Lavement, tells Roderick how her husband Lieutenant Gawky (Roderick's childhood rival) abandoned her. Unable to support his family, the lieutenant left them with the Lavements and went to Germany with his regiment "where he was broke for misbehaviour at the battle of Dettingen; since which time she had heard no tidings of him" (*RR*, 319). Such stories of abandonment by soldier-husbands abroad were numerous in the eighteenth century. *Roderick Random* contains several examples of men being somehow consumed by the military life. By using the 1743 campaign as a focal point, Smollett does distance his fiction from the more recent military events such as Fontenoy and Culloden (1745, 1746). His Scottish heritage made the latter a painful memory and Fontenoy did not serve as the sample of military puffing that Dettingen did.

Postscript on *The Adventures of an Atom*

No study of Smollett's use of the grotesque to address the subject of war could avoid *The Adventures of an Atom* (1769). This political satire is a topical and gross attack on the Whig administration, particularly William Pitt, and not an indictment of the Seven Years' War or of war in general.[60] What makes it so relevant to the present discussion is the grotesque image of the "Legion" or "hydra" (also called the "blatant beast") that represents the public.[61] Herein Smollett effectively conveys his view of how the masses must have either been mad or manipulated for the war effort to be maintained. In a way, the "Legion" image shows the development of a theme that Smollett touched upon in *Roderick Random*—the often perverse relationship between military leaders and their followers.

Pitt is represented by the figure of Taycho, who controls the beast or masses through the magic of rhetoric. Once the beast has been spellbound by Taycho, it indulges in an irrational and obsequious kind of hero worship. For example, driven to promote the glory of its leader above all others, the beast picks up the following cry after the fall of Quebec: "Yaf-frai [General Wolfe] has slain his thousands; Ya-loff [Lord Amherst] has slain his five thousands; but Taycho has slain his ten thousands."[62] The cry parodies the biblical story of how David was triumphantly received by the Israelites after slaughtering the Philistines (I Samuel 18:6–8). Smollett's indignation may be likened to Saul's envy.

That Smollett elected to pursue the political satire beyond the conclusion of the Seven Years' War to the return of Pitt and the Rockingham Whigs contributes to the universality of the "Legion" image. One war has passed, but another looms ahead—the American War of Independence. Smollett focuses on the civil nature of this conflict by pointing to how England's "Legion" is eager to battle its own offspring, "the unnatural monsters," and to be "drenched with the blood of its fellow-subjects."[63]

Smollet's *Atom* may be largely a vicious attack on Pitt, but it also asks the question—who is ultimately responsible for war, the manipulative leaders or that mindless beast, the masses? Smollett leaves the question unanswered, yet he is one of the first to raise it within the context of a British parliamentary democracy. As the eighteenth century wore on, the conventional humanist attitude about war originating from the ambition and vanity of princes (which passed down through the tradition of learned wit to Swift) could no longer explain all. With the rise of a ministerial and parliamentary form of government, the people had to share in the accountability, and the folly of the beast became more apparent. William Cowper may have best expressed the grotesque truth: "But war's a game, which, were their subjects wise, / Kings would not play at."[64]

Smollett's kings, however, do play at war. In *Ferdinand Count Fathom*, the hero, hearing the "strange sound . . . of a human voice imitating the noise of a drum," looks through a prison keyhole and sees Theodore king of C——rs——ca, jailed for debt, and a Major Macleaver, promoted by the king to "general-in-chief," employed in "landing troops upon the Genoese territory":

He then . . . reconnoitered them through the key-hole, and perceived the sovereign and his minister sitting on opposite sides of a deal board table, covered with a large chart or map, upon which he saw a great number of muscle and oister-shells, ranged in a certain order, and at a little distance, several regular squares and columns made of cards cut in small pieces. The prince himself, whose eyes were reinforced by spectacles, surveyed this armament with great attention, while the general put the whole in action, and conducted their motions by beat of drum. The muscle-shells, according to Minikin's explanation, represented the transports, the oyster-shells were considered as the men of war that covered the troops in landing, and the pieces of card exhibited the different bodies into which the army was formed upon its disembarkation.

(*FCF*, 186–87)

When the "grey pease," march along the shore to defend against the invading force, the general orders the oyster-shells to begin a bombardment and performs "the cannonading with his voice" (*FCF*, 187). The attack is successful. And so monarchs, crazed by quixotic pride and ambition, are still quite willing to engage in the sport of kings.

4

Fielding: Military Unruliness, Advancement, and Grandeur

A MILITARY ATMOSPHERE hung over London, indeed all of Britain, during the war years 1739–48 and is reflected in the social background of Fielding's fiction. In the first two sections of this chapter, I will examine the most prominent domestic features of this atmosphere, namely the subjects of military unruliness and preferment. Aside from Booth's service abroad, all of Fielding's military characters and episodes are set in England. As a novelist, Fielding was primarily interested in the domestic social problems of the military and not its performance in the field. However, in various other works Fielding does address, more directly, general ethical issues regarding militarism. There are also passing references of this kind in *Joseph Andrews* and *Tom Jones*, but, with the exception of *Amelia*, the military content of Fielding's fiction is kept on the periphery. Nevertheless, the military characters, incidents, and references in the novels do add up to a substantial commentary.

The use of the grotesque to illuminate Fielding's technique in handling military subjects arises from the incongruities inherent in the general unruliness of the military, the preferment system of purchased commissions, and finally the micro and macro worlds of conflict. Fielding's comic and satiric irony produces a ludicrous response, and yet this response is tinged with an awareness of more disturbing implications. How did Fielding portray and understand the unruly behavior of the troops who threatened civilians? Was their unruliness owing more to their pugnacious spirit or to their billeting with civilians? What kind of officer corps did Fielding see the system of purchased commissions as creating? Finally, how important is conflict in Fielding's comedy, and how are military grandeur and illusion dependent upon language?

Domestic Unruliness

Two specific factors help explain the tension between civilians and military personnel in Fielding's fiction: first, the wholesale disbanding of regiments at the conclusion of a war; and second, the quartering of troops by law in private homes and inns. Martin Battestin and Donald Low have recently pointed out that Fielding was concerned about the civil disorder in London created by the disbandment of no fewer than forty thousand sailors and soldiers after the conclusion to the War of the Austrian Succession.[1] It seems that these men, suddenly released from their strict military occupations and many without prospects in labor or trade, naturally fell into the vices attendant on the idle and especially associated with the military: drunkenness, womanizing, rowdiness, gaming, and riot. The close living conditions of active soldiers and private citizens exacerbated the tension between these two groups. Childs gives us the following overview of the subject:

> Civilians generally hated soldiers. To the reluctant householders who had to billet their unwelcome military guests the regulars must have seemed little more than armed policemen living for next to nothing at the expense of honest townsfolk—anti-social and dangerous parasites . . .[2]

> Soldiers stole, assaulted men and women, plundered, raped and often refused to pay the whole or part of the bill for their billets.[3]

This tension was deeply felt on both sides and long standing. In Otway's comedy *The Souldiers Fortune* (1681), Courtine, a military man, mimics the typical voices of the populace in a counterpoint of hypocritical nicety, "Heaven's bless you, Sir," and scurrilous abuse:

> Ye Lowsy Red-coat rake hells! hout ye Caterpillars, ye Locusts of the Nation, you are the Dogs that would enslave us all, plunder our Shops, and ravish our Daughters, ye Scoundrels.[4]

Civilian-military friction forms an important part of the social background of *Tom Jones*. The irony of military unruliness—depicted so fully in Hogarth's "March to Finchley"—is that, as Childs also points out, "the standing armies of all European states assisted in the maintenance of law and order."[5]

As the inn provides Fielding with a perfect setting for his

wonderfully comic conflicts between the different professions and classes, so such inn scenes frequently include a representative from the military. *Joseph Andrews* contains only passing references to the military, but several of these are noteworthy with respect to the subject of domestic tension. When asked if she would take Joseph into her inn out of charity, Mrs. Towwouse objects with the following squeal: "The Law makes us provide for too many already. We shall have thirty or forty poor Wretches in red Coats shortly."[6] Besides Mrs. Tow-wouse's comments, there is the reference to Betty's predicament or the "ticklish Situation of a Chamber-maid at an Inn, who is daily liable to the . . . Addresses of Fine Gentlemen of the Army, who sometimes are obliged to reside with them a whole Year together" (*JA*, 86). The billeting of soldiers in private homes and inns was the common practice in eighteenth-century England, especially during emergencies like the 1745 uprising, and it created considerable friction between the military and civilian populations. In 1746 a petition to the members of Parliament was made by the County of Lancaster to protest the billeting in Manchester and Salford of "one regiment of foot and one of dragoons, making nine hundred men in both towns . . . and two hundred and fifty women and children belonging to them."[7] These men and their families had been living in Manchester and Salford for over four months going back to the action of Preston. England's only military barracks at this time were located at the Tower, the Savoy, and Hull. It is believed that the building of more was discouraged because the English associated barracks with a tyrannical military state.[8] Thus it comes as no surprise that barracks, as opposed to public billets, were used in Ireland and Scotland. The irony of the situation is straightforward: the military was not trusted to be left concentrated and apart from the civilian population; on the other hand, the quartering of soldiers in public inns and houses created a considerable dislike and fear of the military on the part of the civilians.

Trained in violence and force, military men seem prone to fall into general unruliness when they find themselves in civilian situations. In fact, their exposure to the dangers of the field may make them zealous to enjoy the domestic amusements of wine, women, and whatever. Another example of civilian-military tension occasioned by the billeting of troops occurs when Adams meets a gentleman out hunting who makes an angry comment on the lack of game: "the Soldiers, who are quartered in the Neighbourhood, have killed it all" (*JA*, 131). Hence, one would have expected to see military characters in groups of rowdies like the half-pay captain in the company of the squire who abducts Fanny.

These references cast light on the military episode in *Tom Jones* (*TJ*, bk. 7, chap. 11 to bk. 8, chap. 2). The suspicious landlord "Robin" keeps a watchful eye on the sleeping Jones when suddenly "a violent Thundering at his outward Gate called him from his Seat . . . his Kitchen was immediately full of Gentlemen in red coats, who all rushed upon him in as tumultuous a Manner, as if they intended to take his little Castle by Storm."⁹ These boisterous redcoats force the landlord to furnish them with beer and drive Jones from his slumber. They then get into a "violent Dispute" over who should pay the reckoning, which "seemed to draw towards a military Decision" (*TJ*, 367) when Jones volunteers to pay the bill himself.

Jones also volunteers to join the two companies that are on their way to fight against the Jacobite rebels, and after a day's march they arrive at another inn. While dining with the officers, Jones proves himself a sharper wit than the rough Northerton who suddenly decks his antagonist with a bottle to the head. The landlady's comments to Jones after the companies have left encapsulate the resentment that many innkeepers and civilians felt toward the military:

> I think it is a great Pity that such a pretty young Gentleman should undervalue himself so, as to go about with these Soldier Fellows. . . . And to be sure it is very hard upon us to be obliged to pay them, and to keep 'em too, as we Publicans are. . . . Then there's such Swearing among 'um, to be sure, it frightens me out o' my Wits, I thinks nothing can ever prosper with such wicked People. And here one of 'um has used you in so barbarous a Manner.
>
> (*TJ*, 408)

Battestin notes that, "According to the annual statute against Mutiny and Desertion, the keepers of inns and ale-houses were required to provide food and lodging for the Army at a rate *per diem* of 4d. for a foot-soldier and 1s. for a commissioned officer below the rank of captain" (*TJ*, 408, n. 1).¹⁰

A similar incident occurs at the Upton inn. A party of musketeers arrives with a deserter in its custody; the sergeant demands "his Billets, together with a Mug of Beer" and spreads "himself before the Kitchen Fire" (*TJ*, 505). During the ensuing conversation, the landlord expresses his resentment toward an officer whom he felt had abused his billet privileges: "Here was one quartered upon me half a Year, who had the Conscience to take up one of my best Beds, tho' he hardly spent a Shilling a Day in the House, and suffered his Men to roast Cabbages at the Kitchen Fire, because I would not give them a Dinner on a *Sunday*" (*TJ*, 516). After an exchange of hard words, the sergeant issues a general challenge that is accepted by a coachman, and Fielding mentions that both men had sacrificed as well to "the God of Drink" as "the God of War"—in plain words, "they were both dead drunk" (*TJ*, 517). The pattern of military unruliness repeats itself.

The history of the parliamentary debate of these prescribed allowances in the Mutiny Act reflects the degree of dissension that existed on the subject of the army and its subsistence. The Mutiny Act itself, first passed in 1689, has generally been re-garded as Parliament's grant of a statutory right for a standing army to exist. Because the Mutiny Act had to be renewed every year,[11] this statutory right was considered, by those who gener-ally opposed standing armies (i.e., Tory sympathizers like Swift), temporary, and hence, from their viewpoint, the army had no real legal "standing" status at all. However, in practical terms, there had been a standing army in England since November 1660 when the First Foot Guards were formed, largely on account of Charles II's fears about civil disorder.[12] This origin points to the great irony of the army—as it was perceived and used in the eighteenth century: established to quell civil disorder, the army itself is feared for exactly the same reason. As far as the militias were concerned, they bore notorious reputations for rowdiness and lack of discipline—hence Fielding's aspersions on London's "Trained Bands" (see *JA*, 132, and *TJ*, 37). Dryden's lines on the militia suggest that their unprofessional and unreliable behavior was another long-standing point of ridicule:

> The Country rings around with loud Alarms,
> And raw in Fields the rude Militia swarms;
> Mouths without Hands; maintain'd at vast Expense,
> In peace a Charge, in War a weak Defense;
> Stout once a Month they march a blustering Band,
> And ever, but in times of Need, at hand:
> This was the Morn when issuing on the Guard,
> Drawn up in Ranks and File they stood prepar'd
> Of seeming Arms to make a short essay,
> Then hasten to be Drunk, the Business of the Day.[13]

Such negative depictions of the militia, eager for the play and revelry of the profession, are standard in the literature of the period.

In any case, when the Mutiny Act was passed in 1703, it contained the clause that stipulated the maximum subsistence allowances justices could set. In some cases innkeepers were allowed to pay soldiers (their *per diem* allowance) to lodge elsewhere. What happened is that it was generally agreed through practice that these maxima were in fact the expected allowances. A crisis occurred in 1741 when in John Fortescue's words, "there was a general refusal of innkeepers to supply soldiers with food and forage, owing to the dearth caused by a winter of extraordinary severity."[14] It was therefore within the law for justices to set lower allowances, and they were prevailed upon to do so when it was argued that innkeepers could not afford to provide what they had in the past. Violence had erupted in Wakefield and Ledbury, and the House of Commons began debating a bill at the beginning of 1742 that would fix the daily allowances at four pence for foot soldiers and more as one went up the ranks. The debate was interrupted by the defeat of Walpole and grew quite heated as members vied for future positions. All the traditional arguments, and some new ones, concerning the needs and evils of standing armies were voiced.

Speaking in favor of the bill were Sir William Yonge, Pelham, Winnington, Cocks, and General Wade—on the other side: Sandys, Gybbon, Campbell, Bramstone, Sir John Barnard, and Pulteney. Among the highlights of the debate was Gybbon's insinuation that the "true cause of sending a regiment to quarter upon a borough" is that borough's election of an opposition member. Bramstone remarked that four pence was a luxurious *per diem* sum, enough even to keep one's hair in powder and that "our army has been designed rather to kill the ladies, than to kill the enemies of the country."[15] Exasperated at a debate over what seemed to contain a foregone conclusion, the necessary subsistence of the army, Pelham remarked that when he reflected on the issue he could not "easily conceive by what art it can be made the subject of long harangues, or how the most fruitful imagination can expatiate upon it."[16] Pulteney proved himself equal to the charge of repetition by answering, ". . . surely the repetitions may be excused: for an objection is to be urged in every debate till it is answered, or is discovered to be unanswerable."[17] After some time, an amendment was introduced to fix the allowance at three quarts of small beer or cider a day rather than a monetary sum, which depending on market conditions, may not reflect the subsistence level. As one might predict, this led to differences over what was a "sufficient" amount of small beer a foot soldier could be expected to consume a day. The debate reached the apex of mundane and frivolous wrangling when Velters Cornwall rose to praise the excellence of the cider of his own constituency and to accuse his fellow members of legislating inebriation among the army: "And what outrages and insolencies may not be expected from men trusted with swords, and kept from day to day, and from month to month, in habitual drunkenness by an act of parliament?"[18] Sir William then affirmed that the cider of his native region was "of equal excellence," an assertion that brought forth an invitation from Cornwall to join him at his table with the firm belief that he would find two quarts more than sufficient. Ultimately, Yonge conceded some ground by introducing an amendment of five pints rather than three quarts.[19] All this demonstrates the deep feelings and contentious temperament of the English—especially when it comes to the army and beer.

The tension between civilian and military personnel that naturally arose from the billeting of the latter in public inns was by no means restricted to England. Most European nations routinely quartered soldiers in inns and private homes. One may recall the scene in Smollett's *Peregrine Pickle* (chaps. 53–54) wherein two French officers rudely protest a bill presented to them by an innkeeper on the grounds that they were being overcharged. The innkeeper, who confides to Peregrine that he has actually undercharged them for fear of such a protest, relents because pressing the issue would bring government officials down upon him and ultimately ruin his business. But as much as soldiers caused commotion and discouraged regular customers, recent research has pointed to the great extent that rural French communities were dependent on the military for their economic prosperity.[20]

The havoc raised by military personnel was often of the amorous kind. Farquhar's Captain Plume claims that it is a maxim among recruiting officers "to leave as many recruits in the country as they carry out" (*RO* 1.1.219–20). The standard military amour is usually portrayed as a transient or slapdash affair, and the responsibility is often mutually shared by both male and female as it is with Wickham and Lydia in *Pride and Prejudice*. The boisterous veteran and his doxy in Burns's "The Jolly Beggars" are true comic representatives of the bawdier spirit of military celebration, which is also present at the beginning of Smollett's *Ferdinand Count Fathom*. For obvious reasons, public-house servants were favorite targets of amorous designs on the part of the military. In *Joseph Andrews* readers are told that "an Ensign of Foot" was the first to make an impression on Betty's heart, and that other "officers of the Army" burned for her (JA, 86). Smollett gives us a good example of the brash and disruptive soldier-lover in the character of ensign Gauntlet whose amours reveal "a particular biass [sic] towards married women," a relish he "had adopted in the course of a military education" (PP, 166). Conversely, women like Austen's Mrs. Bennet or Fielding's Mrs. Booby (who finally pushes Joseph out of mind by attaching herself to a young captain in the Dragoons) are shown to be attracted to redcoat men. This attraction to the military man was also frequently expressed on the stage, as in the prologue to Susanna Centlivre's play *The Beau's Duel: Or A Soldier for the Ladies:* "She [Centlivre] thinks't a Crime for any one to dare, / Or hope to gain a Conquest o'er the Fair, / Who ne'er cou'd boast a Victory in War."[21] Centlivre obviously plays to the officers and enlisted men who would have come to see her comedies, as the epilogue to *The Beau's Duel* suggests: "A Soldier is her darling Character."[22] In *Amelia*, Fielding's last novel, Mrs. Williams tells how her heart was won by a Dragoon officer, Cornet Hebbers, who was quartered in her "Neighbourhood," and how he then proved unfaithful.[23] Later there are the schemes of Captain James to make an impression on Amelia. As one would expect, military men were often depicted as fortune-hunters—in the style of a Captain Blifil—and hence Mrs. Harris must be persuaded to consent to Booth's marrying her daughter (A, 74–79). In addition there are more violent types of military lovers. Fanny is abducted by a half-pay "Captain" (JA, 256–59); Jones meets up with Northerton, who has escaped his guard, just when Northerton is about to rape Mrs. Waters (TJ, 496); and Amelia is accosted by two military men in Vauxhall gardens (A, 395–98). Mrs. Waters, however, is not an innocent as seen in the billeting sergeant's account of her past as a regimental belle (see TJ, 514), a role also played by Fathom's mother and the bawd in "The Jolly Beggars." Mrs. Waters's history brings us full circle so to speak insofar as she begins her series of military amours as Jenny Jones departing Allworthy's vicinity with "a recruiting Officer" (TJ, 101).

That the wives of soldiers were often regarded as fair game is seen in Boswell's account of going to bed with a woman who happens to be married to a Prussian guard: "To bed directly. In a minute—over. I rose cool and astonished, half angry, half laughing. I sent her off. Bless me, have I now committed adultery? Stay, a soldier's wife is no wife."[24] Moreover, it should be noted that Fielding did not mean a character like Northerton to represent, as he calls it, "the Officers of our Army in general" (TJ, 522). He bids

The March to Finchley, 8th State, L. Sullivan/W. Hogarth (1761). *Courtesy of the Huntington Library.*

the reader to blame those who gave Northerton his commission, and of course the whole system of military commissions—how they were purchased and how influence was exercised—is a major preoccupation in *Amelia*.

Let us now turn to Hogarth's "March to Finchley," completed in 1750 or thereabouts.[25] The theme of military disorder is, of course, central to the scene here depicted, and the specific similarities between it and the military episode in *Tom Jones* are striking. The print depicts the general chaos of a troop of soldiers on their way to fight against the Jacobites. The scene is packed with all kinds of camp followers, sutlers, and families. The soldiers, paying no attention to their gesturing commander in the middle of the mob, mill about between an ale house on the left and a brothel on the right. The brothel keeper, a recent convert to Methodism, prays for the soldiers to return because they have been so good for business. Most noteworthy are the intoxicated soldier in the lower right who sits in a puddle and reaches for more gin (from a woman who looks like Ferdinand Count Fathom's mother), and his comrades immediately behind him who are all actively engaged in stealing from the civilians. These acts of theft are all connected and set in motion by the soldier who kisses a milkmaid while thrusting his hand rudely into her dress. Thus engaged—and offering little resistance—the maid is oblivious to the companion who pours from her milk container. Meanwhile another soldier points out the theft to a pieman so that he might snatch from his tray. Next to these figures are two other soldiers who have punctured a liquor barrel for their own benefit. On the left there is a soldier urinating against the tavern wall and grimacing with pain from his venereal infection, much to the horror of the woman in the window. In the upper left-hand corner is a boxing match, perhaps a travesty of the greater conflict and designed to show the true pugnacious spirit of the common soldier. The enthusiastic crowd gathered around expresses the idea of human bellicosity as grotesque spectacle.

Robert Moore sees the "elements of comedy" in Hogarth's "March to Finchley" as "the very essence of Fielding's comedy as well":

> At a first hasty glance the multiplicity of characters and action in *Tom Jones,* once the story has taken to the road, suggests a chaos just like the wild disorder of the "March to Finchley." Coleridge has pointed out, however, what everyone now recognizes—that the structure of *Tom Jones* is well-nigh perfect, one of the marvels of English fiction. Likewise, in the field of painting, there has seldom been a more ordered chaos than that of the "March to Finchley."[26]

Hogarth's details have a cumulative effect on beholders and impress them with the same comic-satiric spirit of robust military celebration that can be seen in the soldiers of *Tom Jones,* the Picardy regiment in *Roderick Random,* and the couple in "The Jolly Beggars." The print is dedicated to the king of Prussia and this has generally been recognized as a satirical statement on the lack of discipline for which the British troops were notorious. On being shown the print, George II is reported to have said the following: "I hate bainting and boetry too! Neither the one nor the other ever did any good! Does the fellow mean to laugh at my guards? . . . he deserves to be picketed for his insolence!"[27]

Paulson believes that the "March to Finchley" could have been meant to appeal to both sides in the Mutiny Act debate that had

Detail from *The Times. Plate I*, W. Hogarth (1762). *Courtesy of The British Museum.*

heated up again in the 1749–50 and 1751 sessions (not on account of any changes in the billeting provisions). The depiction of chaos could have been interpreted as Hogarth's support for the Duke of Cumberland and his wish to impose a strict Prussian-like discipline on the troops. On the other hand, the print could also be seen as a negative statement on the commonly expressed view that "the Duke, the incarnation of 'Prussianism,' [already] treated his soldiers 'rather like Germans than Englishmen.' "[28] The second interpretation is a little tenuous, but further support for it can be found ten years after the "March to Finchley" when Hogarth would mock the order and precision of the Norfolk militia in "The Times, I" (1762). John Wilkes pointed to the apparent inconsistency between the chaos of the "March to Finchley" and the unnatural uniformity in "The Times, I" print and defended the importance of strict discipline for the army: "[Hogarth] ought to have known that tho' *l'homme machine* is not sound philosophy, it is the true doctrine of tactics."[29] More-over, Steele's *Spectator* No. 152 gives a good portrait of the soldier's need for a kind of "mechanick Courage which the ordinary Race of Men become Masters of from acting always in a Crowd: They see indeed many drop, but then they see many more alive; they observe themselves escape very narrowly, and they do not know why they should not again."[30] We might defer to Dr. Johnson on the matter, since he wrote one of the most insightful analyses of the common English soldier. Johnson expresses the opinion that the insolence common English soldiers showed during peacetime and in domestic situations stemmed from a stubborn desire for independence and ultimately made them brave and successful in wartime.[31] In short, unruly and bois-terous fellows make better soldiers than mechanical wimps.

The civilian-military tension deriving from the billeting of soldiers in public inns and houses arose from a paradox of fear. On one hand, barracks were feared as a possible instrument of military tyranny. On the other, innkeepers feared that quartered redcoats would drive away civilian business and that regimental debts would not be paid. A standing army was maintained for fear of civil disorder, but ironically soldiers themselves were feared as dangerous rowdies. It is impossible to determine ex-actly where Fielding and Hogarth stood on the politics of mili-tary billets and discipline. Paulson links the ambiguity of *Tom Jones* and the "March to Finchley" in general terms: "For both Fielding and Hogarth the '45 is a metaphor for a clash between ideals of order and stability in the Jacobite's absolute monarchy and the relatively disorderly but very English parliamentary sys-tem of government staggering along under the Hanoverians."[32] More specifically, one can conclude that the interaction between the military and civilians resulting from public billeting was marked by a friction that could be assuaged by the rowdy or commercial designs of the respective parties; soldiers will have their recreation and innkeepers their profits.

Military Poverty and Preferment

Amelia contains Fielding's most sustained commentary on military-civilian interaction. However, Fielding here concen-trates on the desperate plight of the officer who retires on half pay and must struggle against poverty, and Booth *is retired* as his regiment is disbanded after the siege of Gibraltar. A rather dim character, Booth gets quite drunk and falls into his old bad habit

Six-Pence A Day, artist unknown (1775). *Courtesy of The British Museum.*

of gaming. He ultimately goes into debt for fifty pounds to Trent, besides losing his own much-needed twelve guineas. This weakness, not to mention several others, puts his family in dire straits (*A*, bk. 10, chaps. 5–6). The poverty of half-pay or pensioned soldiers and their families was a subject that surfaced in the poetry throughout the period. The speaker of Richardson Pack's "An Epistle from a Half-Pay Officer in the Country" (1714) mourns, in a manner that looks forward to uncle Toby, the peace that has reduced him to half pay and indigence.[33] There are several examples from the second half of the century including the memorable lines from the anonymous poem "The Soldier that has Seen Service" (1788), spoken by the soldier's wife: "Was it for this we left our home / About the troubled world to roam, / To conquer Spain and want a meal?"[34] Then there is the bitter sarcasm on the same subject, as well as that of child officers, in another anonymous poem "The Volunteer" (1791).[35] The latter two examples emphasize familial poverty, an aspect that is central to the satirical print "Six-Pence a Day," which shows a thin and gaunt infantryman surrounded by his indigent family. The infantryman is considerably thinner than the mocking representatives of the lower trades: a chairman, a wagoner, and a chimney sweep—who are all better paid at three, two, and one shillings a day respectively.

Military preferment was often depicted negatively since the system of purchased commissions remained a controversial subject throughout the century. For instance, readers are told that Captain Sentry quits "a Way of Life in which no Man can rise suitable to his Merit" and laments "that in a Profession where Merit is placed in so conspicuous a View, Impudence should get the Better of Modesty."[36] In many cases, a military career was somewhat of a calculated and desperate choice for a second son who was without an estate but who looked to use his connections and financial resources to purchase a suitable commission. Eliza Haywood dramatizes this specific situation in her novel *Betsy Thoughtless*, wherein the younger brother, Francis, eventually secures himself a regimental commission after his fiery character gets him into trouble at university. The various social realities pertaining to commissions are reflected in a variety of ways from Defoe to Austen depending on the views of the novelist.

One may remember that the military episode of *Tom Jones* includes the pitiful story of the lieutenant who served in the ranks for forty years only to suffer the "Mortification to be commanded by Boys, whose Fathers were at Nurse when he first entered into the Service" (*TJ*, 371). That undeserving men could purchase military ranks meant that many of the positions went to those with financial influence, like Squire-turned-Lieutenant Gawky in *Roderick Random*. John C. Miller describes the situation succinctly: "Advancement in the Army was made easy for those whose way was smoothed by wealth. Commissions were bought and sold much like shares on the exchange: prudent parents provided for their children by purchasing them commissions in the army."[37] The weakness of this system was that it treated poorly the soldier who perhaps merited promotion but did not have the financial resources. (There were some exceptions like General Wolfe.) Such soldiers, according to Childs, tended to linger at the rank of lieutenant.[38] Here one thinks specifically of the characters of Lieutenant Lismahago in Smollett's *Humphry Clinker*, Gauntlet in *Peregrine Pickle*, and the lieutenant in *Jonathan Wild* (bk. 4, chap. 7). Godfrey Gauntlet, discovered to be the son of one of Trunnion's trusted sea friends, impresses the commodore and Peregrine to such a degree that they assist him first to an ensign's commission and later to the ranks of lieutenant and captain (*PP*, 164, 364, 586). Then there is the magnanimous effort of Smollett's Mr. M—— who financially backs meritorious gentlemen, several of whom are lost in the War of Jenkins's Ear (*PP*, 709). Laurence Sterne's father remained at the rank of lieutenant for many years, and it is worth noting that Sterne's uncle Toby, who rises as high as captain, expresses a sincere, albeit naive, unwillingness to have considered purchasing a higher commission (see *Tristram Shandy*, vol. 7, chap. 27).

Although an official system of purchased commissions did not exist in the navy, influence and bribery were common practices.[39] On learning that one "Admiral Bower will soon be created a British peer," Commodore Trunnion explodes with the following denunciation that reflects the lack of merit in determining naval preferments:

> Will. Bower a peer of this realm! a fellow of yesterday, that scarce knows a mast from a manger; a snotty-nose boy, whom I myself have ordered to the gun, for stealing eggs out of the hen-coops! and I, Hawser Trunnion, who commanded a ship before he could keep a reckoning, am laid aside, d'ye see, and forgotten! If so be, as this be the case, there is a rotten plank in our constitution, which ought to be hove down and repaired, damn my eyes!
>
> (*PP*, 9)

Smollett is alluding to the early promotion of sea cadets, derisively known at one time as the "King's Letter Boys," over old sea dogs such as Trunnion.[40] The cadet system was established under Pepys's tenure, and its graduates were often depicted as irresponsible and inexperienced. Trunnion goes on to attribute his lack of promotion to his refusal to play the patronage game: "For my own part, d'ye see, I was none of your Guinea-pigs; I did not rise in the service by parliamenteering interest, or a handsome bitch of a wife. I was not hoisted over the bellies of better men, nor strutted athwart the quarter-deck in a laced doublet and thingumbobs at the wrists" (*PP*, 9). This statement suggests that things had not changed since Swift's time. Trunnion resembles the Host in *Joseph Andrews* who was "bred a Sea-faring Man," but unlike Trunnion, the Host is willing to play the game until his hopes fizzle out. He gives up both the game and his naval career when he discovers that his Squire's promises of "A lieutenancy of a Man of War" were never actually made to the Admiralty

(*JA*, 179–80). As a gruff seaman, Trunnion anticipates characters like Captain Mirvan in Burney's *Evelina* (1778), but the type, of course, is older than Smollett. A hilarious conflict between the rough, experienced sea captain and the delicate gentleman officer occurs in Charles Shadwell's play *The Fair Quaker of Deal, or, The Humours of the Navy* (1710).

There was a wide range of desirability as far as military commissions were concerned. First choice probably lay with the prestigious Royal Guards who remained in London to protect the sovereign; it was this regiment that Boswell had his heart set on. Less attractive were the newly raised and soon-to-be disbanded regiments that were quickly thrown into active service abroad. After the glitter and safety of the Royal Guards, service in the lowlands was, as Fortescue points out, usually preferred over colonial postings since the former offered better prospects of plunder while the latter conjured up visions of native barbarism and environmental hardship.[41] Pottle is certainly right in identifying Lord Auchinleck's opposition to Boswell's military aspirations as the prime reason for their never being realized (that and the fact that the war was all but over).[42] Put simply, the favor of granting Boswell a commission could not produce any political obligation on the part of his father.

In the *Champion* paper of 27 November 1739, Fielding distinguishes between two military types. First there are those who obtain higher commissions and "are content to receive from five hundred to two thousand pounds a year, for appearing now and then in a red coat with a sash, in the parks and market-places of this kingdom, and who never saw an enemy."[43] Then there are the poverty-stricken common foot soldiers who "may be seen in St. James's Park in a foggy morning in shabby red and black coats, with open mouths eagerly devouring the fog for breakfast."[44] These portraits form the prototypes for *Amelia*.

The purchase system had the undesirable effect of encouraging a certain portion of society to consider the military profession not so much as a first choice but as a contingency for those who failed at something else. Here one thinks of Wickham in *Pride and Prejudice* who serves with the militia after squandering a clerical career and before Darcy buys him an ensign's commission in a regular regiment. Beside being viewed as a fall-back career, the military also provided an easy means for those with money to manipulate the lives of the poor—at least the plot possibilities of such manipulation were not lost on novelists. In *The Vicar of Wakefield*, Squire Thornhill conveniently removes

Primrose's son George from the scene by arranging and financing his commission in a regiment that is scheduled to go overseas. Miss Jenny's comment on the pusillanimous Captain Weazel in *Roderick Random* succinctly expresses Smollett's criticism of the system: " 'Sdeath the army is come to a fine pass when such fellows as you get commissions" (*RR*, 51). In fact Captain Weazel owes his commission to his former employer, a lord who has to turn Weazel out to please his wife. Fielding's *Amelia* contains another example in the form of a Captain Trent whose rank was purchased for him by his father-in-law in hope that combat would eventually make his daughter a widow. Despite the calls for reform (such as Argyll's famous speech in Parliament, 9 December 1740) and the attempts to at least regulate the bartering, the system of purchased commissions continued with a momentum all its own.

Fielding's objections to purchased commissions are more problematic. First, like Sterne, Fielding came from a military family. The system of purchased commissions, despite its abuses, was firmly established by Marlborough, whom Fielding regarded highly, to keep the control of the army more in the regiments themselves and less in the hands of Parliament. His father served under Marlborough and rose to the rank of lieutenant-general, and his brother Edmund, at the age of seventeen (1733), received an ensign's commission.[45] Second, a percentage of the purchase price both on the part of the seller and the buyer went towards the maintenance of Chelsea hospital (established in 1684 for war veterans) and to help the families of deceased officers.

In *Amelia*, Fielding is deeply concerned not only with purchased commissions but with the plight of the veteran and of war widows and their children. We see the first in the portrait of the disabled war veteran who cannot get into Chelsea Hospital because of a bureaucratic obstacle; Booth meets the veteran in Newgate where the old soldier ends up when he cannot pay his legal fees after being cleared of a theft charge (*A*, 35). Then there is Bob Bound's sister, an officer's widow, whose pension has been withheld by the government for almost two years (*A*, 448–49). Her desperate situation was repeated many times in real life, as suggested by Mary Barber's poem "On Seeing an Officer's Widow distracted who had been driven to Despair by a long and fruitless Solicitation for the Arrears of her Pension" (1734).[46] The incongruity of preferment is poignantly depicted in T. Colley's print entitled "The Comforts—And Curses—of a Military Life" (1781), one side of which depicts the preferred officer drinking

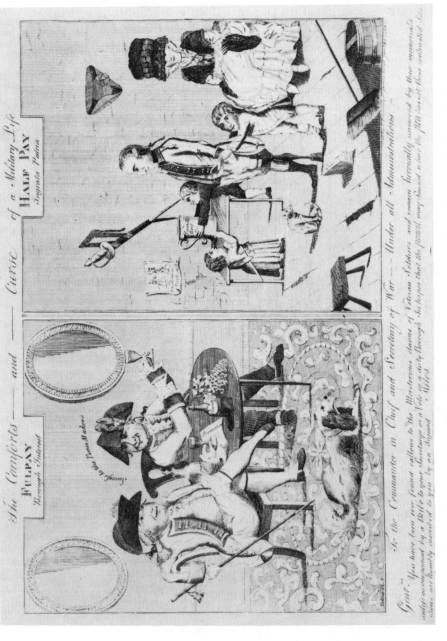

The Comforts—and—Curses of a Military Life, T. Colley (1781). *Courtesy of The British Museum.*

brandy at the club, while the other shows a half-pay officer and his family in dire straits.[47] In *Amelia* it is clear that Fielding's main concern is for the families of military personnel. Obviously, Fielding remembered his own financial difficulties as the son of an unpredictable lieutenant-general who like Booth had an itch for gaming. The image of the struggling military family marks the background of the woman whom Wilson ruins in *Joseph Andrews*: ". . . the Daughter of a Gentleman, who after having been forty Years in the Army, and in all the Campaigns under the Duke of *Marlborough*, died a Lieutenant on Half-Pay; and had left a Widow with this only Child, in very distrest Circumstances: they had only a small Pension from the Government . . ." (*JA*, 206–7). The poverty of war widows and their families was a real social problem in the eighteenth century; hence, to oppose the system of purchased commissions meant, in a sense, opposing whatever assistance was being given these parties.

Despite these facts, Fielding is quite blatant in his criticism of child officers, and abuses were rife. Patrick Murray, fifth Lord Elibank, entered the army in 1706 at the age of three as a commissioned captain![48] According to Fortescue, many of these child commissions were granted on the basis of family need: "In many instances children received commissions in a regiment wherein their fathers had commanded and done good service, either for the relief of the widows, if those fathers had fallen in action, or for a reward if they were still living."[49] Obviously little Patrick would have been only a nominal captain, yet Fortescue records that children as young as twelve actually saw combat in Flanders, one in particular having served with distinction.[50] The plight of Bob Bound in *Amelia*, who stays at the rank of lieutenant for thirty-five years and sees many child-soldiers put over his head, is, as Bowers notes, very similar to that of the good lieutenant in *Tom Jones*. In *Amelia*, one also finds the insolent boy-officer who curses Sergeant Atkinson, and Mrs. Ellison's tirade against "those pretty Masters" that she sees "walking about, and dragging their long Swords after them, when they should rather drag their Leading-Strings" (*A*, 201). This exact image had been brought to life by R. Athwold in a print called "The Military Nurse or Modern Officer," which probably appeared just before Fielding's last novel. Things had not changed by the end of the eighteenth century; the cartoonist Gillray would register the same criticism in his "Hero's Recruiting at Kelsey's;—or—Guard-Day at St. James's" (1797), which depicts a boy officer eating a dessert.

The Military Nurse, or Modern Officer, R. Athwold (1750?). *Courtesy of The
Huntington Library.*

However, it is the plight of Booth that contains Fielding's most sustained commentary on military promotion. Entering the army as an ensign, Booth receives a *gratis* promotion to lieutenant when his regiment adds two companies and his mother-in-law, Mrs. Harris, promises to use her money to purchase a higher rank for him. Thus Booth becomes a captain, but his regiment is disbanded after the siege of Gibraltar. Commissions in permanent regiments were, of course, much better investments than those in "new" regiments that were raised for a specific conflict. However, the scarcity of the former meant that military opportunity really lay with the latter. Defoe's Colonel Jack deserts the permanent Douglas regiment when he realizes that he could "buy a [sic] Colours in any New Regiment" and be a "Gentleman Officer."[51] The image of the military as "genteel Employment" puts one in mind of Lady Booby who mentions to her nephew "that by a Commission in the Army" Joseph Andrews might be put "on the foot of a Gentleman" (*JA*, 301). Military gentility was of particular interest to Defoe because it could be acquired. Defoe's Colonel Jack eventually does quite well, obtaining a company in Dillon's Irish regiment—newly raised for service in the Spanish Succession War—and then a "Lieutenant Colonel" commission.[52] But Colonel Jack moves on to other things and never sees the military as a life-long career. We do not condemn Fielding's Booth for not seeing his way to a commission in a permanent regiment for he is without money or interest, but we might well find him a little dim in how his desire for such a commission makes him an easy dupe and in how he seems completely at a loss to do anything else.

In other words, Booth is the fool among knaves, and as awful as the knaves are, Booth may remain too foolish to earn any sympathy from the reader. He first becomes the dupe of Colonel James who promises to use his interest to obtain Booth a regular commission. It is soon apparent that either James is lying or without the interest he claims to have, and Booth is more than a little obtuse when it comes to realizing that James's real interest lies with Amelia. Booth also fails to recognize the similar intentions of the lord. Booth's best chances rest with Dr. Harrison, who sees a nobleman on Booth's behalf but who is laughed at for criticizing the commission system. One expects that Booth would wise-up somewhat after being enlightened on the real intentions of Colonel James, the lord, and Captain Trent. Captain Trent is actually working for the lord when he suggests that Booth try to pimp his wife to secure a commission. He even admits that that was exactly what he himself did. Unfortunately for Amelia and her children, Booth does not wise-up. When the pathetic and not-too-bright Bob Bound advises Booth to use the money that Amelia raised (to pay off the gaming debt to Trent) to bribe or "touch" a gentleman in the War Office, readers cringe uncomfortably with the knowledge that Booth just might be stupid enough to do it (A, 474–77). And when he does, readers may start to wonder about Amelia, whose support for her fool-husband begins to seem more questionable than admirable.

Booth's dimness forces us to look closely at the so-called merit that is cited on his behalf when it comes to promotion. The most that Amelia or Dr. Harrison can say about his "merit" is that he was twice wounded at the siege of Gibraltar. First he receives a musket ball in the leg; the second wound is a "Contusion from the bursting of a Bomb" (A, 116). In both instances, there is no mention of any unusually heroic or meritorious action; on the contrary, all readers are given is the matter-of-fact observation "so unkind was the Fortune of War" (A, 115), which reads like a statement on the futility of individual endeavor. One is tempted to argue that Booth has no real merit at all. "Military merit," however, seems to have been equated with "experience" in the field. At least this is the meaning that the Duke of Argyll gives to "merit" in his parliamentary speech attacking the purchase system: "And so long as you have officers who have seen service in time of war, which alone is service, you ought not to have recourse to others."[53]

Contemporary accounts of "genteel" officers are extremely revealing insofar as their lack of merit renders them both ill-equipped and reluctant to command in the field or even see action. For instance, "Von Ewald, who served with the British forces in the War of Independence, noted that English officers did not study the art of war whilst in camp—their portmanteaux were filled with bags of hair powder, boxes of sweet smelling pomatum, cards instead of maps, even novels or stage plays."[54] James McGrigor, a regimental surgeon, makes the following observations:

> The army is officered by gentlemen of anything but a studious turn of mind. There is more of gaiety, and perhaps of giddiness, or thoughtlessness, among them, than among any other class. Unless in time of war, their duties on entering the services are slight, and amusement is too often their principal occupation. A great many of them being well born, and all of them gentlemen, they do not look

with much respect to a profession which requires study and close attention, or what they term plodding and drudgery. In fact, not a small portion of them have betaken themselves to the Army from their distaste to study, and some of them from unsteadiness. Their parents have intended them for the church, the law, or some other profession, in which they had the fairest prospect of success; but after their failures in either of these, they have viewed with envy the seemingly easy, gentlemanly life of some officer in the army who happened to have no other object than riding out after the morning parade, or sauntering about a town, ogling and coquetting with the fair who admired his dress and equipment, and who was an object of notice at concerts, theatre, and evening parties.[55]

The military fop, of course, is a stock character, perhaps best represented by Sir Nicholas Dainty and Sir Timothy Kastril in Shadwell's play *The Volunteers*. On the other side, the superficial attraction to a man in uniform is wonderfully expressed by Austen's Mrs. Bennet, who fuels the infatuation that her daughter Lydia has for military men: "I remember the time when I liked a red coat myself very well—and indeed so I do still at my heart."[56] Nobody accounts for surface "scarlet coat" amours better than Mary Wollstonecraft. In *A Vindication of the Rights of Women*, she argues that military officers, like women, are victimized by poor education. According to Wollstonecraft, both learn "manners before morals": "And as for any depth of understanding, I will venture to affirm, that it is as rarely to be found in the army as amongst women. . . . It may be further observed, that officers are also particularly attentive to their persons, fond of dancing, crowded rooms, adventures, and ridicule. Like the *fair sex*, the business of their lives is gallantry.—They were taught to please, and they live only to please."[57] There certainly are enough fictional types of negative military officers ranging from Smollett's Captain Weazel to Austen's Wickham, and many of these do not even seek to please. The positive military character—and here one thinks of Smollett's Lieutenants Bowling and Lismahago, Commodore Trunnion, or Sterne's uncle Toby—are good-natured men who possess a strong sense of duty and do not play the commissions game. One is tempted to put Booth in this category, but there is nothing positive about his naïveté.

As Battestin points out, there are striking resemblances between Booth's misfortunes and those of Fielding's father; both married women whose families opposed the match, both were retired on half pay when their newly raised regiments were disbanded, and both had a special art for financial disaster.[58] On the other hand, Edmund Fielding rose to the rank of lieutenant-general, while Booth remains a mere captain. It seems likely that Fielding meant to criticize the low aspirations and machinations of those who profited by the purchase system while at the same time creating a military character who was so good-natured and naive that he becomes easy prey for the sharpers.

Military commissions in the eighteenth century, like recruiting practices, leave the impression of a martial system that grotesquely feeds on the pecuniary interest of those involved. For the poor unconnected youth struggling to make his way, enlistment serves as an initiation into the low, picaresque world of violence and corruption. In this respect, Smollett is far more satirical than Defoe, who espouses the opportunity offered by the military. For the son without an estate and countless others seeking financial and social status, the commission represents both stability and prestige. Here we find again the positive attitude of Defoe, the negative view of Smollett, and the problematic criticism of Fielding. A military commission often ties up the loose ends of a novel—Wickham's, for instance, at the end of *Pride and Prejudice*. And yet this is not so neat a closure, for the idea of the army staffed with Wickhams is a rather disturbing prospect, especially when one realizes that the good-natured "humourous" soldier, such as Bowling or uncle Toby, is no match for the sharpers and opportunists.

Martial Greatness and Parody

Fisticuffs or the *argumentum ad baculinum* (argument by the rod) is as much a feature of Fielding's comic fiction as it is of Smollett's. An important source for these brawls is Paul Scarron's *Le Roman comique* (bk. 1, chap. 12), wherein one finds the players embroiled in a combat similar to those described in *Joseph Andrews* and *Tom Jones*. Violent fights break out suddenly and repeatedly and yet do no permanent damage. In fact, the pattern of these microcosm wars in Fielding resembles the comedic form. A peaceful even festive group of travelers will be assembled drinking by the fire; a dispute breaks out that leads to blows; peace is eventually restored and the participants make up over a bottle. As the narrator of *Tom Jones* declares, "no Nation produces so many drunken Quarrels, especially among the lower People, as *England*. . . . and as their drunken Mirth generally ends in a Battle, so do most of their Battles end in Friendship" (*TJ*, 253). And it is in *Tom Jones* that these microbattles are set against the ominous macroconfrontation between the advancing Jacobite rebels and the forces of the crown led by the Duke of Cumberland.

There are faint outlines of a micro-macro military theme in *Joseph Andrews*. On the micro level, it is noteworthy to recognize the military incidentals surrounding Joseph's mysterious birth. While still an infant, Joseph is kidnapped from the Wilsons by a gipsy woman who later attaches herself to a drummer of a recruiting party. This drummer, who reappears at the end of the novel as a pedlar, holds the secret of Joseph's birth, which the gipsy relates to him on her deathbed. Believing Joseph to be frail, the gipsies switch him for Fanny Andrews while Gaffar had departed "a Serjeant to *Gibraltar*" and was abroad for "upwards of three Years" (*JA*, 336). As far as the macro dimension goes, there are a few significant references to the events leading up to and including the War of Jenkins's Ear. In the first instance, Adams meets a gentleman who denounces "that Affair of *Carthagena*" (*JA*, 131) at which, he insinuates, the British troops behaved cowardly. The same gentleman also admits to having "disinherited a Nephew who is in the Army, because he would not exchange his Commission, and go to the *West-Indies*," and adds "I believe the Rascal is a Coward tho' he pretends to be in love forsooth" (*JA*, 135)—the situation of course resembles that of Booth at the beginning of *Amelia*, who exchanges his commission in an attempt to avoid going to Gibraltar (see *A*, 92–93). The gentleman's comments lead Adams to cite, in a sound and learned manner, a number of classical instances wherein "a Man might be a Coward at one time, and brave at another" (*JA*, 136). When the gentleman flees at the sound of Fanny's screams, Fielding is not just satirically exposing him to be as hypocritical as those members of Parliament who decided to strike a deal with Walpole,[59] he also presents us with an example of how boisterous rhetoric can be inversely proportional to firm action. The second macro reference is contained in the host's lament that he was the victim of flagrant Spanish aggression and his own country's neglect—a shot at Walpole's avoidance of war with Spain (see *JA*, 179). As mentioned, these international conflicts can be symbolically connected to the burlesque-fisticuffs of the main action. Adams, who continually espouses Christian virtues, is usually the first to start throwing punches when the occasion calls for physical action. And so he does at Tow-wouse, at the rapist who assaults Fanny, at Fanny's later abductor, and mistakenly at Slipslop.

Fielding, of course, is famous for his use of burlesque or the mock-epic to describe scenes of physical violence. Not only do these burlesque passages link the micro and macro themes of discord, they also draw attention to the process of representing violence as spectacle—specifically a spectacle of language. Hence the narrator of *Joseph Andrews* appeals to the muse, "do thou assist me in what I find myself unequal to" (*JA*, 239), and closes with a mocking statement that distances himself from the entire passage: "Thus far the Muse hath with her usual Dignity related this prodigious Battle, a Battle we apprehend never equalled by any Poet, Romance or Life-writer whatever, and having brought it to a Conclusion she ceased; we shall therefore proceed in our ordinary Style with the Continuation of this History" (*JA*, 242). Adams's flight is defended again on the basis of classical parallels. Fielding even incorporates the pervasive element of interruption in the passage by having the narrator suggest that an extended simile to convey Joseph's rescue "would interrupt the Description" and that Joseph himself is "above the reach of any Simile" (*JA*, 241). These self-conscious interruptions serve the same kind of comic purpose as the brawls themselves do; discord suddenly intrudes and suddenly dissolves. Paulson argues that in the churchyard and Upton battles of *Tom Jones* Fielding goes beyond the chase scene in *Joseph Andrews* because, in the former, history is truly presented as a myth-making process.[60]

It is certain that the micro-macro military theme is more central to *Tom Jones* than it is *Joseph Andrews*. In addition to the churchyard brawl, the micro dimension is represented by the fight between Jones and Thwackum and company and, of course, the battle at Upton. The first and last of these are straightforward examples of the mock-heroic. In the fight between Jones and Thwackum, Fielding makes a number of macro references that constitute a commentary on human warfare. When Blifil joins the fight on Thwackum's side, we are told, "The Victory, according to modern Custom, was like to be decided by Numbers" (*TJ*, 262). As Battestin notes, Fielding had facetiously attributed any French success in the war to their greater multitudes.[61]

The subsequent chapter, depicting the unconscious Sophia, is entitled, "*In which is seen a more moving Spectacle, than all the Blood in the Bodies of Thwackum and Blifil and of Twenty other such, is capable of producing*" (*TJ*, 263). It is precisely this notion of "Spectacle" that underlies our delight in Fielding's mock-heroic style and in the sport of battle itself. Battestin points out that Fielding's description of the final positions of the participants, in particular the comparison of Thwackum to "King *Porus*, sullenly submitting to the Conqueror," calls to mind LeBrun's famous series on Alexander's victories that LeBrun did for Louis XIV in 1661–68. The interest in military *tableaux* reflects this popular notion of war as spectacle as we saw in our discussion of Swift. Conquest and power hold a fascination for those who feast on visual representations of so-called great moments in history.

It is also in the subsequent chapter that we find Fielding's aside on the subject of military arms:

> Here we cannot suppress a pious Wish, that all Quarrels were to be decided by those Weapons only, with which Nature, knowing what is proper for us, hath supplied us; and that cold Iron was to be used in digging no Bowels, but those of the Earth. Then would War, the Pastime of Monarchs, be almost inoffensive, and Battles between great Armies might be fought at the particular Desire of several Ladies of Quality; who, together with the Kings themselves, might be actual Spectators of the Conflict. Then might the Field be this Moment well strewed with human Carcasses, and the next, the dead Men, or infinitely the greater Part of them, might get up like Mr. *Bayes's* Troops, and march off either at the Sound of a Drum or Fiddle, as should be previously agreed on.
>
> (*TJ*, 265–66)

The allusion to *The Rehearsal* reminds readers of the difficulties, and often inherent incongruities, of representing the momentous gravity of war in art. Again, the spectator appeal of human conflict is expressed, and this grotesque aspect is only a slight exaggeration of how Louis XV and his entourage viewed the battle of Fontenoy in 1745. Of course the main thrust of the aside is its felicitous identification of how human reason remains in the service of passion insofar as the weapons of war grotesquely escalate the degree of violence that animosity can inflict. Furthermore, as the aesthetics of burlesque depend upon the incongruity, or more accurately the clash, between language and content, so it is that the horror and absurdity of human warfare emanate from the perceived disproportion of bloodshed to cause. Too many die for too little.

The macro dimension of the theme, in the form of the Jacobite uprising, hangs over the middle portion of *Tom Jones*. As we have seen, Jones, without a clear direction or purpose, throws himself in among the Duke's forces as a volunteer. Various incidents and alarms about the advancing rebels or a French invasion serve as continual reminders of this macrowar in the middle portion of the novel (see *TJ*, 367–68, 576–78, 593–94, 635–36, 648, and 654).[62] Sophia is mistaken for the Pretender's mistress, Jenny Cameron, and Jones's intention of joining the Duke's forces is humored by Partridge who reveals Jacobite sympathies and paradoxically nervous fears about a French invasion. The greater macro context to the theme of dissension is alluded to again by the Man of the Hill who discloses his own involvement in Monmouth's futile 1685 uprising. When Jones tells the hermit that "there have been two Rebellions in favour of the Son of King James, one of which is now actually raging in the very Heart of this Kingdom," the hermit's response expresses the grotesque perspective: "[He] then cried, then laughed, and, at last, fell down on his Knees, and blessed God, in a loud Thanksgiving-Prayer, for having delivered him from all Society with Human Nature, which could be capable of such monstrous Extravagances" (*TJ*, 478). Although it is clear that Fielding himself endorsed the anti-Jacobite cause and Jones's own idealism about protecting the Protestant faith—specifically the Anglican Church (see *TJ*, 368), it is not misleading to argue that he entertains the hermit's position while remaining committed to the antirebel cause. In other words, one can imagine a detached or distanced perspective and at the same time support a particular side in the fray, just as Swift ridicules war and yet remains loyal to the Tory cause in Part 1 of *Gulliver's Travels*. The debate between Partridge and Jones on the merits of joining the anti-Jacobite forces (*TJ*, 628–31) has the same ambiguous tension—naive idealism (honor) versus practical cowardice—as may be found in the brief encounter between Prince Hal and Falstaff before the battle of Shrewsbury (*I Henry IV* 5.1). Fielding steers away from making an extended and explicit statement on the Jacobite rebellion in *Tom Jones*. The novel remains primarily about its hero who almost gets swept into a monstrous conflict but whose personal romantic quest takes him away from it.

In the same fashion, but to a lesser degree, the action of *Jonathan Wild* is set against the hostilities with France that preceded the War of the Austrian Succession. Here Fielding presents the reader with French sea captains who are more humane than their English counterpart. The first French captain sets Wild adrift for his attempted rape of Mrs. Heartfree and protects the latter from further umbrage until his vessel is taken by an English man-of-war. Mrs. Heartfree receives little better treatment from the English captain than she did from Wild, who is meanwhile rescued by a second French vessel. Back on En-

glish soil, Wild takes immediate steps to have his rescuer seized.
Such is true martial greatness in a world in which all is fair.
Throughout *Jonathan Wild,* the reader is pointed to parallels
between the greatness of a thief and that of a military conqueror
such as Alexander the Great or Caesar.[63] Wild also justifies
murder to Marybone by referring to "those glorious heroes, who,
to their immortal honour, have massacred whole nations."[64]
These allusions to the sphere of macro war echo the words of
Macheath's gang member, Jemmy Twitcher, who declares that
"What we win, Gentlemen, is our own by the Law of Arms, and
the Right of Conquest."[65] While individual murder remains a
criminal offense, nationally sanctioned murder remains per-
missible according to international law, even that of Grotius.

The idea of military grandeur and its linguistic properties was
a major concern of Fielding's. In *The Tragedy of Tragedies,* we
learn that the great Tom Thumb is about to march on stage with
the head of his rival, Grizzle, underarm, when suddenly, Noodle
announces that Tom has been swallowed by a cow:

> *Noodle.* Oh! Monstrous, dreadful terrible, Oh! Oh!
>   Deaf be my ears, for ever blind, my Eyes!
>   Dumb be my Tongue! Feet lame! All Senses lost!
>   Howl Wolves, grunt Bears, hiss Snakes, shriek all ye Ghosts!
> *King.* What does the blockhead mean?
> *Noodle.* I mean my Liege
>   Only to grace my Tale with decent Horror.[66]

Grotesque language fitted to grotesque action is the heroic formula for military spectacle, and the last line in the passage even
includes a direct echo of Dryden's *Cloemenes.* In his poem "Of
True Greatness," Fielding puts forward an unconvincing distinction between the false grandeur of Alexander and its genuine
manifestation in Marlborough. Alexander's exploits amount to
nothing other than horrific bloodshed described in terms of the
epic grotesque:

> Behold, the Plain with human Gore grow red,
> The swelling River heave along the Dead.
> See, through the Breach the hostile Deluge flow,
> Along it bears the unresisting Foe:
> Hear, in each Street the wretched Virgin's Cries,
> Her Lover sees her ravish'd as he dies.[67]

In contrast, Marlborough's conquests, achieved by "defensive
Arms," are said to have "Sav'd Millions by each noble Life they

lost" (lines 100–102). If there is a distinction to be made between the two military leaders, which there certainly is, it evaporates in the formality of Fielding's traditional rhetoric. More distinguished is the author's aside in *Tom Jones* about habit lessening the horror of certain professional activities, such as those of the lawyer Dowling or the "Professors of Human Bloodshedding, who in their Trade of War butcher Thousands, not only of their Fellow Professors, but often of Women and Children, without Remorse" (*TJ*, 658). The aside heightens in irony when the author points out that these professionals may also be very decent individuals when they are not practising their trade: ". . . even these . . . in Times of Peace, when Drums and Trumpets are laid aside, often lay aside all their Ferocity, and become very gentle Members of civil Society" (*TJ*, 658). So it goes. Similarly, when one senses that a battle description repeats the customary images of slaughter in stock similes and language, its pure shock value decreases.

Like Swift, Smollett, and Sterne, Fielding engaged in polemical battles of his own and frequently resorted to warfare metaphors in his journals. He first compared the writer to the soldier in *The Champion* paper of 27 November 1739, but it is really in "A Dialogue between Alexander the Great and Diogenes the Cynic" that Fielding explores the organic similarities between military conquerors who seek physical dominance and satirists who wish to persuade their readership of a certain point of view. Like those of Lucian and Prior, Fielding's dialogue is a lively and succinct form for expressing general thoughts on art and military achievement. Diogenes maintains the Shaftesbury position that sees the profession of satire as ultimately having the most beneficent objective—the moral reformation of man. Alexander stubbornly insists that his profession can boast of real material accomplishment—physical conquest, but Diogenes remains unconvinced. Frustrated, Alexander then claims that Diogenes possesses the same "Greatness of Soul" as he does and offers to use his army to inflict punishment on the *"Athenians"*, who have attacked Diogenes's philosophy.[68] The prospect of physical revenge appeals to Diogenes, who reveals his human side in accepting Alexander's offer, yet he continues to insult the Macedonian. In turn, Alexander reveals his affinity with the cynic in that he admires and envies Diogenes's "Obstinacy."[69] The roles of the conqueror and the satirist come together.

It is easy to see the connections between the subject of military unruliness and the micro-macro theme. But one must conclude that Fielding did not seem to have a clear opinion on the issue of military discipline; nor are his satiric comments on the system of purchased commissions without their complications. Through family history and personal belief, Fielding was led to honor the memory of Marlborough and to support a strong military as a defense against civil insurrection and foreign invasion. What is clear, however, is that in his fiction Fielding allowed himself the opportunity to explore both the absurdities of human conflict and ultimately the grotesque nature of humankind's fascination with military grandeur. Finally, Fielding was always ready to call attention to and celebrate the shortcomings of human attempts to capture a sense of this grandeur in language.

5

Sterne: Military Veterans and "Humours"

The Charm of the Military Veteran

LAURENCE STERNE WAS charmed by the military character. This charm obviously had its roots in family history; Sterne's father served as an ensign in Chudleigh's Foot Regiment and saw action in the Spanish Succession War after which he was posted to Jamaica.[1] Although Sterne went to live with relatives in York who raised him, he never lost the soft heart that he had for the military veteran and that inspired the incomparable figure of uncle Toby. Sterne's love for the military character is explicitly stated in *A Sentimental Journey* when Yorick steps into a box at the Comic Opera and sees a "kindly old French officer" sitting there quietly by himself:

> I love the character, not only because I honour the man whose manners are softened by a profession which makes bad men worse; but that I once knew one—for he is no more . . . Captain Tobias Shandy, the dearest of my flock and friends, whose philanthropy I never think of at this long distance from his death—but my eyes gush out with tears. For his sake, I have a predilection for the whole corps of veterans . . .[2]

This passage suggests that the creation of uncle Toby was inspired by Sterne's acquaintance with a soldier he knew through his father, or by Roger Shandy himself whom Sterne described as an innocent. However Sterne came by his character, uncle Toby remains one of the most, if not the most, single quixotic figures in English literature by virtue of the complexity of his military "humour."

Yorick encounters several veterans in *A Sentimental Journey*, and their military stories tend to be colored by a somber sense of misfortune. First, there is the Calais monk who alludes to "some military services ill requited," which resulted in his abandoning "the sword" (*SJ*, 102). Then there is, of course, Yorick's valet who had been a regiment drummer: "La Fleur had set out early in life, as gallantly as most Frenchmen do, with serving for a few years; at the end of which, having satisfied the sentiment, and found moreover, That the honour of beating a drum was likely to be its own reward, as it open'd no further track of glory to him—he retired . . ." (*SJ*, 124–25). Yorick's hiring of La Fleur, who "could do nothing in the world but beat a drum and play a march or two upon the fife" (*SJ*, 124), is motivated solely by a sense of benevolence that is more than fairly recompensed by La Fleur's good nature and company. Finally, there is the "old soldier" beggar "who had been campaign'd and worn out to death in the service," to whom Yorick gives "a couple of sous" (*SJ*, 133), and the Chevalier de St. Louis who is selling "*patès*" at Versailles (*SJ*, 209–11). The latter is a victim of regimental disbandment, and when the king learns of his plight, which the old soldier suffers without a harsh word, "he broke up his little trade by a pension of fifteen hundred livres a year" (*SJ*, 211). All of these portraits are infused with that endearing sentimentality that few novelists other than Sterne can successfully manage.

The situation in England resembled that of France. Hence despite the services offered by institutions like the *L'Hôtel des Invalids* or Chelsea Hospital, it was generally thought that veterans were not well treated for their sacrifices. In Hogarth's "The Times, Plate II" (engraved 1762 or 1763, published 1790), the spray of water that symbolizes government assistance completely misses a group of maimed war veterans. John Collier's "The Pluralist and Old Soldier" (1763) is a dialogue between a begging veteran who lost a leg at Guadeloupe and has not received his pension and a "well-fed pluralist" who tells the veteran to be-gone.[3] For those invalids who, for whatever reason, were refused admission to Chelsea or who did not receive pensions, the government did nothing except give them the right to beg in public. The veteran and his family described in the poem "The Volunteer" (1791) endure all kinds of miseries that culminate in a most inglorious end: "Some merciful volley then shatters a leg, / And his crutches procure him permission to beg."[4]

Consequently, it is not surprising that sentimental portraits of military veterans are quite common in the eighteenth century.[5] There seem to be two extreme types: the loquacious soul who, like uncle Toby, is always anxious to verbalize his experience; and the rather silent or pithy stoic whose experience has a significance that lies beyond language. Examples of the first include Goldsmith's "broken soldier" from "The Deserted Vil-

Detail from *The Times. Plate II,* W. Hogarth (engraved 1762 or 1763; published 1790). *Courtesy of The British Museum.*

lage," who sits by the good preacher's fire "and talked the night away; / Wept o'er his wounds, or tales of sorrow done, / Shouldered his crutch, and shewed how fields were won."[6] "The Old General" (1740), by Sir Charles Hanbury Williams, contains a portrait that is very close to uncle Toby's "humour":

> If you name one of Marlbro's ten campaigns,
> He tells you its whole history for your pains:
> And Blenheim's field becomes by his reciting,
> As long in telling as it was in fighting.[7]

Another comic example is Goldsmith's Mr. Hardcastle who is all too eager to command attention with his stories of Marlborough and Prince Eugene. The same type can be seen in satiric prints such as Bunbury's "Fought His Battles All O'er Again" (see the Frontispiece). One might also think of Defoe's Colonel Jack who "lov'd to talk to Seamen and Soldiers about the War" and from whom he imbibes an oral history, as Jack says,

> . . . those old Soldiers and Tars love to talk with me too, and to tell me all the Stories they could think of, and that not only of the Wars then going on, but also of the Wars in *Oliver's* time, the Death of King *Charles* the first, and the like.
>
> By this means, as young as I was, I was a kind of an Historian, and tho' I had read no Books . . .[8]

The soldier who has had to face life-or-death situations on a daily basis bears an experience that demands extraordinary attention and discourse.

Because language cannot adequately contain the meaning of the military experience, veterans are often portrayed as lapsing into cliché or being somewhat distant and silent. A veteran of the battle of Dettingen delights Boswell's curiosity for a moment with simple comments like, "Salvation is promised to those that die in the field."[9] Another example of this type is the old soldier whom Wordsworth describes in *The Prelude*.[10] The poet is walking home one summer evening when he encounters an "uncouth shape" (bk. 4, line 387); becoming curious, he looks more closely to see a "meagre man" standing alone "in military garb" and eventually presses the veteran with questions (bk. 4, lines 393, 398):

> His history, the veteran, in reply,
> Was neither slow nor eager; but, unmoved,
> And with a quiet uncomplaining voice,
> A stately air of mild indifference
> He told in a few plain words a soldier's tale—
>
> (bk. 4, lines 417–21)

Wordsworth prompts the veteran to "speak of war, battle and pestilence" (bk. 4, line 437), and the old man's response gives the impression of a resigned stalwartness:

> He all the while was in demeanour calm,
> Concise in answer; solemn and sublime
> He might have seemed, but that in all he said
> There was a strange half-absence, as of one
> Knowing too well the importance of his theme,
> But feeling it no longer.
>
> (bk. 4, lines 440–45)

The veteran's parting words, spoken with a "ghastly mildness in his look" (bk. 4, line 458), reflect the humble faith and strength that Wordsworth admired in many of his rustic figures: "My trust is in the God of Heaven, / And in the eye of him who passes me!" (bk. 4, lines 459–60). There is a heroic sense of resolution and strength that attaches itself to such figures who suffer hardship and often mutilation and yet who are not embittered. An excellent example is the begging veteran with the wooden leg who is described in *The Citizen of the World*, Letter 119. The "intrepidity and content" of the veteran despite his misfortune impress his beholders who subsequently acknowledge that "an habitual acquaintance with misery is the truest school of fortitude and philosophy."[11] Moving from the particular to the universal, one could claim that the pervasiveness of war in history immunizes us against its horrific barbarism and cruelty.

Several prototypes for Sterne's uncle Toby can be found, beginning with Shadwell's Captain Blunt, whose companions are forever reliving past battles (see *The Volunteers*). Yet Shadwell's veterans feature the hard celebrating and resolve that look ahead more to the "Sodger Laddie" and "doxy" of Burns's "The Jolly Beggars" than they do *Tristram Shandy*. In contrast to Sterne's meek Toby, Burns's "Sodger Laddie" is a rollicking ex-trooper:

> And now tho' I must beg, with a wooden arm and leg,
>   And many a tatter'd rag hanging over my bum,
> I'm as happy with my wallet, my bottle and my Callet,
>   As When I us'd in scarlet to follow a drum.[12]

The grotesque depiction of the veteran often includes references to lost limbs. Nelson recognizes the black humor in Burns's "Jolly Beggars" and in an Irish song in which a woman facetiously comments on how "queer" her soldier-beau looks on his return:

> You haven't an arm and you haven't a leg,
> You're an eyeless, noseless, chickenless egg;
> You'll have to be put with a bowl to beg:
> Och, Johnny, I hardly knew ye![13]

Goldsmith chose to mingle the sentimental with an abrupt style, and this combination makes him more like Sterne—as in the following picture in *Threnodia Augustalis*:

> The hardy veteran after struck the sight,
> Scarr'd, mangl'd, maim'd in every part,

Lopp'd of his limbs in many a gallant fight,
In nought entire—except his heart.[14]

Major Matchlock of *The Tatler* may also have figured into the genesis of Sterne's Captain Shandy. Matchlock "has all the Battles by Heart" and is held "in great Esteem" among his fellow tatlers.[15]

However, it is not until Steele's Captain Sentry—Matchlock's counterpart in *The Spectator*—a "Gentleman of great Courage, good Understanding, but invincible Modesty,"[16] that we discover a "humourous" military character who is modest and delicate rather than brash and boisterous. His military "humour" is, of course, animated whenever he has an occasion to indulge in military history. Like so many of Sterne's military veterans, Captain Sentry is noteworthy for how his lack of preferment has not left him embittered, as the Spectator himself remarks: ". . . I never heard him make a sower Expression, but frankly confess that he left the World because he was not fit for it."[17] Sentry, however, is an extremely sketchy figure (Matchlock, a ghost). Smollett's Commodore Trunnion seems to rate as the first fully realized military quixotic in the English novel. Yet Trunnion, actually falls into the category of the old sea dog, not known for modesty.[18] Seamen represent a separate subgroup insofar as their peculiar roughness and ignorance of social refinements were standard jokes.

This survey brings us back to Sterne. The especially intriguing feature of *Tristram Shandy* is how Sterne puts the reader in the awkward position of feeling sorry for uncle Toby because the Peace of Utrecht ends the War of the Spanish Succession, and the end of the war means the end of uncle Toby's miniature reenactments on the bowling green. Uncle Toby and Corporal Trim get their pleasure out of recreating Marlborough's campaigns and battles as accurately as they can; their harmless play depends upon, and is not merely tied to, the real war.[19] (In this sense the bowling green campaigns are different from Wemmick's castle.) After the peace is announced, Walter Shandy cannot resist executing a subtle "back-stroke" at his brother's hobbyhorse that expresses the paradox beautifully: "Never mind, brother *Toby* . . . by God's blessing we shall have another war break out again some of these days; and when it does,—the belligerent powers, if they would hang themselves, cannot keep us out of play."[20] As much as the reader may find uncle Toby (or Captain Shandy) endearing, and as much as his hobbyhorse is amusing, the notion of wanting "another war"—or of seeing the present one continued, which describes Toby's exact desire—is perfectly disturbing.

The grotesque best explains this paradoxical structure as well as the military theme that is an integral part of the Shandean dialectic. Not surprisingly, both Wolfgang Kayser and Mikhail Bakhtin single out Sterne as a writer of the grotesque. Kayser points to how the grotesque is more appropriate than a number of other descriptive generic terms, including satire, for identifying Sterne's art: "I emphatically subscribe to the classification of Sterne as a writer of the grotesque, for the categories of humor, satire, and irony . . . fail to do full justice to the form and content of *Tristram Shandy*."[21] According to Bakhtin, Sterne stands out as an eighteenth-century writer who continues the carnival elements of the grotesque.[22] Laughter, which Bakhtin sees as the key carnival element, clearly dominated the corresponding element of fear in the medieval grotesque, reached a climax in the fiction of Rabelais, and then gradually became extinct when the romantic grotesque exorcised the "comic" and intensified the "terrifying world."[23] Sterne is the exception who writes neither condemnatory satire nor pure romantic sentimentality but rejuvenates a kind of saturnalia that is akin to Rabelais's world. Although a few critics have already linked *Tristram Shandy* to the grotesque, their comments tend to address Sterne's general tragicomic sentimentalism or his disjointed narrative form as opposed to the military subject.[24] In *Tristram Shandy*, the bowling green hobbyhorse represents war as a ludicrous game; conversely, the battle wound represents war as fearful destruction.

The modern theory of the grotesque as a ludicrous-fearful duality differs slightly from the primary meaning that the English word "grotesque" had during the eighteenth century. Johnson defined "Grotesque" as "Distorted of figure; unnatural; wildly formed"—a meaning that reflects the pejorative connotations that the word then had.[25] The adjectival sense of "grotesque" as unnatural is still current (OED #2) and remains somewhat pejorative in connotation.[26] Sterne himself seems to use "grotesque" in this way (but without a clearly pejorative connotation) when Tristram self-consciously introduces his portrait of Corporal Trim.[27] It is also interesting to note that after the second installment of *Tristram Shandy* appeared in 1761, a writer for the *Critical Review* associated Sterne's humor with the "grotesque" and raised the subject of laughter as being worthy in and of itself:

Every body had heard of the different species of humour; grave humour and gay humour, genteel humour and low humour, natural humour and extravagant humour, grotesque and buffoonery. Perhaps these two last may be more properly stiled the bastards of humour than the power itself, although they have been acknowledged and adopted by the two arch priests of laughter *Lucian* and *Rabelais*. They deserve to be held illegitimate, because they either desert nature altogether, in their exhibitions, or represent her in a state of distortion. Lucian and Rabelais, in some of their writings, seem to have no more purpose in view, unless the design of raising laughter may in some cases be thought a moral aim.[28]

For Sterne, raising laughter certainly was a moral aim, or at least laughter could serve a therapeutic function and partially redeem mankind.[29] The art of cultivating laughter is the art of recognizing the comic in life, in Walter Shandy's words, "Every thing in this world . . . is big with jest . . . if we can but find it out" (*TS*, 1:470). This is the point at which the two senses of "grotesque" meet; what is perceived as unnatural (according to an erroneous assumption about rational behavior as a norm) and fearful may also be seen as ludicrous. Shandeism, therefore, squares with Bakhtin's profound view of carnival laughter as a kind of instinctive folklore celebration of the more frightening aspects of our existence such as death and war—a celebration of the ludicrous, of inexorable birth-death cycles.

Sterne was sensitive to a double-edged effect, similar to that of the grotesque, in laughter itself, and this sensitivity is at the heart of why "satire," as it is usually defined, inadequately accounts for how the military theme is treated in *Tristram Shandy*. When two parties feel that they are *laughing together* they also feel like allies insofar as they accept a common ludicrous point even if they themselves are the object of it. On the other hand, if one of the two feels *laughed at*, then offense and animosity may result. Sterne is eager to enjoy true comedic laughter but aware that human nature, as sensitive as it is, is often fearful about being the victim of insolence. Tristram tells the reader that uncle Toby's bowling green campaigns could be a satire against the magnificent pomp and ceremony with which Louis XIV took the field, except that uncle Toby could not insult anyone. Ironically, the very denial of satiric intent only raises the subject of satiric possibility, which is as far as Sterne means to go. Military ostentation can be seen as ludicrous. Likewise, Tristram does not mean to characterize "the militiating spirits of [his] country" (*TS*, 1:360) in uncle Toby. And one must not forget that the novel is dedicated to William Pitt, the champion of the British cause in the Seven Years' War, which went on while Sterne was bringing out the first three installments of *Tristram Shandy*. The Dedication recommends that Pitt take the novel "into the country" where it may beguile him "of one moment's pain" for when a man laughs "it adds something to this Fragment of Life" (*TS*, 1:i). Despite these qualifications and the military background of his father, Sterne nevertheless ridicules the human propensity for fragmentation and conflict, but he does not do so with any vain desire to laugh man out of his folly. Uncle Toby's wish to continue the war strikes a fearful chord and no more. Sterne's belief is that redemption lies in laughter itself, and if Tristram is writing against anything, it is, as he says, "the spleen" (*TS*, 1:360).

Still, laughter is extremely volatile as Trim is well aware when he proposes it as a means of disarming the daunting gravity of courting Widow Wadman: "All womankind . . . love jokes; the difficulty is to know how they chuse to have them cut; and there is no knowing that, but by trying as we do with our artillery in the field, by raising or letting down their breeches, till we hit the mark" (*TS*, 2:753). The highest role one can hope to play in the fallen world is that of the self-sacrificing butt, which is what Yorick does in *Tristram Shandy*: ". . . he chose rather to join in the laugh against himself" (*TS*, 1:20).[30] Conflict arises, however, when others are not willing to join in the comic fun for most consider a joke directed at them to be a declaration of war:

> . . . it happens, that a person laugh'd at, considers himself in the light of a person injured, with all the rights of such a situation belonging to him; and when thou viewest him in that light too, and reckons up his friends, his family, his kindred, and allies,—and musters up with them the many recruits which will list under him from a sense of common danger;—'tis no extravagant arithmetic to say, that for every ten jokes,—thou hast got a hundred enemies.
>
> (*TS*, 1:31)

When it is considered inappropriate or made at somebody's expense, humor can create rather than alleviate tension. The idea of laughing at another—satirizing an individual for example—recalls Hobbes's view of laughter as being a "sudden glory" derived from a feeling of superiority.

Sensitivity is the key to uncle Toby's Cervantic attraction,[31] for his military affectation or "humour" constitutes a sharp Jonsonian ridicule. This parodox of being a man-at-arms and yet a man so harmless, innocent, and naive puts Toby at the center of

Sterne's grotesque rendering of the military theme in *Tristram Shandy*. The military veteran who possesses a blind professional simplicity and kindness of heart emerges as a character type in eighteenth-century fiction, the very opposite of the *miles gloriosus*. Uncle Toby, however, may be the most lovable of these characters; he literally cannot hurt a fly. On the other hand, he may be the most unnerving as well, insofar as his perverse wish to continue the war is concerned.

War Games and Wounds

Laughing at a serious subject like war seems callous and bound to offend, but it is here that Sterne's subtlety plays such an important role. Neither Tristram nor the reader ever laugh directly at war; we laugh at the hobbyhorse, and the hobbyhorse is both a mock-heroic of adult play and a travesty of the War of the Spanish Succession. As Rabelais's Picrocholine War is both a mock-allegory of a lawsuit in Rabelais's home village, according to Bakhtin, and a satire against the aggressiveness of Charles V, so Sterne's uncle Toby is both a man at play and a man at arms.[32] For those who, like uncle Toby, feel themselves to be emotionally caught up in the military spirit, to go to war is—grotesquely or unnaturally enough—an expression of love. Toby defends his wish to continue the war by arguing that it is based on his love of honor and liberty (see TS, 2:557, 753). Violence is sometimes necessary to curb greater violence. Sterne's madcap narrator may describe uncle Toby's "amours" as the "choicest morsel" of his story (TS, 1:401), but the bowling green reenactments clearly form another key episode that Sterne could have expanded if he had felt more hobbyhorsical. What the reader gets in the novel, according to Tristram, is only a "sketch" of uncle Toby's entire "campaigns" (TS, 2:536), which Tristram is considering to publish as a separate work and which he estimates will, by itself, consist of three books.

Uncle Toby's hobbyhorse is the epitome of war as play or game. The reality of war is symbolized by Toby's war wound, and it is important to see the connection between the two. Toby's hobbyhorse originates from his attempt to communicate the circumstances that led to his horrific wound at the siege of Namur. The wound is as horrific as Sterne could have made it—a piece of a parapet breaks off and hits Toby in the groin, crushing his hip bone and confining him to his room for four years. It is an unheroic and freak accident that can only be blamed on the conflict itself, since the parapet was presumably hit by British artillery. But it is the diction of technicalities that plagues poor Toby (and his audience) more than anything else, when he tries to explain his sacrifice both to himself and the world: the "distinctions between the scarp and counterscarp,—the glacis and covered way,—the half-moon and ravelin" (TS, 1:94) are too much to handle. Language fails. Toby confuses himself as much as his audience and is in danger of sliding into fatal despair when he suddenly gets the idea to consult a map.

Ichnography appeals to the demand of the mind for rational explanation, and here Peter Stevick's comments are relevant: "Uncle Toby's fortifications and battle diagrams are, among other things, his defense against the possibility that his function, as part of the 'prodigious armies in Flanders,' may have been meaningless or incomprehensible."[33] As an individual soldier, Toby plays less than a "miniature" role in the siege of Namur. But explaining how he was injured is crucial to him for in Tristram's words, "The history of a soldier's wound beguiles the pain of it" (TS, 1:88). One map leads to another, to the science of fortifications, and then to the hobbyhorse itself, which Toby rides with all his love away from death's door.[34] His play-fantasy constitutes the essence of how the grotesque mode is used to address the subject of war, because it effectively distances the reader (and Toby too for that matter) from the reality of battle. I have already discussed the board war game in *Ferdinand Count Fathom* essentially as a wish-fulfillment being played out by King Theodore— the occupation of Genoese territory. For uncle Toby, the bowling green imitation is his mission.

It has been suggested that uncle Toby's miniature reenactments may have derived from Sterne's possible knowledge of "raree" or puppet shows.[35] Reenactments of military victories were popular parts of theatrical entertainments; for instance, the battle of Dettingen (in particular, George Darraugh's recapture of an English standard) was reproduced several times on the London stage in August 1743.[36] The main difference, however, between such shows and Toby's fun on the bowling-green is that the latter constitutes a private hobby that can produce great personal pleasure at the risk of public embarrassment. (Toby, however, is too far gone to be self-conscious about the puerility of his hobby.) The more important, albeit obvious, source for the bowling green reenactments is the military miniature, those wonderful toy soldiers and artillery pieces that were often given to monarchs-to-be to play with and were eventually mass-produced for the public

Miniature cannon and limber (ca. 1770). *Courtesy of the Colonial Williamsburg Foundation.* Miniatures of this type were made as models or ornaments for retired military officers.

about the time Sterne was writing *Tristram Shandy*.[37] These miniatures were constructed out of papier-mâché, cardboard, and wood carvings; tin eventually became the most common material. Some miniatures were elaborately mechanized. Louis XIII and his war-loving successor had mechanical soldiers designed by none other than Vauban himself, the famous French military engineer; they "moved, marched, fired, shot and retreated."[38] The wood carvers of southern Germany even produced a splendid "movable fortress," which reminds one of uncle Toby's changeable model town (*TS*, 2:539–40).

Although there is no direct evidence linking Sterne to military miniatures, it is clear that through his father he would have known many soldiers and people in the military coterie who could have collected them.[39] Miniature artillery pieces were often given to veterans. The significance of the miniature as a reproduction is its abstract nature, which it shares with military history and tableaux. In his discussion of Charles LeBrun and battle painting, Norman Bryson claims that "one sees a marked tendency towards a signification that is highly abstract": "the model here is the war-room. . . . a simulacrum of the battlefield, the war-room is also its real theatre . . . nothing essential is lost."[40] For the military strategist, this "simulacrum" allows one to be indifferent to the materiality of armies: "the martial body is enciphered, made into a statistical entity, a vortex of abstract force."[41] As a veteran and soldier's soldier, Toby is certainly not indifferent to the flesh, but only when it appears as such, as in the case of LeFever; otherwise, the bowling green campaigns are nothing but abstract games.

Before proceeding any further, one should note that there are *no* miniature soldiers on uncle Toby's bowling green. Toby and Trim are in effect toy soldiers or play as such in wielding spade and shovel to cut the breaches in the walls or in arranging the artillery pieces to copy the steps of the actual siege carried on by their commander Marlborough. Their commitment to reproducing the actual events of the war forms the key to the novel's theme of automatism or *l'homme machine*, because uncle Toby's hobby-horsical joy is to play out a reproduction that is entirely under the control of a greater force. To match exactly the real campaign is Toby's order, and a military man to the core (which is to say a puppet on strings), he thrills in the carrying out of that order without question and as perfectly as he can. This mechanical aspect can also be linked to the grotesque, which according to Kayser often shows a world in the process of dissolution—a world in which the human body is reduced to a marionette or automaton.[42] A commitment to duty, not the intellect, makes a good soldier, as suggested by uncle Toby's remark about the "*Walloon* Officer at the battle of *Landen*, who had one part of his brain shot away by a musket-ball,—and another part of it taken out after by a *French* Surgeon; and, after all, recovered, and did his duty very well without it" (*TS*, 1:173). The mechanical feature of uncle Toby's hobbyhorse is Sterne's subtle way of identifying the comic in military discipline and behavior. Furthermore, Toby and Trim's obsession with sequential detail and precision also reflects the discursive emphasis of military history. One thinks of Marlborough himself, who personally directed de Vos's representations of troop deployments in the Blenheim tapestries so that they coincided as accurately as possible with the Duke's own memories.

Uncle Toby's habitual association of whatever might be uttered by others (e.g., moisture, lashings) with his own military experience is perhaps the more central part of his mechanical "humour," which has traditionally been explained by Sterne's adaptation of Lockean epistemology.[43] Northrop Frye aptly describes the comic quality of the mechanical in his comments on "blocking character" or the Jonsonian "humour": "The principle of the humour is the principle that unincremental repetition, the literary imitation of ritual bondage, is funny. . . . Repetition overdone or not going anywhere belongs to comedy, for laughter is partly a reflex, and like other reflexes it can be conditioned by a simple repeated pattern."[44] The mechanical aspect of uncle Toby's behavior can also be seen as the element that connects the ludicrous antics of the bowling green campaigners with Sterne's greater comic vision of human conflict. As we have seen, the tradition of learned wit includes a comic stoicism with regard to war and natural catastrophes (plagues, floods, famines, etc.) that arises from a sense that these phenomena are part of inevitable cycles (see *AM*, 2:127).[45] Tristram alludes to the cyclical theory of war that was part of the popular culture of the Renaissance: "... *war begets poverty, poverty peace*" (*TS*, 1:72) and continues thus—peace begets prosperity, prosperity envy, and envy leads back to war. Writing on the subject of Sterne and late eighteenth-century ideas of history, Stuart Peterfreund claims, "Cyclicality ... was in general viewed with a sentiment ... approaching comfort arising from familiarity."[46] Again as we saw with Swift, a cyclical or determined view lends itself to the comic; the certain swings of fortune might as well be accepted, even celebrated. Henri Bergson's identification of the "mechanical" in human behavior as being the source of the comic or ludicrous can easily be extended to this cyclical theory.[47] If it is inevitable that humankind will fall into conflict, then we have nothing to do but continue on our merry way, stay in motion, and make the best peace we can—as Tristram does in France during the Seven Years' War.

When Tristram is arrested in Volume 7 for not paying a post fee to French officials, Sterne seems to be mock-heroically representing the Seven Years' War, or France's attempt to confine British expansion. In spite of the dedications to Pitt, who opposed the peace treaty of 1763 because he considered it too generous towards France, Sterne suggests that everyone should be willing to sacrifice something to obtain peace: "AND SO THE PEACE WAS MADE;—And if it is a bad one—as Tristram Shandy laid the corner stone of it—nobody but Tristram Shandy ought to be hanged" (*TS*, 2:638). In *A Sentimental Journey*, Yorick is detained in Paris specifically on account of the war. When a passport is finally issued to him to allow him to continue, it is issued to "let Mr. Yorick, the king's jester, and his baggage, travel quietly along" (*SJ*, 228). Again, humor is, for Sterne, the best way to make peace with the world and go merrily forward.

In *An Essay on Man*, Pope alludes to the justification of human suffering that is based on the hypothesis that mortal afflictions are part of some greater divine plan. The Miltonic echo, "Laugh where we must, be candid where we can; / But vindicate the ways of God to man," forms the rationale for Pope's later lines on war:

> Who knows but he, whose hand the light'ning forms,
> Who heaves old Ocean, and who wings the storms,
> Pours fierce Ambition in a Caesar's mind,
> Or turns young Ammon loose to scourge mankind?[48]

As pointed out in the introduction, the scourge theory of war, like the cyclical, was a popular Renaissance belief and derived from both classical and biblical sources. Satire has also been called a scourge,[49] and in this punitive function it may again be linked to war. If the cyclical or mechanical view of war possesses a ludicrous kind of inevitability, then the scourge theory conversely may be said to imply a kind of fearful expectation of punishment. Therefore, the combination of a sense of the inevitable and the idea of divine wrath, which can be located in Clarendon and Voltaire as well as Pope, incorporates the basic ludicrous-fearful dichotomy of the grotesque.

Lockean epistemology and a cultural sense of war memory run deep; furthermore, their relationship is given to sentimentalism. Cultural war memories are triggered by a variety of sensory phenomena that have historic properties (e.g., old battlefields, national music, roll calls). Thus Boswell contemplates the battle of Culloden on his trip to Scotland with Johnson:

> There is a certain association of ideas in my mind upon that subject [battle of Culloden], by which I am strongly affected. The very Highland names, or the sound of a bagpipe, will stir my blood and fill me with a mixture of melancholy, and respect for courage; and pity for the unfortunate, and superstitious regard for antiquity; and inclination for war without thought; and, in short with a crowd of sensations.[50]

Sterne keeps the reader well away from the possibility of such melancholy by emphasizing the "humourous" quality of Toby and Trim. Still, the reader is never allowed to forget the reality of battle as represented by the war wound, and this maintains the necessary fearful-ludicrous duality.

Like his master, Corporal Trim has been maimed by war. He was hit in the knee by a "musket-bullet" at the battle of Landen. Trim likes to see the positive side of his fate, and his remarks may actually be Sterne's way of subtly satirizing the inadequate pensions awarded to veterans, especially the disabled: "that the shot which disabled me at the battle of Landen, was pointed at my knee for no other purpose, but to take me out of his [King William's] service, and place me in your honour's [uncle Toby's], where I should be taken so much better care of in my old age" (TS, 2:693). Uncle Toby and Trim are so proud of their wounds that the only real dispute that arises between them is "Whether the pain of a wound in the knee is not greater than a wound in the groin" (TS, 2:696). For them the pain is emblematic of their love of country and freedom or of the highest principles of humanity. This paradoxical relationship between love and war is central to *Tristram Shandy*.[51]

Hence, however ludicrous the mechanical aspect of war can be, Sterne uses the war wound motif to remind his readers of what is fearful about war—the pain and injury suffered by so many. Besides Captain Shandy and the corporal, there are a number of other figures in the novel who have been victimized by battle: LeFever, his son, and even Cervantes—whose "wither'd stump" is referred to in Tristram's "Invocation" (TS, 2:780). (Cervantes's left hand was mangled at the battle of Lepanto—lucky for us it was not his right!). Their maimed bodies are living proof of the unnatural injury of war. When Tristram defends his purpose in the novel, he claims that uncle Toby's wound "is a wound to every comparison of that kind" (TS 1:360), and one may interpret this ambiguous statement in two ways: it is either of the military kind or of the groin kind. One is probably safe in saying that Sterne wants the reader to associate the two within the greater symbolic structure of the novel; the threat of castration, which is what Toby's wound signifies, reflects the danger that war poses to the human species. Tristram's wound also represents the threat of castration; the curtain falls while he is relieving himself at the window. And Tristram's can also be called a war wound; for after all the curtain only falls because Trim has taken and melted down the weights on the sash-window pullies to add a few cannon to the bowling green artillery. As much as Sterne makes his readers laugh, he can also make them wince.

Adding to the bowling green miniatures becomes a subtle means for Sterne to express what seems to be a clear yet indirect indictment of the cost of war. As with all hobbies, the bowling green campaigns are sure to incur some expense. Trim wants to use a pair of "jack boots" to make "two mortar pieces for a siege next summer" and this arouses some objection from Walter Shandy. It turns out that the "jack boots" date back to the civil wars and were worn by Roger Shandy "at the battle of *Marston-Moor*" (*TS*, 1:241–42); this confers a sentimental value on the boots, and Walter does not want to part with them. When uncle Toby offers his brother ten pounds for the boots, his brother goes into a harangue about how much money has been spent outfitting the bowling green. But uncle Toby will not be easily denied in his campaign: ". . . 'tis for the good of the nation" (*TS*, 1:242). Walter Shandy relents at this good-natured, yet absolutely mad, response. Sterne dissolves the distance created by the hobbyhorse fantasy whenever it serves his purpose. Trim enthusiastically melts down a good part of uncle Toby's rain gutters and spouts and even his pewter shaving basin, "going at last, like *Lewis* the fourteenth, on to the top of the church, for spare ends" (*TS*, 1:451).[52] Sterne does not want to upset his reader unduly. The sash-window incident throws a scare into the bowling green campaigners and suspends their fun but only temporarily. Likewise, one might say that on the surface Sterne's novel keeps us laughing, for the action certainly remains comic even if we laugh nervously at times.

Surely one of the most exquisite features of Sterne's art as a comic novelist is the yoking of the vulgar with the heroic. When the news of Tristram's misfortune at the window arrives in the parlor, uncle Toby is giving an account of the battle of Steenkirk to Yorick, who more than any other character enjoys seeing others in full gallop on their hobbyhorses. Yorick draws Toby into the full vigor of his spirit by allowing him to indulge himself in the particulars of "the strange conduct of count *Solmes* in ordering the foot to halt, and the horse to march where it could not act; which was directly contrary to the king's commands, and proved the loss of the day" (*TS*, 1:452). Enter Trim all in a panic about how he is responsible for Tristram's injury. Toby gallantly contests for the blame by insisting that Trim was only following orders, and this leads Yorick to draw an analogy between the historical account and the hobbyhorsical crisis: "Had count *Solmes*, *Trim*, done the same at the battle of *Steenkirk*, said *Yorick*, drolling a little upon the corporal, who had been run over by a dragoon in the retreat,—he had saved thee" (*TS*, 1:453). Yorick knows that such a remark will only give the pair a chance to escape, momentarily at least, from the immediate crisis back into their glorious remembrances. This they do and the climax comes when Trim blames Solmes for his wound for "had we drub'd them soundly at *Steenkirk*, they would not have fought us at *Landen*" (*TS*, 1:454). The subject of blame relates directly to the immediate crisis concerning Tristram's injury. Although Trim goes too far in accusing Solmes, both Trim and Toby feel responsible for the fall of the curtain. Sterne's point is clear enough: life is a confused muddle of intent and accident.

The History of Discord and the Discord of History

As mentioned, part of Toby's military "humour" is to indulge in the history of King William's wars at every opportunity. This fascination with battles and sieges is clearly understandable according to the "curiosity value of grotesque art," which Clayborough claims "is considerable."[53] The bizarre and monstrous attracts and fixes the human eye, a circumstance that is evident when the citizens of Strasbourg all follow the stranger with the huge nose and later find that their city has fallen into French hands (TS, 1:323–24). It may be remembered that much of the attractiveness of military art and the theater of war lies in their monstrous symmetry and conformity: uniforms, parades, and—of course—fortifications. Tristram, himself, is disappointed that he could not "take an exact survey of the fortifications" of Calais, which he calls "the strongest in the world" (TS, 2:583). But conversely the human imagination is also drawn in numerous ways to the monstrosity and spectacle of violence. For Toby, military history is resplendent with unnatural heroism and glory. And although his single-track enthusiasm strikes the reader as ludicrous, the eighteenth-century tactic, about which he and Trim get so worked up, of advancing right up to the opposing line and drawing the enemy fire before discharging one's own musket is itself fraught with the fearful: "some regiments . . . marched up boldly . . . and received the enemy's fire in their faces, before any one of their own platoons discharged a musket" (TS, 1:454). This standard procedure of withholding one's fire amounted to a battle of nerve to see which side could control the fear of its individual soldiers—sacrifice the few to achieve the greater objective (see "Introduction," pp. 23–24).

Moreover, to be enjoyed to the full, an enthusiasm must be shared; the *raconteur* must have an audience. Corporal Trim and Captain Shandy have each other, and their friendship forms one of the main sentimental lines of the novel. The delight with which they describe past battles reaches a climax when they are addressing Yorick on how to fight the French: "There is no way but to march cooly up to them,—receive their fire, and fall in upon them, pell-mell—Ding dong, added *Trim.*—Horse and foot, said . . . uncle *Toby.*—Helter skelter, said *Trim.*—Right and left, cried . . . uncle *Toby.*—Blood an' ounds, shouted the corporal;— the battle raged,—*Yorick* drew his chair a little to one side for safety . . ." (*TS*, 1:454–55). Because the soldier's profession involves such awesome performances of duty in the face of death, it is natural for the military to amuse themselves, and others, with stories of their trade. In Book 12 of *The Metamorphoses*, Nestor entertains the Greeks after a day of slaughter by relating the battle between the Lapithae and the Centaurs. Militarism feeds on its own history. When Yorick decides to entertain Toby by reading him Rabelais's account "of the battle fought single hands betwixt *Gymnast* and captain *Tripet*," uncle Toby brims with anticipation and requests that Trim be called in since "the description of a battle, will do the poor fellow more good than his supper" (*TS*, 1:462–63). Yorick's Rabelaisian joke is lost on the pair because for them the story of a battle should be the story of heroic love and sacrifice. Moreover, it comes as no surprise that Toby's favorite biblical passage is the siege of Jericho. The history of a military event may, as Tristram believes, beguile a veteran's pain, and this notion offers some explanation for the profusion of military memoirs and accounts from all ages. It may also partially account for the military emphasis in what Bryson defines as the lowest level of historiography—a narrative that "consists almost exclusively in a listing of battles, and where the work of history as an interpretative discipline is at a minimum."[54] Literary parodies of such historiography include Gulliver's accounts of Europe to the Brobdingnagian king and later to his Houyhnhnm master, and Toby's campaign stories.

Toby answers the charge of cruelty against the soldier's profession when he justifies his reasons for wanting to continue the war. Based on the irreconcilable plurality of the world, his justification is irrefutable: " 'Tis one thing, from public spirit and a thirst of glory, to enter the breach the first man . . . and 'tis another thing to reflect on the miseries of war: (*TS*, 2:556). One cannot debunk the ideals of soldiery by pointing to the horrible consequences of war. Those satirists who do exercise too much wit and not enough judgment. H. J. Jackson points out that uncle Toby's defense "was taken from an outright attack upon war in Burton's *Anatomy* and observes, "Sterne inverted the bias . . . when he transposed the passage into *Tristram Shandy*."[55] This is true, but Jackson may dismiss Toby's defense too easily. For Sterne and Burton, war is a terribly complex and ambiguous issue. Burton certainly rages against the soldier's profession in his tirade, but later in the "Satyricall Preface" he actually says that the world is so fraught with madness that what it needs more than anything is "another Attila [or] Tamberlane" (*AM* 1:96). And Toby's idea of his military role involves nothing but benevolence: "what is it, but the getting together of quiet and harmless people, with their swords in their hands, to keep the ambitious and the turbulent within bounds?" (*TS*, 2:557). Shaftesbury makes one of the most lucid statements on how "most savage" war ironically brings out the most heroic affections:

> 'Tis strange to imagine that war, which of all things appears the most savage, should be the passion of the most honest heroic spirits. But 'tis in war that the knot of fellowship is closest drawn. 'Tis in war that mutual succour is most given, mutual danger run, and common affection most exerted and employed. For heroism and philanthropy are almost one and the same. Yet by a small misguidance of the affection, a lover of mankind becomes a ravager; a hero and deliverer becomes an oppressor and destroyer.[56]

As paradoxical as Toby's martial benevolence is, England under William of Orange did feel a responsibility to help curtail the aggression of Louis XIV.

The military theme in *Tristram Shandy* is characterized by this kind of contradiction. Sterne may satirize man's fallen nature but he also accepts and even celebrates the stubborn endurance of human folly. Although uncle Toby is a perfect simpleton, it is his very simplicity that puts him in touch with the naturalness of his role in the world. When his heart follows the beat of a drum, he believes that in sallying forth he is answering the great end of his creation. And so he is, at least in his own eyes. Uncle Toby is also a Carlylean man of action and duty; according to him, a benevolent deity will judge in the end: "God Almighty is so good and just a governor of the world, that if we have but done our duties in it,—it will never be enquired into, whether we have done them in a red coat or a black one" (*TS*, 2:506). The camaraderie of soldiers transcends conflict, and conflict remains an integral part of the world.

The Shandy brothers can be seen as representatives of an archetypal dialectic or discord that manifests itself in the Shandy parlor, a microcosm of the world theater. Walter will talk of philosophical matters, the Captain military, and other than a few tolerances on the part of the former never the twain shall meet. While Tristram is being born, uncle Toby mounts his hobbyhorse and begins a discourse on the relative merits of the ravelin and the demibastion. His brother cannot hold his irritation:

> By the mother who bore us!—brother *Toby* . . . here you have got us, I know not how, not only souse into the middle of the old subject again:—But so full is your head of these confounded works, that tho' my wife is this moment in the pains of labour,—and you hear her cry out,—yet nothing will serve you but to carry off the man-midwife [Dr. Slop]. . . I wish the whole science of fortification, with all its inventors, at the Devil;—it has been the death of thousands,—and it will be mine, in the end.
>
> (TS, 1:129–30)

Images of birth and death mingle together. Uncle Toby may be his brother's worst provoker, but he also cannot hurt a fly, and when he sends his brother a tender and innocent glance, Walter Shandy melts with shame. Although a soldier by profession, Toby himself usually responds to provocation by smoking his pipe or whistling Lilliburlero. Whistling is a good way to reach a cease-fire in a hostile exchange of words, but the song Lilliburlero is ironically a mockery of Irish Catholics (the satirical content perhaps accounts for its popularity among the military; see *TS*, 3:113–15). In any case, Sterne's positive comic vision can be seen in the fact that while the Shandy brothers rarely communicate outside of a few sentimental moments, their differences never lead to a lasting or serious conflict. Uncle Toby may interrupt his brother's exposé on the radical moisture to recall the rain-drenched siege of Limerick, but his brother cannot stay angry. The larger characters on the world stage have the same propensity for inadvertent provocation but without the fraternal sentiment. Interrupting his own characters, Tristram gives the reader an anecdote about how Francis I sought to strengthen the understanding between France and Switzerland. Ironically misunderstanding results, and instead of achieving closer relations, the two countries find themselves in a state of war (TS, 1:357–59).

For Sterne as for many other comic writers, language miscarries. In fact, Tristram's "Well might *Locke* write a chapter upon the imperfections of words" (*TS*, 1:429—which of course Locke did, *Essay*, bk. 3, chap. 9) is the keynote of the novel and guides an analysis of its abundant war metaphors. Uncle Toby and Trim advance on the widow Wadman and Bridget from two flanks, but a breakdown in communications between the male pair leads to another hilarious misconception. Touched by the widow's inquisitiveness about the particulars of where he received his wound, Toby thinks about his map, "You shall lay your finger upon the place" (TS, 2:773). To him the widow's query is proof of her humanity, and so it is, but in more of a physical than idealistic context. In the end, uncle Toby's wound remains as bewitching and obscure to the reader as it does to the widow.

Tristram describes the courtship in the language of "Love militancy" (TS, 2:673) or in terms of war metaphors, a practice that goes back at least as far as Ovid and that reminds us of the love-war paradox. Like war, love or courtship often takes on the semblance of a game. Reminiscent of Mrs. Waters's "artillery of love" in that famous seduction scene of *Tom Jones* (bk. 9, chap. 5), widow Wadman uses her "eye" as a "cannon" and succeeds in blowing up uncle Toby, whose heart has been left vulnerable after the demolition of Dunkirk. Putting a hand on his breast, the gallant veteran turns to Trim and murmurs, "She has left a ball here" (TS, 2:712). The language of "Love militancy" is an accurate means of identifying the aggressive party—normally the male but not in this case. Despite his profession, uncle Toby is neither aggressive nor suspicious. It is Trim who devises a plan of attack and who recognizes the proximity between what he and his master have dedicated their lives to and what hits uncle Toby so unexpectedly: "Love . . . is exactly like war, in this; that a soldier, though he has escaped three weeks compleat o' Saturday-night,—may nevertheless be shot through his heart on Sunday morning" (TS, 2:700). Once inside her parlor, uncle Toby walks right up to the widow as he would to the French and blurts out that he is in love. As devotion to liberty and justice inspires Toby to fight under William of Orange, so he handles his courtship as if it were a military decree.

Furthermore, Sterne uses Trim to draw attention to the more physical connection between war and love when Trim relates the story of how love burst upon him "like a bomb" as a fair Beguine nurse rubbed "every part" of his frame (TS, 2:700, 703). However, Sterne does not just degrade the subject of physical love as uncontrollable passion; it is life, the life of us all and the life of Tristram's book. If war threatens the human species, love saves it, or in the words of Mrs. Shandy, "keeps peace in the world . . . [and] replenishes the earth" (TS, 2:721). (Mrs. Shandy, largely ignored by Tristram, represents the maternal figure of love and life.) But this kind of love can also cause war as Swift suggests in the "Digression of Madness" (*Tale of a Tub*, sec. 9). The Trojan War rates as the greatest mythic example of love-begetting-war in

Western literature, and the only harsh word that uncle Toby ever speaks in his life regards Helen of Troy whom he calls a "bitch" (TS, 2:556) for her part in that conflict.

War metaphors pervade Sterne's novel and suggest that the Shandean universe is a dialectic, that reality is not a state of flux but a state of conflict. To Walter Shandy, the speculative philosopher, it is imperative "to investigate truth and fight for her on all sides," but truth is known "not to surrender herself sometimes up upon the closest siege" (TS, 1:271, 282). Bombarded with all kinds of connected thoughts whenever he continues his *Tristra-paedia*, Walter Shandy discovers that "the life of a writer . . . was not so much a state of *composition*, as a state of *warfare*" (TS, 1:447). To Tristram, whose book is an elaborate improvisation on Locke's philosophy, the world is about equal in its stock of wit and judgment; wit leads to satire and conflict, but judgment makes "up matters as fast as ever they went wrong" (TS, 1:229). When another communication miscarries at Tristram's christening, Walter Shandy wails that "heaven has thought fit to draw forth the heaviest of its artillery against me" (TS, 1:353–54). Siege and fortification, aggression and defense, are the rhythms of the world.

While recounting uncle Toby's bowling green campaigns, Tristram mentions that "the most memorable attack in the whole war" was fought during the siege of Lille, it being "the most gallant and obstinate on both sides,—and . . . the most bloody too, for it cost the allies themselves that morning above eleven hundred men" (TS, 2:543). The grotesque formula for how man views war partially lies in the implied apposition between memorable, gallant, obstinate, and bloody. The more blood, the more memorable; the more bizarre or irrational, the more curious. Sterne is only playing with the reader when he has Tristram say that he cannot resist giving the reader a fifty-page description of the "most memorable" (TS, 2:584) siege of Calais—a threat that he does not carry out. But there is a very serious side to Walter Shandy's last harangue, which begins as a lament on the grotesque side of physical love and turns into an attack on the glorification of war. Accordingly, the first part is addressed to Mrs. Shandy, the maternal figure of love, and the second to uncle Toby, the fraternal figure of fragmentation:

> That provision should be made for continuing the race of so great, so exalted and godlike a Being as man . . . I still think and do maintain it to be a pity, that it should be done by means of a passion which bends

down the faculties . . . continued my father, addressing himself to my mother . . . and makes us come out of our caverns and hiding-places more like satyrs and four-footed beasts than men.

. . . .

—The act of killing and destroying a man, continued my father raising his voice—and turning to my uncle Toby—you see, is glorious—and the weapons by which we do it are honourable—We march with them upon our shoulders—We strut with them by our sides—We gild them—We carve them—We inlay them—We enrich them—Nay, if it be but a *scoundril* cannon, we cast an ornament upon the breech of it.

(TS, 2:806–7)

Despite the serious side, the harangue reasserts the comicality of life and death and rates as the most memorable run in Walter Shandy's oration. Lila Graves cites the "satyrs" reference in her argument that there is a "coherent imagistic pattern" of "man/beast references" in the novel; she then relates this pattern to Locke's attack on the doctrine of distinct essences and belief that there are no perfect divisions between man/beast or rational/irrational beings.[57] As Tony Tanner suggests, humankind is in reality more grotesque and less rational than we think.[58] The indictment of the glorification of war is, of course, a universal theme, yet one that has a special significance in an age that saw the lavish decorative art of Marlborough's Blenheim Palace and the *Salon de la Guerre* at Versailles. Keeping with the Shandean dialectic, Sterne has both uncle Toby and Yorick ready "to batter the whole hypothesis to pieces" (TS, 2:807) before Obadiah interrupts with his Cock and Bull story, the finale.

Walter's last harangue remains unanswered, and the silence on the part of Toby and Yorick, while preserved only through Obadiah's timely interruption, has the effect of implicating the reader in the statement itself. It may be said, therefore, that Sterne's closing segment climactically recapitulates the ludicrous and fearful incongruity of human discord by moving beyond the Shandy parlor and involving the greater audience of the novel. And as much as most readers feel the tickle of Shandean laughter in *Tristram Shandy*, uncle Toby's naive idealism and wish to continue the war will never cease to give them a gentle shudder as well.

Conclusion: The Last Line of Fortification

ON 13 JULY 1764 Boswell was in Potsdam and saw Frederick the Great inspecting his troops. The giddy enthusiasm expressed in Boswell's journal entry is noteworthy:

> I then went to the Parade. I saw the King. It was a glorious sight. He was dressed in a suit of plain blue, with a star and a plain hat with a white feather. He had in his hand a cane. The sun shone bright. He stood before his palace, with an air of iron confidence that could not be opposed. As a loadstone moves needles, or a storm blows the lofty oaks, did Frederick the Great make the Prussian officers submissive bend as he walked majestic in the midst of them. I was in noble spirits, and had a full relish of this grand scene which I shall never forget. I felt a crowd of ideas. I beheld the king who had astonished Europe by his warlike deeds.[1]

Despite the visual delight of such scenes, there is a certain Lilliputian quality to military parades that strikes one as ludicrous. After seeing King Frederick with his white feather and cane, Boswell spent much of that day listening to the war stories of two of his native countrymen: Captain Scott of the Prussia regiment and a traveling companion by the name of Macpherson. They dined together, played billiards, and went for a walk. Nothing is so amusing as the military *raconteur*; Boswell enjoyed himself thoroughly:

> Never were fellows more jolly. Scott gave us stories of Prussian wars, and Macpherson of American ones. I saw that the Prussian officers live just as well as others; and for the common soldiers, they placed themselves on a seat before the guard-room and sung most merrily. My ideas of the value of men are altered since I came to this country. I see such numbers of fine fellows bred to be slaughtered that human beings seem like herrings in a plentiful season. One thinks nothing of a few barrels of herring, nor can I think much of a few regiments of men. What am I then, a single man? Strange thought! Let it go.[2]

Strange thought indeed! But to liken soldiers to herring may well come naturally to somebody who aspired to the officer rank.

There is a facetious humor in the generalizing simile, the recognition of individual minuteness, and the easy close, "Let it go." Yet what strikes one most is the sense of absolute spontaneity and frankness. These features breathe life into Boswell's journal and make it a truly entertaining and revealing document— human thought, at once so uncanny and familiar.

On the other hand, this glimpse into the mind of a man who just might have received his precious commission is rather disturbing. In a similar way, the grotesque captures us in an intensely ambivalent aesthetic experience. We may inwardly laugh, but we then feel guilty for doing so. The interaction of the ludicrous and the fearful generates the life of the grotesque, and the grotesque is a mainstay of the human imagination.

The science of war had made considerable advancements with militaristic monarchs like Lewis *le grand* and Frederick the Great. Their strategies and tactics laid the path for the carnage of Waterloo (a battle claimed to have been won on the playing fields of Eton)—no better opportunity for the facetious. Byron, of course, rose to the occasion more than once but perhaps best in his picture of Saint Peter and the celestial gate's examining "board":

> This was a handsome board—at least for heaven;
>   And yet they had even then enough to do,
> So many conquerors' cars were daily driven,
>   So many kingdoms fitted up anew;
> Each day too slew its thousands six or seven,
>   Till at the crowning carnage, Waterloo,
> They threw their pens down in divine disgust—
> The page was so besmear'd with blood and dust.[3]

Byron's Augustan frame of mind definitely shows in "The Vision of Judgment," which was written about five years after the "crowning carnage," but Byron was certainly not the only writer during the Romantic period to use the grotesque mode to address the subject of war (although he and Sir Philip Sidney may be the only writers mentioned in this study to find a soldier's death). Whenever the human imagination is distanced from the reality of battle, the potential for the grotesque exists. At almost thirteen hundred lines, "Civilized War" (1798) by Joseph Fawcett may well be the longest English discursive poem devoted entirely to the subject of human bellicosity. It features a number of aspects of the war-grotesque association but is clearly at the "terrible" side of the spectrum. The ghoulishness of victory celebrations is depicted at some length:

> All to the feast, the Feast of Blood! repair.
> The high, the low, old men and prattling babes,
> Young men and maidens, all to grace the feast,
> Light-footed trip,—the feast, the Feast of Blood![4]

In his poem "Fears in Solitude" (also published in 1798), Coleridge expresses a similar disdain for how people made war into a popular diversion: "The best amusement for our morning meal!"[5] Here, however, we see that Coleridge focuses specifically on the 1798 threat of a French invasion and hence the fearful aspect, emphasized in the title, has completely pushed out any sense of the ludicrous that might come with a greater view of historical recurrence. In other respects, "Fears in Solitude" contains subjects that are standard in grotesque depictions of war. For instance, there is condemnation of military jargon, "our dainty terms for fratricide" that are nothing but "empty sounds" without substance or real meaning.[6] This idea is then neatly joined to the possibility of divine retribution which is akin to the war-as-scourge view:

> Therefore, evil days
> Are coming on us, O my countrymen!
> And what if all-avenging Providence,
> Strong and retributive, should make us know
> The meaning of our words, force us to feel
> The desolation and the agony
> Of our fierce doings?[7]

The cyclical theory of war is clearly behind Coleridge's 1796 poem "The Destiny of Nations." Coleridge is also more removed from the immediate Napoleonic threat in his poetical dramatization "A War-Eclogue," which features satanic laughter and a wild exchange between the three allegorical sisters "Fire, Famine, and Slaughter." Published the same year as "Fears in Solitude," this short dramatization shows the range of response that is possible from a man who five years earlier had to be bought out of the cavalry by his family because he could not stay on his horse!

The comic images of "Boney" and "John Bull" appear frequently in the graphic satire of Gillray (whose father lost an arm at Fontenoy), Rowlandson, and Cruikshank. Rowlandson illustrated *The English Dance of Death* (1815), which includes a section entitled "The Battle," wherein it is argued that war, far more than disease, is the true "power that thins the human race."[8] The illustration for "The Battle" depicts Death firing a cannon with slain soldiers and horses piling up on the ground. Rowlandson also illustrated Alfred Burton's popular doggerel poems, *The Military Adventures of Johnny Newcome* (1816) and *The Adventures of Johnny Newcome in the Navy* (1818), which made fun of the naive soldier and sailor respectively. Some poets drew the especially tragic "intestinal" parallel between the conflict with the colonies and the civil wars in the previous century. John Freeth's "Bunker's Hill, or the Soldier's Lamentation" (1780?) expresses a soldier's fond nostalgia about fighting the French.[9]

It is a long way from the Lilliput-Blefuscu war to the "most memorable attack" on uncle Toby's bowling green, yet so much of the ground in between begins to look familiar. One of the general conclusions we can make is that a definite continuity of ideas and modes exists in eighteenth-century grotesque portrayals of war. The continuity is largely due to the dependence of the grotesque on literary convention, yet this dependence also involves the wit or aesthetic energy of variation. Standard epic-battle motifs from the *Iliad* and the *Aeneid* and the learned wit of Renaissance humanists form the mainstream of this convention. Already steeped in the grotesque, epic-battle motifs were moved a little further toward the comic. This movement is important when understood according to Peckham's belief that "artistic behavior" concerns itself with the capacity to evade "the sentimentalities of comedy and of tragedy."[10] In Sterne, it is more accurate to say that vacillation replaces evasion. It might also be mentioned that with the exception of Smollett and one or two others, the writers examined in this book all knew war from second-hand, often third-hand literary sources rather than first-hand experience.

While the ludicrous-fearful duality constitutes the essential feature of the grotesque, we may also recognize many others: the playful attitude, exaggeration and deformity, and a self-conscious delight in spectacle and paradox. War is marked by many of the same features: strategy, ostentation, and escalation. Likewise, the grotesque has close affinities with the idea of satiric attack. What one ultimately has is an organic relationship between content and form, a relationship that can be mythically traced to the Fall of humankind; for as Baudelaire reminds us, the Fall ushers in both the misery of our debasement, so obvious in human conflict, and the potential for laughter.[11] Ironically, laughter is god-like and redeems us or raises us back up. But only when we can put a certain distance between ourselves and our misery, can we join, and only temporarily, the laughter of the gods.[12] This uplift, which is never completely free of fear and guilt, is what I have analyzed. Swift sees the petty nature of war's escalation and the spectacle of violence in historical discourse. Smollett reveals the grim realities about military service—not only the horrors of a colonial expedition but also how eighteenth-century armies consumed the indigent and how officer glamor enticed commission-seeking fops. Fielding focuses on the domestic military subjects of unruliness and preferment with the macroconflict always in the background. Sterne delights in the military "humour" and reminds us of its Cervantic nobility and comedy. To generalize horribly, Swift and Smollett laugh at humankind as if it were something alien; Sterne and Fielding laugh at the human in us all.

Those at the cutting edge of literary theory remind us that the grotesque is no longer the trendy term it was in the 1960s, yet a truly worthwhile critical vocabulary should survive trends. My method has been more eclectic than novel. I have drawn from the various approaches of Ruskin, Kayser, Bakhtin, and others for two reasons: one, it is perhaps time to take stock and synthesize the theory we have as opposed to improvising a new language for traditional ideas; and two, applicability must remain the first and foremost criterion for any theory. As far as theory can help readers understand their responses to texts, and help explain why part of one text is reminiscent of another, the grotesque is a valuable generic category with no mean background.

We might briefly sketch out a few of the ways that the war-grotesque association continues in nineteenth- and twentieth-century literatures. For Carlyle's Teufelsdröckh, Marchfeld, sight of "thy Wagrams and Stillfrieds" (Napoleonic and medieval battles respectively) is an apt place to meditate on centuries of escalated conflicts and destructive wars, and Teufelsdröckh does so in the language and imagery of the grotesque. He even alludes to the ridiculous smoking duel between Smollett's Captain Minikin and Major Macleaver (see *FCF*, chap. 41). Although Teufelsdröckh's meditation comes in the "Centre of Indifference" of *Sartor Resartus*, it seems to involve more ambivalent tension than indifference—namely, the tension between the language of misanthropy, "those red mould heaps . . . the Shells of Man," and that of reaffirmation, "unwearied Nature . . . from the very car-

cass of the Killer, [will] bring Life for the Living."[13] Having
perspective on the greater pattern as opposed to just the individual event is important here, as it is in the Nietzschean celebration
of eternal recurrence. On the most caustic side, Washington Irv-
ing, in *A History of New York* (bk. 1, chap. 5), repeats Swift's
ironic attack on aggressive colonization or conquest by "RIGHT
OF EXTERMINATION." The word "right" in this context may
well be an ironic reference to the work of moralists like Grotius.
Mark Twain's *A Connecticut Yankee in King Arthur's Court* concludes with a holocaust battle that points to the catastrophic
consequences of employing modern technology in war. The picaresque hero who must go to war to earn a living resurfaces in
Thackeray's *Barry Lyndon*, and Barry deserts the British army
only to be pressed into the Prussian.

It could easily be argued that the so-called black humor of
recent novelists would be equivalent to the grotesque modes
discussed in this study. The absurd situations in *Catch-22* follow
ad infinitum; rhetorical exuberance contributes to the overall
impression of madness as it does in Swift and Smollett. Vonnegut's haunting line in *Slaughterhouse-Five*, "So it goes,"[14]
strikes the same stoic chord that is ultimately heard in the Shandean universe. Then there is Anthony Burgess's *Napoleon Sym-
phony*, which contains the same low festive language in its battle
descriptions as one finds in *Roderick Random*. Some of Evelyn
Waugh's fiction, including the war trilogy—*Sword of Honour*—
may be understood according to the same grotesque patterns
found in Fielding. Perhaps the single most important modern
work for embodying the grand comic myth of discord is *Finnegans Wake* which sports a rich, archetypal series of war trav-
esties: Shem and Shaun, Butt and Taff, Mutt and Jute,
Wellingdone and Lipoleum, Caesar and Brutus, Sigtrygg and
Brian Boru, and Buckley and the Russian general.[15]

Finnegans Wake brings us full circle insofar as it is based on
Giambattista Vico's *Corso-Recorso*—the Enlightenment's most remarkable theory of recurrence. Three months after seeing Frederick on parade, Boswell saw the destruction in Dresden caused by
the Prussian bombardment of that city in the siege of 1760. No
trace of his earlier wide-eyed wonder at the Prussian monarch
remained: "I strolled about and viewed the city. It is finely built
of freestone. It gave me great pain to see the ruins made by the
Prussian bombardments. I hated the barbarous hero. He was
under no necessity to bombard Dresden. It was from mere spite
that he did it."[16] While the external trappings of military pom-

posity are ludicrous, the grim reality of war remains fearful. Nor is there an easy way to reconcile the two.

But never mind trying to reconcile momentous incongruities. What about the confusing science of fortification? So much rational and geometric planning to ease those dark primordial anxieties! Swift, Smollett, and especially Sterne all mocked the newfangledness and jargon of modern military terms. One of the most delightful instances of this linguistic-militaristic labyrinth comes in a letter that Lady Mary Wortley Montagu sent Lady Mar from Leipzig (21 November 1716):

> This is a fortify'd Town, but I avoid ever mentioning fortifications, being sensible that I know not how to speak of 'em. I am the more easy under my ignorance when I refflect that I am sure you'l willingly forgive the Omission, for if I made you the most exact description of all the Ravelins and Bastions I see in my travells, I dare swear you would ask me, What is a Ravelin? and what is a Bastion?[17]

The amount of resources that went into building fortifications in the late seventeenth and eighteenth centuries is absolutely astounding. Obviously, nations felt terribly insecure. And although we can only laugh at what must have been heated arguments over just how many ravelins and where best to place them, we are no better off now at defending ourselves from ourselves.

Humor, it must be admitted, is the last line of defense, especially when all else fails. It must also be admitted that interest in the battle of Fontenoy and the War of Jenkins's Ear has long since been overshadowed by the subsequent occurrence of many more spectacular conflicts. According to Quincy Wright, 147 wars took place between 1763 and 1941,[18] and no doubt we could count many more since—all the more reason for Democritus to laugh harder now than he would have for Burton: "What would he [Democritus] have said to see, hear, and read so many bloody battles, so many thousands slain at once, such streams of blood able to turn mills" (*AM*, 1:55). Surely if St. Augustine was at a loss to convey the horrors of war in language (see *The City of God* 3.26 and 19.7) we could hardly hope to do so now. Moreover, humankind's love of extravagant military reproductions has not diminished, to judge from the war games, complete with calculated odds and permutations, and miniatures, hand-painted in the bright uniforms of long ago, that fill hobby stores. Curiously enough, the monthly trade magazine for the military player, *Miniature Wargames*, features a picture of a cavalry charge against Marlborough's redcoats on the cover of its July 1988 issue.[19]

Whenever we can get away from the groans of the dying and join the laughter of the gods, we remember that, in the tradition of Rabelais and Sterne, laughter is therapeutic as well as derisive. Konrad Lorenz, the noted social scientist, even manages to end his study *On Aggression* with an avowal of optimism because he has "confidence in the great and beneficial force of humour."[20] Another modern theorist who tries to be optimistic about humanity's future bases his argument on the old love-war paradox. Franco Fornari claims that with the destructive power of today's technology men will no longer be able to go to war for love, because all—including the love object—must necessarily perish.[21] There is rationale here, as with most theories, but there is also a catch. Anybody who goes to war for love has to be mad in the first place—a *Furioso* or a simpleton. The energies of humor are as irrational and ungovernable as those of conflict. Art we can command, motley may be worn—but primitive forces command us, and those rough beasts will have their hour. So if one should feel tempted or laughed into complacency by Lorenz's desperate and suspect optimism, there is always Swiftian ridicule to laugh us out of what little confidence one can have in the applications of science.

Abbreviations

A Henry Fielding. *Amelia*. Edited by Martin Battestin. Introduction and notes by Fredson Bowers. Middletown, Conn.: Wesleyan University Press, 1984.

AM Robert Burton. *The Anatomy of Melancholy*. Edited by Holbrook Jackson. 3 vols. 1932. Reprint. London: Everyman, 1968.

FCF Tobias Smollett. *Ferdinand Count Fathom*. Edited by Damian Grant. London: Oxford University Press, 1971.

G&S Jonathan Swift. *A Tale of A Tub &c.* [including *The Battle of the Books*]. Edited by A. C. Guthkelch and D. Nichol Smith. 2d ed. London: Oxford University Press, 1958.

Ham *Hamlet. The Riverside Shakespeare*. Edited by G. Blakemore Evans. Boston: Houghton Mifflin, 1974.

HC Tobias Smollett. *The Expedition of Humphry Clinker*. Edited by Lewis M. Knapp. London: Oxford University Press, 1966.

JA Henry Fielding. *Joseph Andrews*. Edited by Martin Battestin. Introduction by Fredson Bowers. Middletown, Conn.: Wesleyan University Press, 1967.

Poems *The Poems of Jonathan Swift*. Edited by Harold Williams. 2d ed. 3 vols. Oxford: Clarendon Press, 1958.

PP Tobias Smollett. *The Aventures of Peregrine Pickle*. Edited by James L. Clifford. Revised by Paul-Gabriel Boucé. Oxford: Oxford University Press, 1983.

PW *Jonathan Swift: The Prose Works*. Edited by Herbert Davis. 14 vols. Oxford: Basil Blackwell, 1941–68.

PWPS *The Prose Works of Sir Philip Sidney*. Edited by Albert Feuillerat. 4 vols. 1912. Reprint. Cambridge University Press, 1963.

RO   George Farquhar. *The Recruiting Officer.* Edited by Michael Shugrue. Lincoln: University of Nebraska Press, 1965.

RR   Tobias Smollett. *The Adventures of Roderick Random.* Edited by Paul-Gabriel Boucé. Oxford: Oxford University Press, 1979.

SJ   Laurence Sterne. *A Sentimental Journal Through France and Italy by Mr. Yorick.* Edited by Gardner D. Stout, Jr. Berkeley and Los Angeles: University of California Press, 1967.

T   Tobias Smollett. *Travels Through France and Italy.* Edited by Frank Felsenstein. Oxford: Oxford University Press, 1981.

T&C   John Dryden. *Troilus and Cressida, or Truth Found too Late: A Tragedy.* In vol. 13 of *The Works of John Dryden.* Edited by Maximillian E. Novak, George R. Guffey, and Alan Roper. Berkeley and Los Angeles: University of California Press, 1984, 217–355, 497–565.

TJ   Henry Fielding. *The History of Tom Jones, A Foundling.* Edited by Fredson Bowers. Introduction and notes by Martin Battestin. Middletown, Conn.: Wesleyan University Press, 1975.

Tro   *Troilus and Cressida. The Riverside Shakespeare.* Edited by G. Blakemore Evans. Boston: Houghton Mifflin, 1974.

TS   Laurence Sterne. *The Life and Opinions of Tristram Shandy, Gentleman.* Vols. 1–3 of *The Florida Edition of the Works of Laurence Sterne.* Edited by Melvyn New, Joan New, Richard A. Davies, and W. D. Day. Gainesville: University Presses of Florida, 1978–84.

Notes

Introduction: Fontenoy and Theory

1. Francis Henry Skrine, *Fontenoy and Great Britain's Share in the War of the Austrian Succession: 1741–48* (London: Blackwood, 1906), 171. For a discussion of the various versions of this incident, see Skrine, *Fontenoy*, 171–72; and J. W. Fortescue, *A History of the British Army* (London: Macmillan, 1910), 2:115–16.

2. Skrine, *Fontenoy*, 172.

3. Ibid.

4. Fortescue, *History of the British Army* 2:115.

5. Ibid.

6. Jeffrey Beusse, "An Investigation of the Value of Genre Analysis," *Interpretations: Studies in Language and Literature* 7 (1975): 44–46.

7. Alastair Fowler, *Kinds of Literature: An Introduction to the Theory of Genres and Modes* (Cambridge: Harvard University Press, 1982), 65–66.

8. See Quincy Wright, *A Study of War* (Chicago: University of Chicago Press, 1942), vol. 1, tables 34, 35, and 36. The seven major European wars are the two coalitions against Louis XIV (1672–78, 1688–97), the War of the Spanish Succession (1701–13), the War of the Quadruple Alliance (1718–20), the War of the Austrian Succession (1739–48), the Seven Years' War (1756–63), and the Napoleonic Wars (1793–1802).

Other conflicts between 1660 and 1800 that involved Britian include the Anglo-Dutch naval wars (1665–67, 1672–74), the Monmouth and Jacobite Rebellions (1685, 1715–16, 1745–46), the War of Jenkins's Ear (1739–41), which merged with the Austrian Succession War, and the American Revolutionary War (1775–83).

For a description of Britain's role in these wars, see Fortescue, *History of the British Army*, vols. 1, 2, and 3. For an analysis of the structure of the British army in this period, see ibid.; Clifford Walton, *A History of the British Standing Army: 1660–1700* (London: Harrison and Sons, 1894); John Childs, *The Army of Charles II* (London: Routledge and Kegan Paul, 1976); John Childs, *The Army, James II and the Glorious Revolution* (Manchester: Manchester University Press, 1980); John Childs *The British Army of William III* (Manchester: Manchester University Press, 1987); and R. E. Scouller, *The Armies of Queen Anne* (Oxford: Oxford University Press, 1966).

The best general study of European armies and their relations with civilians is John Childs, *Armies and Warfare in Europe: 1648–1789* (New York: Holmes & Meier, 1982). For a concise and focused description of the eighteenth-century British army, see Colonel H. C. B. Rogers, *The British Army of the Eighteenth Century* (London: George Allen & Unwin, 1977). The best general description of military strategy is David Chandler, *The Art of Warfare in the Age of Marlborough* (London: Hippocrene, 1976). On the arms of the period, see Anthony Kemp, *Weapons and Equipment of the Marlborough Wars* (Poole, Dorset: Blanford Press, 1980). For the specific subject of military training, see J. A. Houlding, *Fit for Service: The Training of the British Army, 1715–1795* (Oxford: Clarendon Press, 1981); and for the militia, consult J. R. Western, *The English Militia in the Eighteenth Century: The Story of a Political Issue, 1660–1802* (London: Routledge & Kegan Paul, 1965).

9. On the origins of the "grotesque" and its application to literature, see Frances K. Barasch, *The Grotesque: A Study in Meanings* (The Hague: Mouton, 1971); Wolfgang Kayser, *The Grotesque in Art and Literature*, trans. Ulrich Weisstein (Bloomington: Indiana University Press, 1963), 24–95; and Arthur Clayborough, *The Grotesque in English Literature* (Oxford: Clarendon Press, 1965), 1–62.

10. For instance, see David Evett, "Mammon's Grotto: Sixteenth-Century Visual Grotesquerie and Some Features of Spenser's *Faerie Queene*," *English Literary Renaissance* 12, no. 2 (1982): 180–209.

11. See *The Shakespearean Grotesque: Its Genesis and Transformations* (Oxford: Clarendon Press, 1971), 4, 20–27.

12. Mikhail Bakhtin, *Rabelais and His World*, trans. Helene Iswolsky (Cambridge: MIT Press, 1968).

13. Bakhtin, *Rabelais*, 447–48.

14. Neil Rhodes, *Elizabethan Grotesque* (London: Routledge & Kegan Paul, 1980), 42.

15. Clayborough, *Grotesque*, 112–57.

16. Tony Tanner, "Reason and the Grotesque: Pope's *Dunciad*," in *Essential Articles for the Study of Alexander Pope*, ed. Maynard Mack, rev. ed. (Hamden, Conn.: Archon, 1968), 828–31.

17. "Grotesque Renaissance," *The Complete Works of John Ruskin*, eds. E. T. Cook and Alexander Wedderburn (London: George Allen, 1904), 11:151–54.

18. Ruskin, "Grotesque" 11:151.

19. Ruskin, "Grotesque" 11:161–76.

20. See Lee Byron Jennings, *The Ludicrous Demon* (Berkeley and Los Angeles: University of California Press, 1963), 17; and Sylvie Debevec Henning, "La Forme IN-Formante: A Reconsideration of the Grotesque," *Mosaic* 14, no. 4 (1981):118.

21. Kayser, *Grotesque*, 180.

22. Clayborough, *Grotesque*, 74.

23. Joan DeJean has used the idea of a Vauban-style fortification as a military metaphor to describe literary ambiguity in Rousseau, Laclos, and Sade; see *Literary Fortifications: Rousseau, Laclos, Sade* (Princeton: Princeton University Press, 1984).

24. Jennings, *Demon*, 17.

25. Michael Steig makes this point in "Defining the Grotesque: An Attempt at Synthesis," *Journal of Aesthetics and Art Criticism* 29, no. 2 (1970): 258.

26. Morse Peckham, "Art and Disorder," *The Triumph of Romanticism: Collected Essays* (Columbia: University of South Carolina Press, 1970), 279–80.

27. Thomas Wright, *A History of Caricature and Grotesque in Literature and Art* (London: Virtue Brothers & Co., 1865), 2. Wright's notion of caricature or the grotesque is equivalent to punitive satire. The primitive rudiments of the grotesque that he induces are very close to Robert Elliott's work on satire and its connection to the ancient curse; see *The Power of Satire* (Princeton: University of Princeton Press, 1960).

28. Thomas Hobbes, *Leviathan*, ed. Michael Oakeshott (Oxford: Basil Blackwell, 1946), 36, 82. It has been argued that Locke ultimately held a Hobbesian view on the natural state of humankind. See Richard H. Cox, *Locke on War and*

Peace (Oxford: Clarendon Press, 1960). The relation between deformity and laughter or the comic was, of course, made by Aristotle in *The Poetics* 5.1.

29. Ruskin, "Grotesque" 11:151–61.

30. Northrop Frye, "Norms, Moral or Other, in Satire: A Symposium," *Satire Newsletter* 2 (Fall 1964): 9.

31. J. Huizinga, *Homo Ludens: The Play-Element in Culture* (Boston: Becan Press, 1950), 89–140.

32. Childs, *Armies and Warfare*, 76. See also Chandler, *Art of Warfare*, 107–8.

33. Chandler, *Art of Warfare*, 162–63.

34. For a discussion of how limited warfare was in the latter half of the seventeenth and eighteenth centuries, or in the period after the Thirty Years' War (1618–48) and before the Napoleonic era, see Childs, *Armies and Warfare*, 1–27.

35. For ostentatious uniforms, see Childs, *Armies and Warfare*, 73–74.

36. See Roger Caillois, *Man, Play, and Games*, trans. Meyer Barash (New York: Free Press of Glencoe, 1961).

37. See Childs, *Armies and Warfare*, 45, 61–62; and Scouller, *Armies of Queen Anne*, 102–25.

38. Fortescue, *History of the British Army* 1:591.

39. Hugo Grotius, *The Law of War and Peace*, trans. Francis W. Kelsey, intro. James Brown Scott (1925; reprint, Carnegie Endowment for International Peace, New York: Bobbs-Merrill, 1962), 20.

40. Childs, *Armies and Warfare*, 98–100.

41. Lord Ligonier, quoted in Rex Whitworth, *Field Marshal Lord Ligonier: A Story of the British Army, 1702–1770* (Oxford: Clarendon Press, 1958), 158.

42. Tobias Smollett, *The Reprisal: or, the Tars of Old England, Plays and Poems* (London: T. Evans and R. Baldwin, 1777), 177.

43. [Thomas] D'Urfey, *The Campaigners: or, The Pleasant Adventures at Brussels* (London: A. Baldwin, 1698), 6–7.

44. Quoted by Fortescue, *History of the British Army* 1:444. Fortescue's history is rich with fictionalized statements that perpetuate this myth of "genteel" decorum. On arriving in Nottingham as a prisoner of war, Tallard was apparently addressed by a butcher: "Welcome to England. I hope to see your master here next year." Fortescue, 1:448. Count Bellair in *The Beaux' Stratagem* may well be based on Tallard.

45. See Humphrey Bland, *A Treatise of Military Discipline* (1727), in *English Historical Documents: 1714–1783*, eds. D. B. Horn and Mary Ransome (London: Eyre & Spottiswoode, 1969), 615: " . . . those who preserve their Fire the longest, will be sure to Conquer." Chandler, *Art of Warfare*, 126, 133; and Childs, *Armies and Warfare*, 126, also discuss this tactic.

46. Kayser, *Grotesque*, 183, 198.

47. See Antonia Fraser, *A History of Toys* (London: Spring Books, 1972), 18, 86, 102.

48. "To the Reader," *A Military Dictionary. Explaining All difficult Terms in Martial Discipline, Fortification, and Gunnery* (London: J. Nutt, 1702).

49. Alexander Pope, *Memoirs of the Extraordinary Life, Works, and Discoveries of Martinus Scriblerus*, written in collaboration by members of the Scriblerus Club, ed. Charles Kerby-Miller (New York: Russell & Russell, 1966), 99, 195–96.

50. *The Spectator*, No. 2, ed. Donald F. Bond (Oxford: Clarendon Press, 1965), 1:12.

51. Childs, *Armies and Warfare*, 110: "This disconcerting experience occurred at Fontenoy in 1745, when the British and Hanoverian infantry regiments had to stand in line and watch the cannon balls from the French enfilading cannon bound toward them."

52. [M. D'Assigny], *A Collection of the Brave Exploits and Subtil Stratagems of Several Famous Generals Since the Roman Empire* (London: S. Heyrick, 1686), 129.

53. Paul A. Jorgensen, *Shakespeare's Military World* (Berkeley and Los Angeles: University of California Press, 1956), 199.

54. See *Aeneid* 8.703: "*quam cum sanguineo sequitur Bellona flagello* [while Bellona follows her with bloody scourge]." *Virgil*, trans. H. Rushton Fairclough, 2 vols., Loeb Classical Library (1935, 1934; reprints, London: Heinemann, 1965, 1966); all subsequent citations are to this edition. See also Lucan's *The Civil War* 7.568: "*Sanguineum veluti quatiens Bellona flagellum* [like Bellona brandishing her bloody scourge]." In *Lucan: The Civil War*, trans. J. D. Duff, Loeb Classical Library (1928; reprint, London: Heinemann, 1962).

55. *St. Augustine: The City of God*, vol. 1, bk. 1, chap. 1, trans. George E. McCracken (London: Heinemann, 1957); all subsequent citations are to this edition.

56. See *Times Literary Supplement*, 17 February 1916, 82; 24 February 1916, 94; 2 March 1916, 105; and 30 March 1916, 153. Sallust, a Roman historian, refers to the theory in his comments on Rome: "But when this new community had grown in numbers, civilization, and territory, and was beginning to seem amply rich and amply strong, then, as is usual with mortal affairs, prosperity gave birth to envy. As a result, neighbouring kings and peoples made war upon them. . . ." *Sallust: The War with Catiline* 6, trans. J. C. Rolfe, Loeb Classical Library (1931; reprint, London: Heinemann, 1965).

57. "Therefore thus saith the Lord God of hosts, O my people that dwellest in Zion, be not afraid of the Assyrian: he shall smite thee with a rod, and shall lift up his staff against thee, after the manner of Egypt.

For yet a very little while, and the indignation shall cease, and mine anger in their destruction.

And the Lord of hosts shall stir up a scourge for him according to the slaughter of Midian at the rock of Oreb: and as his rod was upon the sea, so shall he lift it up after the manner of Egypt."

58. [Justus Lipsius], *War and Peace Reconciled*, trans. N. Wanley (London: 1672), 80.

59. Clarendon, Edward Hyde, Earl of, *The History of the Rebellion and Civil Wars in England*, ed. W. Dunn Macray (Oxford: Clarendon Press, 1888), 1:2.

60. Sir George Clark, *War and Society in the Seventeenth Century* (Cambridge: Cambridge University Press, 1958), 23.

61. See Bernard Mandeville, *The Fable of the Bees*, ed. F. B. Kaye (1966; reprint, Oxford: Clarendon Press, 1924), 2:17–18, 21, 22, 32, 118–23.

62. Hobbes, *Leviathan*, 82.

63. "Guerre," *Dictionnaire Philosophique, Oeuvres Complètes de Voltaire*, (Paris: Garnier Frères, 1879), 19:318, 321. For a thorough discussion of Voltaire's complex and often contradictory views on war, see Henry Meyer, *Voltaire on War and Peace* (Banbury: Voltaire Foundation, 1976).

64. "A Comparative View of Races and Nations," *The Collected Works of Oliver Goldsmith*, ed. Arthur Friedman (Oxford: Clarendon Press, 1966), 3:80–81.

65. *Collected Works of Oliver Goldsmith* 3:81.

66. Plato, *The Republic* 5.16–17, trans. Paul Shorey (London: Heinemann, 1930), 1:495–501.
67. Henry Fielding, *The Jacobite's Journal and Related Writings*, ed. W. B. Coley (Middletown, Conn.: Wesleyan University Press, 1974), 110.
68. For a discussion of war and French fiction, see Adrienne D. Hytier, "The Battle in Eighteenth-Century French Fiction," *Eighteenth-Century Life* 8, no. 1 (1982): 1–13.
69. *Windsor Forest*, lines 325–26, in *Alexander Pope: Pastoral Poetry and An Essay on Criticism*, ed. E. Aura and Aubrey Williams (London: Methuen, 1961), 180.
70. Frederich Schiller, *Naive and Sentimental Poetry and On the Sublime*, trans. Julis A. Elias (New York: F. Ungar, 1967), 145–46.

Chapter 1. Tradition and Proliferation

1. This theory seems to be generally accepted by Milton scholars. See James A. Winn, "Milton on Heroic Warfare," *Yale Review* 66 (1976): 79.
2. Ibid., 81–82: "The second day's battle is, for Milton, modern warfare. As J. H. Hansford has established, the maneuver by which the rebel angels march forward concealing their artillery comes from Ward's *Animadversions of Warre* (1639), which Milton knew well." See J. H. Hansford, "Milton and the Art of War," *Studies in Philology* 18 (1921): 232–66. The most extensive study of Milton and war is James A. Freeman, *Milton and the Martial Muse: "Paradise Lost" and European Traditions of War* (Princeton: Princeton University Press, 1980).
3. Michael Lieb, *The Dialectics of Creation: Patterns of Birth and Regeneration in "Paradise Lost"* (Amherst: University of Massachusetts Press, 1970), 107.
4. *Literary Works of Matthew Prior*, eds. H. Bunker Wright and Monroe K. Spears (Oxford: Clarendon Press, 1959), 1:422: "Throughout the whole Iliad, the Gods and Goddesses falling out, calling Names, and Cuffing is extremely ridiculous."
5. Robert Burton, *The Anatomy of Melancholy*, ed. Holbrook Jackson (1932; reprint, London: Everyman, 1968), 1:60; all subsequent citations are to this edition (hereafter cited as *AM*). Burton's marginal note refers to "*De benef. lib. 2, cap. 16.*" See "*De Beneficiis 7,*" in *Seneca: Moral Essays*, trans. John W. Basore, Loeb Classical Library (1928; reprint. London: Heinemann, 1964), 3:460–63. A harsher criticism of Alexander can be found in Seneca's "On the Value of Advice 94," in *Seneca: Epistulae Morales*, trans. Richard M. Gummere, Loeb Classical Library (1917; reprint, London: Heinemann, 1962), 3:50–53.
6. For a discussion of Johnson's dual perspective on war, see Lionel Basney, "Samuel Johnson and the Psychology of War," *Midwest Quarterly* 16, no. 1 (1974): 12–24. Johnson's questioning of the morality behind the struggle for new world colonies is addressed by Donald J. Greene in, "Samuel Johnson and the Great War for Empire," *English Writers of the Eighteenth Century*, ed. John H. Middendorf (New York: Columbia University Press, 1971), 37–65.
7. *Boswell's Life of Johnson*, George Birkbeck Hill, ed., revised and enlarged edition by L. F. Powell, (Oxford: Clarendon Press, 1971), 3:265–66.
8. *Boswell's Life of Johnson* 4:319.
9. Samuel Johnson, "*Idler, No. 22,*" *The Idler and Adventurer*, W. J. Bate, John M. Bullitt, L. F. Powell, eds. (New Haven: Yale University Press, 1963), 319.

10. Samuel Johnson, *Political Writings*, ed. Donald Greene (New Haven: Yale University Press, 1977), 369.

11. *Candide, ou l'optimisme*, ed. René Pomeau, *Les OEuvres Complètes de Voltaire* (Oxford, Taylor Institution: The Voltaire Foundation, 1980), 48:223.

12. *Collected Works of Oliver Goldsmith* 2:73.

13. Johnson, *Political Writings*, 370.

14. Johnson, *Political Writings*, 371.

15. *Homer: The Iliad*, trans. A. T. Murray, 2 vols., Loeb Classical Library (1924, 1925; reprint, London: Heinemann, 1965, 1939), 11.161–62; all subsequent citations are to this edition.

16. *The Unfortunate Traveller*, in *The Works of Thomas Nashe*, ed. Ronald B. McKerrow, rev. F. P. Wilson (Oxford: Basil Blackwell, 1958), 2:232.

17. Rhodes, *Elizabethan Grotesque*, 42. See also Rhodes's discussion of the Carnival-Lent combat in Rabelais, 82–85.

18. Bakhtin, *Rabelais*, 193–94.

19. Samuel Butler, *Prose Observations*, ed. Hugh De Quehen (Oxford: Clarendon Press, 1979), 239

20. John Arbuthnot, *The History of John Bull*, eds. Alan W. Bower and Robert A. Erickson (Oxford: Clarendon Press, 1976), 10.

21. Samuel Johnson, "The Vanity of Human Wishes," *Poems*, ed. E. L. McAdam with George Milne (New Haven: Yale University Press, 1964), lines 175–78.

22. Ibid., lines 185, 188.

23. Johnson, *Political Writings*, 115.

24. *Collected Works of Oliver Goldsmith* 3:17.

25. Ibid., 3:18.

26. Ibid., 3:20.

27. Ibid., 3:21.

28. George Farquhar, *The Recruiting Officer*, ed. Michael Shugrue (Lincoln: University of Nebraska Press, 1965), 1.1.1–7; all subsequent citations are made to this edition (hereafter cited as *RO*).

29. *The Poems and Songs of Robert Burns*, ed. James Kinsley (Oxford: Clarendon Press, 1968), 1:195–98.

30. [Charles Shadwell], *The Fair Quaker of Deal, or The Humours of the Navy* (London: Knapton, 1710), 3–5.

31. [Charles] Shadwell, *The Humours of the Army* (London: Knapton, 1713).

32. Farnham, *Shakespearean Grotesque*, 13, 28, 50.

33. "Hanno, Thrasymachus," in *The Colloquies of Erasmus*, trans. R. Thompson (Chicago: Chicago University Press, 1965), 14.

34. *St. Augustine: The City of God*, bk. 3, chap. 18.

35. Francis Bacon, *The Essayes or Counsels, Civill and Morall*, ed. Michael Kiernan (Cambridge: Harvard University Press, 1985), 97.

36. *Troilus and Cressida, or Truth Found too Late: A Tragedy*, in *The Works of John Dryden*, vol. 13, ed. Maximillian E. Novak, George R. Guffey, Alan Roper (Berkeley and Los Angeles: University of California Press, 1984), 5.2.62–71; all subsequent citations are made to this edition (hereafter cited as *T&C*).

37. George Villiers, Duke of Buckingham, *The Rehearsal*, ed. D. E. L. Crane (Durham: University of Durham Press, 1976), 1.1.28, 39, 46–48; all subsequent citations are made to this edition.

38. "Preface," *Amphitryon*, in *The Works of John Dryden*, ed. Earl Miner, George R. Guffey, Franklin B. Zimmerman (Berkeley and Los Angeles: University of California Press, 1976), 15:224.

39. Johnson, "Vanity," lines 239–40.

40. *Works of Thomas Nashe* 2:231.

41. Rhodes, *Elizabethan Grotesque*, 22.

42. *The Defence*, in *The Prose Works of Sir Philip Sidney*, ed. Albert Feuillerat (1912; reprint, Cambridge: Cambridge University Press, 1963), 3:20; all subsequent citations to *The Defence of Poesie* and the *New Arcadia* are made to this edition (hereafter cited as *PWPS*).

43. It might be added that the formality of the heroic couplet may itself lead the poet to grotesque elegance, as in Johnson's description of Xerxes's inglorious retreat: "The daring Greeks deride the martial show, / And heap their vallies with the gaudy foe." "Vanity," lines 235–36.

44. Sidney visited Florence when he was in Italy in 1574 but spent most of his time in Venice and Padua. See John Buxton, *Sir Philip Sidney and the English Renaissance* (London: Macmillan, 1964), 65.

45. John Pope-Hennessy, *The Complete Works of Paolo Uccello* (London: Phaidon Press, 1950), 22.

46. William Rose, "Introduction," to Hans Jacob Christoffel von Grimmelshausen, *Simplicissimus, The Vagabond*, trans. A. T. S. Goodrick (London: George Routledge, 1912), xvi.

47. See Jorgensen, 1–34. Voltaire obviously mocks this convention at the beginning of Chapter 3 in *Candide*.

48. See John J. O'Connor, "Physical Deformity and Chivalric Laughter in Renaissance England," in *Comedy: New Perspectives*, ed. Maurice Charney, *New York Literary Forum* 1 (Spring 1978): 69–70; Dorothy Connell, *Sir Philip Sidney: The Maker's Mind* (Oxford: Clarendon Press, 1977), 118, n. 1; and Alan D. Isler, "Sidney, Shakespeare, and the 'Slain-Notslain'," *University of Toronto Quarterly* 37, no. 2 (1968): 184.

49. See Marvin Herrick on Madius's essay *De Ridiculis* (1550) in *Comic Theory in the Sixteenth Century* (Urbana: University of Illinois Press, 1964), 38. Even though Herrick believes that Sidney had never read Madius, it is clear that Sidney had absorbed this *turpitudo-admiratio* duality from classical or other sources and had practised it in the *Arcadia* episodes dealing with the slaughter of the rebels.

50. L. P. Wilkinson, *Ovid Recalled* (Cambridge: Cambridge University Press, 1955), 163.

51. John Dryden, "A Discourse Concerning the Original and Progress of Satire," *Essays of John Dryden*, ed. W. P. Kerr, 2 vols. (New York: Russell & Russell, 1961), 2:93.

52. *Ovid: Metamorphoses*, bk. 12, trans. Frank Justus Miller, vol. 2, Loeb Classical Library (1916; reprint, London: Heinemann, 1964); all subsequent citations are made to this edition.

53. Sir Philip Sidney, *The Countess of Pembroke's Arcadia (The Old Arcadia)*, ed. Jean Robertson (Oxford: Clarendon Press, 1973), 308.

54. See Alexander Pope, *The Iliad of Homer: Books I–IX*, ed. Maynard Mack (London: Methuen, 1967), 252–54.

55. Samuel Parker, "Homer in a Nutshell" (London: 1700), ii.

56. Connell, *Philip Sidney*, 118, n. 1, cites this reference to support her argument "that Sidney was following a literary not a political convention."

57. See Montague Summers, "Introduction" and notes to *The Rehearsal* (Stratford-Upon-Avon: Shakespeare Head Press, 1914), xi, 62–69, 121–22, 141–42. Any reader of Defoe's *Memoirs of a Cavalier* knows exactly what Bayes means by "dull prolixity." Montague Summers's list of heroic plays and their

sequels that featured elaborate sieges and battles includes *The Siege of Rhodes* (Part One, 1656; Part Two, 1662), Crowe's *Destruction of Jerusalem* (1677, both parts), and of course Dryden's two-part *Conquest of Granada* (1670).

58. Pope, "Preface," *The Iliad of Homer: Books I–IX*, 12.
59. Alexander Pope, *The Art of Sinking in Poetry*, ed. Edna Leake Steeves (New York: King's Crown Press, 1952), 84.
60. Samuel Butler, *Hudibras*, ed. John Wilders (London: Oxford University Press, 1967), 1.1.1–6.
61. Butler, *Hudibras* 3.2.686–89.
62. *Literary Works of Matthew Prior* 2:870. For the poem itself, see 1:139–51.
63. [William] Congreve, "A Pindarique Ode, Humbly Offer'd to the King On His Taking Namure," (London: Jacob Tonson, 1695); and [William] Pittis, "An Epistolary Poem to N. Tate . . . Occasioned by the taking of Namur," (London: R. Baldwin, 1696).
64. "Reflections on the Poems Made upon the Siege and Taking of Namur, &c." (London: M. Whillock, 1696), 3.
65. "Reflections on the Poems," 5.
66. *Literary Works of Matthew Prior* 1:226.
67. Tom Brown, *Amusements Serious and Comical and Other Works*, ed. Arthur L. Hayward (New York: Dodd, Mead and Company, 1927), 231–41.
68. *Collected Works of Oliver Goldsmith* 1:193.
69. Ibid., 1:194.
70. "Blenheim," *The Whole Works of Mr. John Philips* (London: J. Tonson, 1720), 40–41.
71. "The Campaign," in *The Miscellaneous Works of Joseph Addison*, ed. G. C. Guthkelch (1914; reprint, London: G. Bell and Sons, 1978), 1:170, line 466.
72. *Lucian's Dialogues*, trans. Howard Williams, Bohn's Classical Library (London: George Bell and Sons, 1888), 115.
73. *Literary Works of Matthew Prior* 1:609, 612.
74. Ibid., 1:661.
75. Christopher Marlowe, *Tamburlaine the Great*, pt. 2, ed. Una Ellis-Fermor, rev. ed. (London: Methuen, 1951), 1.4.81, 82.
76. Marlowe, *II Tamburlaine* 1.4.89–90, 92–95.
77. *Herodotus*, trans. A. D. Godley, Loeb Classical Library (1921; reprint. London: Heinemann, 1971), bk. 3, sec. 151, 2:185.
78. Thomas Carlyle, *Frederick the Great* (London: Chapman & Hall, 1888), 6:38.
79. Skrine, *Fontenoy*, 172.
80. Voltaire, quoted by Carlyle, *Frederick the Great* 6:48–49. Many of the details in this paragraph are from Voltaire's account.

Chapter 2. Swift: War and History, the Rhetoric of the Grotesque

1. Robert C. Gordon, "Jonathan Swift and the Modern Art of War," *Bulletin of Research in the Humanities* 83 (1980): 187–202.
2. See Clayborough, *Grotesque*, 112–57.
3. Peter Steele, *Jonathan Swift: Preacher and Jester* (Oxford: Clarendon Press, 1978), 222.
4. Patrick Gleeson, "*Gulliver's Travels* as a Version of the Grotesque" (Ph.D.

diss., University of Washington, 1964). Also of interest is Hamida Bosmajian, "The Nature and Function of the Grotesque Image in Eighteenth-Century English Literature" (Ph.D. diss., University of Connecticut, 1968). Bosmajian analyzes only *A Tale of a Tub* in his chapter on Swift, but this is probably because of Gleeson's earlier work on the *Travels*.

5. Carole Fabricant, *Swift's Landscape* (Baltimore: Johns Hopkins University Press, 1982), 186.

6. *The Poems of Jonathan Swift*, ed. Harold Williams, 2d ed. (Oxford: Clarendon Press, 1958), 1:6, lines 1, 19; all subsequent citations to Swift's poetry are to this edition (hereafter cited as *Poems*).

7. Swift seems to draw upon the cyclical and scourge theories of war. First, Louis is likened to a "Gilded Meteor" that will "Stay but a little while and down again 'twill come"; then he is compared to a "fearful Star" that was "Sent by just heaven to threaten Earth / With war . . ." (*Poems* 1:10, lines 122, 133–34).

8. Only once again would Swift attempt a eulogy for a military figure, the egregious "Peace and Dunkirk" (1712) written for Lady Masham's brother Major-General John Hill. *Poems* 1:167–69. Hill is probably remembered more for his botched attempt on Quebec in 1711 than the surrender of Dunkirk.

9. Jonathan Swift, *A Tale of A Tub &c.*, eds. A. C. Guthkelch and D. Nichol Smith, 2d ed. (London: Oxford University Press, 1958), 162; all subsequent citations to *A Tale* and *The Battle of the Books* are to this edition (hereafter cited as "G&S").

10. W. A. Speck, "Swift and the Historian," *Proceedings of the First Münster Symposium on Jonathan Swift*, eds. Hermann J. Real and Heinz J. Vienken (Munich: Wilhelm Fink Verlag, 1985), 261. In one of his later poems, "The Great Question Debated" (1729), Swift humorously plays with the notion of female attraction to military officers in having the Lady of the poem, Mrs. Acheson, express her desire to see Hamilton's "Bawn" turned into "a *Barrack*" rather than a "*Malt-House*" so that she might be entertained with some gallant company (*Poems* 3:866, 867, lines 3, 6): "But, if you will give us a *Barrack*, my Dear, / The *Captain*, I'm sure, will always come here" (*Poems* 3:868, lines 31–32).

11. See F. P. Lock, *The Politics of "Gulliver's Travels"* (Oxford: Clarendon Press, 1980) 30, 87, 144. When Temple cites this doctrine to introduce his focus on the character of William the Conqueror, he does so without humour. See *The Works of Sir William Temple*, (London: 1720), 2:582.

12. Bakhtin, *Rabelais*, 19–20, 315–36.

13. Kayser, *Grotesque*, 182–83. See also Farnham's discussion of the medieval grotesque illustrations that depict elaborately intertwined animal, vegetable, and human forms; *Shakespearean Grotesque*, 4, 11, 28, 34.

14. Swift makes another endorsement of Hobbes's philosophy about human society as a state of warfare in his poem, "On Poetry" (1733): "*Hobbes* clearly proves that e'ery Creature / Lives in a State of War by Nature" (*Poems* 2:651, lines 319–20).

15. Bakhtin, *Rabelais*, 5; and Bakhtin, *The Dialogic Imagination*, ed. Michael Holquist, trans. Caryl Emerson and Michael Holquist (Austin: University of Texas Press, 1981), 308–9.

16. *Works of Sir William Temple* 2:540: " . . . according to the usual Circle of human Affairs, War ended in Peace, Peace in Plenty and Luxury, these in Pride, and Pride in Contention, till the Circle ended in new wars."

For a discussion of war and cyclical theories of history, see G. W. Trompf, *The Idea of Recurrence in Western Thought: From Antiquity to the Reformation*

(Berkeley and Los Angeles: University of California Press, 1979), 70–73, 166–67, 228, 288–89.

Swift's views on history are discussed in W. A. Speck, 257–68; Lock, *The Politics of "Gulliver's Travels"*, 32, 39, 144–47; *Swift's Tory Politics* (London: Duckworth, 1983), 150–52; Myrddin Jones, "A Living Treasury of Knowledge and Wisdom: Some Comments on Swift's Attitude to the Writing of History," *Durham University Journal* 36 (1974): 180–88; J. W. Johnson, "Swift's Historical Outlook," *Journal of British Studies* 4, no. 2 (1965): 68–69; and J. W. Johnson, *The Formations of English Neo-Classical Thought* (Princeton: Princeton University Press, 1967), 44–49.

This cyclical theory of war was part of popular folklore during the Renaissance. Marston based his play *Histrio-Mastix* on it; allegorical figures succeed one another, according to the cycle, in the manner of a morality play. See Jorgensen, *Military World* 192–93; Sir George Clark, *War and Society*, 130–50; and J. R. Hale, *Renaissance War Studies* (London: Hambledon, 1983), 354.

17. *Lucan: The Civil War*, 1.160–70.

18. See Scouller, *Armies of Queen Anne*, 107–8, 341.

19. Childs, *Armies and Warfare*, 111.

20. Philip Pinkus, "Swift and the Ancients-Moderns Controversy," *University of Toronto Quarterly* 29, no. 1 (1959): 51.

21. For other low domestic similes in *The Iliad*, see 12.421–26 and 20.251–55.

22. For a discussion of Shakespeare's Thersites as an incarnation of the grotesque, see Farnham, *Shakespearean Grotesque*, 129–38.

23. See *The Examiner*, Nos. 16 and 27, *The Prose Works of Jonathan Swift*, ed. Herbert Davis, 14 vols. (Oxford: Basil Blackwell, 1939–68), 3:19–24 and 3:80–85; all subsequent citations to Swift's prose works other than *A Tale* and *The Battle* are to this edition (hereafter cited as *PW*). See also the satiric poems "The Widow and her Cat" (1712), "The Fable of Midas" (1711–12), and "A Satirical Elegy On the Death of a Late Famous General," *Poems*, 1:151–58, 1:295–97. Swift draws attention to the Duke's apparent avarice in connection to the bequest of Blenheim Palace and other grants made to him by the crown.

24. For a discussion of the Swift-Marlborough controversy, see Michael Foot, *The Pen and the Sword* (London: Macgibbon & Kee, 1957) and Irvin Ehrenpreis, *Swift: The Man, His Works, and the Age* (London: Methuen, 1962, 1967, 1984), 2:493–541.

25. It is the serious tone of *The Conduct* that sharpens the sarcasm. On Britain's allies not carrying their share of the financial burden, Swift writes: "It is therefore to be hoped, that his *Prussian* Majesty, at the end of this War, will not have the same grievous Cause of Complaint, which he had at the Close of the last; that his Military-Chest was emptier by Twenty thousand Crowns, than at the Time that War began" (*PW*, 6:33).

Swift also allows his humorous fancy some exercise: "If all this, I say, be our Case, it is a very obvious Question to ask, by what Motives, or what Management, we are thus become the *Dupes* and *Bubbles* of Europe? Sure it cannot be owing to the Stupidity arising from the coldness of our Climate, since those among our Allies, who have given us most Reason to complain, are as far removed from the Sun as our selves" (*PW*, 6:40).

26. Peter Steele twice comments at length on this passage; see Steele, *Jonathan Swift*, 25–29, 53–54.

27. Ehrenpreis, *Swift: The Man, His Works, and The Age* 3:445–46.

28. *The Correspondence of Jonathan Swift*, ed. Harold Williams (Oxford: Clarendon Press, 1963), 3:207.

29. David Oakleaf discusses the subject of distortion in the *Travels* and connects the ideas of distance, detachment, and enjoyment as they relate to Swift's depiction of war; see "Trompe l'Oeil: Gulliver and the Distortions of the Observing Eye," *University of Toronto Quarterly* 53 (Winter 1983/84): 169.

30. Bakhtin, *Rabelais*, 228.

31. Jenny Mezciems maintains that Swift's treatment of war in the *Travels* recalls that of Renaissance writers like More, Erasmus, and Rabelais. See "Swift's Praise of Gulliver: Some Renaissance Background to the *Travels*," in *The Character of Swift's Satire: A Revised Focus*, ed. Claude Rawson (Newark: University of Delaware Press, 1983), 268: "War has . . . a particular centrality as the ultimate folly and the symbol of a divided society." The one Renaissance writer to be added to this list is of course Burton, who continues the tradition of Erasmus.

32. This passage also anticipates Voltaire's "Un million d'assassins enrégimentés"; see *Candide*, chap. 20.

33. Louis A. Landa, "'A Modest Proposal' and Populousness," *Eighteenth-Century English Literature: Modern Essays in Criticism*, ed. James L. Clifford (London: Oxford University Press, 1959), 109.

34. See *AM* 1:59; and Erasmus, *Opera Omnia* (Hildesheim: Georg Olms Verlagsbuchhandlung, 1961), 4:634A. See also Spenser's and Ariosto's respective metaphorical references to the evil cannon: *The Faerie Queene* 1.7.13 and *Orlando Furioso* 9.91.

35. The Lindalinian rebellion, which has always been interpreted as an allegory of Swift's successful protest against the copper half-penny, is described in the three additional paragraphs handwritten in Ford's copy of the first edition. *PW*, 11:309–10.

36. See Gordon, "Jonathan Swift," 195–97, on the "bayonet" and other modern weapons or systems. In *The Intelligencer* No. 9, Swift mocks society's faddish infatuation with military figures and ridicules the pervasive use of military language as indicative of a poor education. See *PW*, 12:49.

37. One might say the same thing about both descriptions—that there is an art about their *ut pictura poesis* quality that can, according to Sidney's own *Defence*, "delight," even if the subject matter is "horrible, as cruel battailes [are]" (*PWPS*, 3:30).

38. Bakhtin, *Rabelais*, 25, 211, 217, 447–48; and Bakhtin, *Dialogic Imagination*, 237, 308–9.

39. For more illustrations, see Correlli Barnett, *Marlborough* (London: Eyre Methuen, 1974), 167, 174–75.

40. For information on Laguerre as a decorative painter, see Edward Croft-Murray, *Decorative Painting in England: 1537–1837* (London: Country Life, 1962) 1:61–68; 1:250–54; Margaret Whinney and Oliver Millar, *English Art: 1625–1714* (Oxford: Clarendon Press, 1957), 302–6.

41. George Farquhar, *The Beaux' Stratagem* 4.1.282–87, ed. Charles N. Fifer (Lincoln: University of Nebraska Press, 1977), 85–86.

42. For a discussion of this kind of pictorial history and its relation to English poetry, see Jean H. Hagstrum, *The Sister Arts: The Tradition of Literary Pictorialism and English Poetry from Dryden to Gray* (Chicago: University of Chicago Press, 1958), 307–9. Steele ridiculed the military tableau and the use of Alexander as a subject in *The Tatler*, No. 209, ed. Donald F. Bond (Oxford: Clarendon Press, 1987) 3:107: "It is the great Use of Pictures to raise in our

Minds either agreeable Idea's [sic] of our absent Friends, or high Images of eminent Personages. But the latter Design is, methinks, carried on in a very improper Way; For to fill a Room full of Battle-Pieces, pompous Histories of Sieges, and a tall Hero alone in a Crowd of insignificant Figures about him, is of no Consequence to private Men."

43. Norman Bryson, *Word and Image: French Painting of the Ancien Régime* (Cambridge: Cambridge University Press, 1981), 34–39.

44. Ibid., 35, 36.

45. Alan Wace, *The Marlborough Tapestries at Blenheim Palace* (London: Phaidon, 1968), 19.

46. Ibid., 23–24.

47. Ibid., 26.

48. Bakhtin, *Rabelais*, 34, and Bakhtin, *Dialogic Imagination*, 237.

49. Claude J. Rawson, *Gulliver and the Gentle Reader: Studies in Swift and Our Time* (London: Routledge & Kegan Paul, 1973), 102.

50. Northrop Frye, *Anatomy of Criticism* (Princeton: Princeton University Press, 1957), 236. See also Frye's comments on "intellectual exuberance," 311–12.

51. See Mezciems, "Swift's Praise," 263–64; "A central concern in each writer [More, Erasmus, and Rabelais] is war, not merely as an extreme effect of human pride and greed but as a destructive perversion unique to the human species."

52. *The Complete Poems of John Wilmot, Earl of Rochester*, ed. David M. Vieth (New Haven: Yale University Press, 1968), 99.

53. For an analysis of the *Travels* in the context of this debate, see Gordon, "Jonathan Swift," 187–91. For the debate itself, see Lois G. Schwoerer, *No Standing Armies!* (Baltimore: Johns Hopkins University Press, 1974). Although the first Mutiny Act of 1689 (which, like the military budget, had to be approved every year by Parliament) is often cited as the statutory recognition of a standing army in England, Childs points out that Charles II had actually maintained a small standing force from 1661 onwards. See Childs, *The Army of Charles II*, 15–20; and Fortescue, *History of the British Army* 1:337. Lock describes the annual Mutiny Acts as creating the "fiction that the army was not a 'standing' one." Lock, *Swift's Tory Politics*, 131.

Z. S. Fink argues that the stability of Brobdingnagian civil affairs is Swift's endorsement of a classical political theory based on a balance of power, and that the militia forms a part of this balance; see "Political Theory in *Gulliver's Travels*," *English Literary History* 14 (1947): 158–61. His reading is valid but the stability offered by the militia must be seen against the long-term pattern of conflict that Gulliver perceives in Brobdingnagian history (*PW*, 11:138).

54. See "An Argument Shewing, that a Standing Army, with Consent of Parliament, is not Inconsistent with a Free Government" (1698), in *Daniel Defoe*, ed. James Boulton (New York: Schocken Books, 1965), 35–50; and Prior's "A New Answer to An Argument Against a Standing Army" (1697), *Literary Works*, 1:159–60. Both were responses to John Trenchard's attack, "An Argument Shewing, that a Standing Army is Inconsistent with a Free Government . . ."

55. In the "Kingdom of *Tribnia*," which Gulliver encounters in Part 3, we find the association between the "Plague" and a "standing Army" as the former is considered to be a code for the latter (*PW*, 11:191). This is Swift's updated adaptation of the conventional metaphor that likened the plague to an invading army—see Thomas Dekker's *The Wonderfull Yeare* (1603).

56. This is one of the commonest epic tropes. See the *Iliad* 17.361; and *Aeneid* 9.455–56, 12.690–91.

57. One is reminded of Swift;'s *Examiner* No. 14 on "Political Lying," wherein he refers to the political manipulation of the press by saying that a government could contrive to have a military defeat spoken of as if it were a victory (*PW*, 3:10).

58. Ehrenpreis sees the king of Brobdingnag as a mouth-piece for Swift's former patron Sir William Temple. *The Personality of Jonathan Swift* (Cambridge: Harvard University Press, 1958), 94.

59. *The Decline and Fall of the Roman Empire*, ed. J. B. Bury (London: Methuen, 1909), 1:84.

60. *Works of Sir William Temple* 1:232: "After all that has been said of Conquerors or Conquests, this must be confessed to hold but the second Rank in the Pretensions to Heroic Virtue, and that the first has been allowed to the wise Institution of just Orders and Laws, which frame safe and happy Governments in the World. The designs and Effects of Conquests, are but the Slaughter and Ruin of Mankind, the ravaging of Countries, and defacing the World: Those of wise and just Governments, are preserving and encreasing the Lives and Generations of Men, securing their Possessions, encouraging their Endeavours, and by Peace and Riches improving and adorning the several scenes of the World."

61. Bryson, *Word and Image*, 36.

62. Ehrenpreis, *Swift: The Man, His Works and The Age* 2:62.

63. Jones, "Living Treasury," 185, 187. Myrddin Jones argues that, unlike Part 2 of the *Travels*, which reveals Swift's concern with "political partisanship" in history (i.e., Gulliver's Whig view of England and her past), Part 3 shows history in its "sheer unreliability" insofar as the historian is excited by "his own prestige and power."

64. Kayser, *Grotesque*, 183–84.

65. See *Works of William Temple* 1:204, 211, 229–31.

66. Bakhtin, *Rabelais*, 25, 211, 217.

67. Other possible influences include Altdorfer's "The Battle of Issus." Altdorfer's painting depicts both Alexander's and Darius's armies with a striking brilliance of uniform detail and density.

68. Barnett, *Marlborough*, 273. The most detailed study of Blenheim is David Green, *Blenheim Palace* (London: Country Life, 1951).

69. Gervase Jackson-Stops, *The English Country House: A Grand Tour* (Boston: Little, Brown and Company, 1985), 35.

70. Ibid., 34.

71. "On Blenheim House," *The Oxford Book of Eighteenth-Century Verse*, ed. David Nichol Smith (1926; reprint, Oxford: Clarendon Press, 1946) 205.

72. *The Complete Works of Sir John Vanbrugh*, ed. Geoffrey Webb, (London: Nonesuch Press, 1928), 4:45, 46.

73. *Oxford Book of Eighteenth-Century Verse*, 205; and "[A Character]," *Minor Poems*, ed. Norman Ault and John Butt (London: Methuen, 1954), 358, lines 13–14.

74. Pope to [Martha] Blount, 6 August 1718, *The Correspondence of Alexander Pope*, ed. George Sherburn (Oxford: Clarendon Press, 1956), 1:480.

75. Morris R. Brownell, *Alexander Pope & the Arts of Georgian England* (Oxford: Clarendon Press, 1978), 305–17, 381–83. See also James R. Aubrey, "Timon's Villa: Pope's Composite Picture," *Studies in Philology* 80, no. 3 (1983): 325–48.

76. Polybius relates war's haphazard and predictable aspects; see Trompf, *Idea of Recurrence*, 70–73.

77. Miriam Starkman suggests that Swift may be alluding to "Admiral Russell, who was suspected of treason in the Battle of La Hague in 1692." See *Gulliver's Travels and Other Writings*, ed. Miriam Starkman (New York: Bantam, 1962), 196.

78. Starkman, *Gulliver's Travels*, 197.

79. See Ehrenpreis, *Swift: The Man, His Works, and the Age* 2:509–10.

80. Edmund Burke, *A Philosophical Enquiry into the Origin of Our Ideas of the Sublime and Beautiful*, ed. J. T. Boulton (London: Routledge and Kegan Paul, 1958), pt. 2, sec. 8–9, 73–74.

81. Rawson discusses this passage; see *Gulliver and the Gentle Reader*, 15–17, 50–52. One thinks of Candide and Martin the Manichean who leisurely witness a sea battle: " *qu'on eut le plaisir de voir le combat tout à son aise.*" *Candide*, 203. The most extensive analysis of this spectator subject is Carole Fabricant's *Swift's Landscape*, chap. 5, "The Spectator in the Landscape," esp. 175–76, 198–99.

82. Fortescue, *History of the British Army* 1:357.

83. Clayborough, *Grotesque*, 72–73.

Chapter 3. Smollett: The Grotesque View of Military Service

1. Tobias Smollett, *Ferdinand Count Fathom*, ed. Damian Grant (London: Oxford University Press, 1971), chaps. 3, 4; all subsequent citations are to this edition (hereafter cited as *FCF*).

Alexander A. Parker suggests that Smollett may have modeled these opening scenes on Quevedo's *El Buscón* (1626) in which one finds a similar "disreputable" mother; see *Literature and the Delinquent: The Picaresque Novel in Spain and Europe: 1599–1753* (Edinburgh: Edinburgh University Press, 1967), 128. Also similar is Grimmelshausen's second novel *Courasche* (1670), the heroine of which becomes amorously involved with several military characters.

Ferdinand's paternity can only be ascribed to the British army at large since his mother made it her business to comfort the amorous needs of all and hence could not identify the father of her son. Her status as regimental belle resembles that of Mrs. Waters in Fielding's *Tom Jones* and the "doxy" in Burns's "The Jolly Beggars."

2. On camp-sutlers, see Childs, *Armies and Warfare*, 111. It may well be that Smollett based Ferdinand's mother on the notorious Mrs. Christian Davies or "Mother Ross," a female soldier during Marlborough's campaigns who turned camp cook and then queen of the sutlers after her sex was discovered and whose memoirs have been attributed by some to Defoe. See also Scouller, *Armies of Queen Anne*, 226, 283. Another possible source is the female camp-sutler and babe in the lower right-hand corner of Hogarth's "March to Finchley"; the babe is depicted as reaching for the gin that the sutler is in the process of giving to an inebriated soldier. This detail is similar to how Ferdinand's mother feeds her baby son gin.

3. And conversely, her act of plunder against a member of her own side, an "officer of the hussars" (*FCF*, 16), results in her death when the officer fires a hidden pistol as she is about to strip him of a Turkish standard.

The reward reaped by Ferdinand's mother for saving Count Melvil bears a resemblance to an incident recorded by "Mother Ross." By her own fictional account, "Mother" or "Kit" Ross was promised a handsome reward by the injured Colonel Gossedge, whom she had saved from the battlefield only to see die three days later. See [Daniel Defoe], *The Life and Adventures of Mrs. Christian Davies, Commonly Called Mother Ross* (London: Peter Davies, 1928), 113.

Paul-Gabriel Boucé connects Ferdinand's low military birth to that of Scipio in *Gil Blas; see The Novels of Tobias Smollett*, trans. Antonia White (London: Longman, 1976) 85–87. While this connection is valid (it might be added that Gil Blas himself is the son of a retired soldier), Ferdinand's adoption into Count Melvil's military family bears a closer similarity to Don Alphonso's beginnings. Don Alphonso, a foundling, is taken in and raised by Baron Steinback, an officer of the German guard. Like Ferdinand, Don Alphonso makes his entrance into the world as a soldier (*Gil Blas*, bk. 4, chap. 10).

4. For a sensible view of this polemical debate, one should consult Boucé who remarks that the "picaresque battle—or rather anti-picaresque battle—is far from over as far as Smollettian studies are concerned." Paul-Gabriel Boucé, "Smollett's Pseudo-picaresque: A Response to Rousseau's Smollett and the Picaresque," *Studies in Burke and His Time* 14, no. 1 (1972): 74. After mentioning a few model pieces that demonstrate a "healthy concern for a more refined analysis of the picaresque elements at play in Smollett's novels," Boucé warns that "the existence of such sundry *elements*, in varying proportion" should not lead scholars to label Smollett "a 'picaresque' writer."

The leading challenge to the view that Smollett is a picaresque novelist is made by G. S. Rousseau, "Smollett and the Picaresque: Some Questions about a Label," *Studies in Burke and His Times* 12, no. 3 (1971): 1886–1904. Rousseau argues that only *Roderick Random* meets some requirements of the picaresque; see 1890.

Frank J. Kearful, who ultimately concludes that the application of the term "picaresque" to eighteenth-century English fiction must occasion "such qualifications as to negate its usefulness," also recognizes that both Grimmelshausen's *Simplicissimus* and Smollett's *Roderick Random* portray "the barbarism and inhumanity of war through the eyes of an innocent . . ."; "Spanish Rogues and English Foundlings: On the Disintegration of Picaresque," *Genre* 4, no. 4 (1971): 389, 388.

5. For discussions of these two novels and the association of the picaresque with war, see Parker, 74–98; Richard Bjornson, *The Picaresque Hero in European Fiction* (Madison: University of Wisconsin Press, 1977), 134–35, 177–79; and Harry Sieber, *The Picaresque*, Critical Idiom #33 (London: Methuen, 1977), 34–35, 69.

6. A summation of the typical picaro's life is made by Cadwallader in *Peregrine Pickle:* "In short, I have travelled over the greatest part of Europe, as a beggar, pilgrim, priest, soldier, gamester, and quack; and felt the extremes of indigence and opulence . . ." Tobias Smollett, *The Adventures of Peregrine Pickle*, ed. James L. Clifford, revised Paul-Gabriel Boucé (Oxford: Oxford University Press, 1983), 386; all subsequent citations are to this edition (hereafter cited as *PP*).

7. Tobias Smollett, *The Adventures of Roderick Random*, ed. Paul-Gabriel Boucé (Oxford: Oxford University Press, 1979), 95; all subsequent citations are to this edition (hereafter cited as *RR*).

8. See Louis L. Martz, "Smollett and the Expedition to Carthagena," *PMLA* 56 (1941): 435; and Lewis M. Knapp, "The Naval Scenes in *Roderick Random*," *PMLA* 49 (1939): 595.

As the narrator, Roderick himself admits to keeping a diary on the expedition. In an incident that seems to be borrowed from Fielding's *Joseph Andrews* (bk. 2, chap. 11), Roderick's diary—written in Greek—is used as evidence of a secret code in his spy trial. See *RR*, 174–76.

9. Martz, 443. See also his book, *The Later Career of Tobias Smollett* (Hamden, Conn.: Archon Book, 1967), 183–84.

10. Martz, "Smollett and the Expedition to Carthagena," 444–45.

11. Henry Veits, M.D., "Smollett, the 'War of Jenkins's Ear' And 'An Account of the Expedition to Cartagena,' 1743," *Bulletin of the Medical Library Association* 28 (1940): 178–79. According to Veits, the "Account" was first published anonymously in 1743, edited later by Smollett and included in the *Compendium* in 1756.

12. Daniel Defoe, *Colonel Jack*, ed. Samuel Holt Monk (London: Oxford University Press, 1965), 104. See also *Memoirs of a Cavalier* for Defoe's positive view of the military profession. Defoe apparently served in Monmouth's army in the 1685 rebellion.

As an orphan Jack is given title "Colonel" by his nurse to distinguish him from another orphan whose name also happens to be Jack and who is called "Captain." See Defoe, *Colonel Jack*, 4–5. The title enhances Jack's sense of self-worth and gentility—as his nurse tells him, " . . . none but Gentlemen are ever made Colonels; besides *says she*, I have known Colonels come to be Lords, and Generals, tho' they were Bas——ds at first."

13. Defoe, *Colonel Jack*, 183. The military episodes in *Colonel Jack* constitute a typical example of that ambivalence between moral duty and material gain for which Defoe is famous. For a history of recruiting practices, see Walton, *Standing Army*, 468–69, 479–95, and Childs, *Armies and Warfare*, 45, 60–61.

14. Boucé, *Novels of Tobias Smollett*, 263. For a detailed history of the press-gang in the eighteenth century, see J. R. Hutchinson, *The Press-Gang: Afloat and Ashore* (London: Eveleigh Nash, 1913). For a more recent discussion, see N. A. M. Rodger, *The Wooden World: An Anatomy of the Georgian Navy* (London: Collins, 1986), 164–82. One might also note Lady Bellaston's scheme to dispose of Tom Jones by arranging for him to be pressed (*Tom Jones*, bk. 16, chap. 8).

15. See Boucé's summary of the case of Alexander Broadfoot; *Novels of Tobias Smollett*, 278.

16. Such a play-bill is reproduced in Hutchinson, *Press-Gang*, facing 188; at the top is the statement, "Lieutenant Kelley, Lieutenant King, and Lieutenant Bevis, Pledge their Words of Honour, that no Seaman whatever shall be molested by their People, on Play-Nights, from the Hours of Four in the Afternoon to Six the following Morning, after which time the indulgence ceases."

17. Trading vessels were the greatest sufferers of the press-gang. See Hutchinson, *Press-Gang*, 78.

18. Fortescue, *History of the British Army* 1:591.

19. Although, as chance would have it, Colonel Jack is unable to pursue his immediate scheme after he deserts, he is never apprehended or anxious about being caught. When one considers the high level of anxiety, even paranoia, among Defoe's narrators—Colonel Jack himself becomes paranoid about his association with the 1715 Jacobite Rebellion—this lack of concern suggests that desertion was committed in a casual manner.

20. Chandler, *Art of Warfare*, 71. See also Walton, *Standing Army*, 488, 534–35, 542; Scouller, *Armies of Queen Anne*, 292–309; and Childs, *Armies and Warfare*, 70–73.

Fortescue, *History of the British Army* 2:32, gives us the following portrait of the negative recruit: "The standard of the recruit, socially and morally, appears at the accession of George the First to have sunk to the level of the worst days of Elizabeth, of the Restoration, or of William the Third. It is abundantly evident that the ranks were filled in great measure by professional criminals, who passed from regiment to regiment, spreading everywhere the infection of discontent, debauchery, and insubordination. The noxious weeds of desertion and fraudulent enlistment flourished with amazing exuberance, and no severity of punishment had power to root them out."

21. Flavius Vegetius Renatus, *De Re Militari*, trans. Lieutenant John Clarke (Harrisburg, Pa.: Stackpole Books, 1944), 71: "However, the best judges of the service have always been of the opinion that daily practice of the military exercises is much more efficacious in preserving the health of an army than all the art of medicine."

22. Smollett's "Account" repeats the same horrific description and even includes more grotesque details; see "An Account of the Expedition Against Carthagena," in *The Complete Works of Tobias Smollett*, ed. Thomas Roscoe (London: George Bell, 1887), 610: " . . . they wallowed in filth . . . nothing were heard but groans, lamentations, and the language of despair."

23. John R. McNeill, "The Ecological Basis of Warfare in the Caribbean: 1700–1804," in *Adapting to Conditions: War and Society in the Eighteenth Century*, ed. Maarten Ultee (Tuscaloosa, Ala.: University of Alabama Press, 1986), 35. McNeill summarizes, "As tropical infections were much more lethal than combat, the ability to withstand disease often proved more important than martial prowess"; ibid., 39.

24. Ibid., 42.

25. See Boucé's notes, *RR*, 458.

26. Critics have pointed out that this scene is a comment upon the *in abstracto* wounds studied at surgeon's hall; see Boucé, *Novels of Tobias Smollett*, 113.

27. *Shakespeare's Ovid, Being Arthur Golding's Translation of "The Metamorphoses"*, ed. W. H. D. Rouse (New York: Norton, 1966), 12.478.

28. *Works of Thomas Nashe* 2:231.

29. Ibid., 4:267. From Languet, *Chronicle* (Cooper, 1565, fol. 275v).

30. *The Diary of Samuel Pepys*, 8 June 1665, ed. Robert Latham and William Matthews (London: Bell, 1972), 6:122.

The severed head becoming a projectile is vaguely reminiscent of how Aiantes cuts off the head of Imbrius in the *Iliad* 13.200–205 and sends it "rolling through the throng like a ball . . . before the feet of Hector."

31. "The Second Advice to a Painter for drawing the History of our navall busynesse," lines 183–84, *Andrew Marvell: Complete Poetry*, ed. George de F. Lord (New York: Modern Library, 1968). However, other editors consider Marvell's authorship of the poem to be doubtful. The lines are noted by Pepys's editors. Scott repeats this grotesque motif of the splattered brains of the apparently brainless in his mock-elegy for the Laird of Balmawhapple; *Waverly*, chap. 47.

This *ut pictura poesis* verse epistle was used again by A. Marvell, Junior, in 1740 to satirize the pacifists and praise Admiral Vernon; see "Satirical and Panegyrical Instructions to Mr. William Hogarth, Painter, on Admiral Vernon's Taking Porto Bello With Six Ships of War Only" (London: H. Goreham, 1740).

32. Angus Ross, "The 'Show of Violence' in Smollett's Novels," *The Yearbook of English Studies*, vol. 2, ed. T. J. B. Spencer and R. L. Smallwood (London: Modern Humanities Research Association, 1972), 120.

33. Alice Green Fredman, "The Picaresque in Decline: Smollett's First Novel," *English Writers of the Eighteenth Century*, ed. John H. Middendorf

(New York: Columbia University Press, 1971), 203. Fredman goes on (205) to call this bombardment scene with Roderick tied to the deck "the paradigm of the vision of Roderick Random's world," which is the very opposite of the wanton cruelty of the picaresque: "It is a stunning example of the vision, and a horrifying vision too; it could drive a man mad. Nothing could be further from the picaresque vision than this."

34. On the unexaggerated veracity of Roderick's account of the Cartagena expedition, see Boucé, *Novels of Tobias Smollett*, 266–79.

35. See Smollett, *The Complete Works*, 605.

36. Joanne Lewis Lynn, "Configurations of the Comic Grotesque in the Novels of Tobias Smollett" (Ph.D. diss., University of California, Irvine, 1974), 82.

37. Ibid., 81–82.

38. On the inexperience of the troops, see Fortescue, *History of the British Army* 2:58–59, 78. "His regimental officers were, without exception, young and inexperienced, while some few of them, who had obtained their commissions through political jobbery, are described as the most abandoned wretches of the town."

39. "Duke of Argyll's Speech on the Army," 9 December 1740, *Cobbet's Parliamentary History of England* (London: T. C. Hansard, 1812), 11:894–910.

40. As Boucé notes, this is a verbatim translation of Lucan, *The Civil War* 1.125–26, and as Lucan goes on to say that it is impossible to tell who "had the fairer pretext for warfare"—or *"Quis iustius induit arma, / Scire nefas"* (1.127–28)—so it is impossible for Roderick to decide who is more blameworthy.

41. When Sir Launcelot Greaves is in the insane asylum, he hears a raving military commander issuing a series of impetuous orders; see Tobias Smollett, *The Life and Adventures of Sir Launcelot Greaves*, ed. David Evans (London: Oxford University Press, 1973), 185–86: "Bring up the artillery—let Brutandorf's brigade advance—detach my black hussars to ravage the country—let them be new-booted—take particular care of the spur-leathers—make a desert of Lusatia—bombard the suburbs of Pera—go, tell my brother Henry to pass the Elbe at Meissen with forty battalions and fifty squadrons—so ho, you major-general Donder, why don't you finish your second parallel?—send hither the engineer Schittenbach—I'll lay all the shoes in my shop, the breach will be practicable in four and twenty hours—don't tell me of your works—you and your works be damn'd—."

42. Boucé makes this important point in his response to Rousseau: ". . . the genuine picaro has little or no choice between right or wrong, for if he wishes to survive he has to obey the clamorous visceral urges of an empty belly." Boucé, "Smollett's Pseudo-Picaresque," 76.

43. Tobias Smollett, *The Expedition of Humphry Clinker*, ed. Lewis M. Knapp (London: Oxford University Press, 1966), 36–37; all subsequent citations are to this edition (hereafter cited as *HC*).

44. The location of this kind of moral vision in *Humphry Clinker* is made by Philip Stevick who applies game theory to Smollett's novels. According to Stevick, *Roderick Random* and *Peregrine Pickle*, largely picaresque in content, involve *agon* (competition) and *mimicry*; only *Humphry Clinker* shows evidence of *eutrapelia*, a balance and harmony between a fondness for the playful and an appreciation of the serious. See "Smollett's Picaresque Games," *Tobias Smollett: Bicentennial Essays Presented to Lewis M. Knapp*, ed. G. S. Rousseau and P. G. Boucé (New York: Oxford University Press, 1971), 126–30.

45. Robert Hopkins, "The Function of the Grotesque in *Humphry Clinker*," *Huntington Library Quarterly* 32 (February 1969): 173.

Boucé has pointed to the similarity between the scarred Lismahago and

Lesage's Captain Chinchilla who "had left an eye at Naples, an arm in Lombardy, and a leg in the Low Countries"; Boucé, *Novels of Tobias Smollett*, 85. *Gil Blas*, trans. Tobias Smollett (New York: Thomas Y. Crowell, n.d.), bk. 7, chap. 12, 409.

46. Boucé claims that there is more structural unity in *Roderick Random* than has been generally thought; see Boucé, *Novels of Tobias Smollett*, 100, 103.

47. Tobias Smollett, *Travels Through France and Italy*, ed. Frank Felsenstein (Oxford: Oxford University Press, 1981), 104; all subsequent citations are to this edition (hereafter cited as *T*).

48. The criticism was repeated in Smollett's translation of Voltaire; see *T*, 376, n. 9.

49. *Boswell's Life of Johnson* 2:226–27.

50. Henry Fielding, *Amelia*, ed. Martin Battestin, introduction and notes by Fredson Bowers (Middletown, Conn.: Wesleyan University Press, 1984), 365; all subsequent citations are to this edition (hereafter cited as *A*).

51. Tobias Smollett, *The History of England* (London: D. S. Maurice, 1823), 3:108.

52. Ibid.

53. Ibid., 3:107.

54. Ibid., 3:108.

55. *London Magazine* (July 1743), 346.

56. Ibid. I have not been able to find this line in D'Avenant's works.

57. *The Idler*, No. 20, 62.

58. *The Idler*, No. 30, 94–95.

59. Lynn, "Configurations," 83.

60. For the most detailed examination of the political satire, see Wayne Joseph Douglas, "Smollett and the Sordid Knaves: Political Satire in *The Adventures of an Atom*" (Ph.D. diss., University of Florida, 1976). For a review of the possible influences on Smollett's *Atom*, see Martz, *The Later Career of Tobias Smollett*, 90–103.

61. Smollett uses these three terms synonymously throughout the *Atom*. Douglas traces the "Legion" to Mark 5:9 and the "blatant beast" to *The Faerie Queene*, bk. 6; see Douglas, "Smollett," 94–97. Boucé refers to the mob as a "protean character" in the work; Boucé, *Novels of Tobias Smollett*, 38. There are also a number of critical commentaries on mobs in *Humphry Clinker*.

62. Tobias Smollett, *The History and Adventures of an Atom*, in *Complete Works*, 916.

63. Smollett, *The Atom*, *Complete Works*, 966.

64. "The Winter Morning Walk," lines 187–88, in *The Poetical Works of William Cowper*, 4th ed., ed. H. S. Milford, rev. Norma Russell (London: Oxford University Press, 1934).

Chapter 4. Fielding: Military Unruliness, Advancement, and Grandeur

1. See Martin C. Battestin, "General Introduction," *Amelia*, ed. Martin Battestin (Middletown, Conn.: Wesleyan University Press, 1984), xxxiii, and Donald Low, "Mr. Fielding of Bow Street," in *Henry Fielding: Justice Observed*, ed. K. D. Simpson (London: Vision and Barnes & Noble, 1985), 16.

2. Childs, *Armies and Warfare*, 175.

3. Ibid., 186. See also Scouller, *Armies of Queen Anne*, 253–92. One again thinks of Farquhar's Sergeant Kite: "I at last got into the army, and there I learned whoring and drinking" (*RO* 3.1.118–19).

4. *The Souldiers Fortune*, 1.1.201, 208–11, in *The Works of Thomas Otway*, ed. J. C. Ghosh (Oxford: Clarendon Press, 1932), 2:101–2.

5. Childs, *Armies and Warfare*, 175.

6. Henry Fielding, *Joseph Andrews*, ed. Martin Battestin, introduction Fredson Bowers (Middletown, Conn.: Wesleyan University Press, 1967), 56; all subsequent citations are to this edition (hereafter cited as *JA*).

7. "Petition to the Members of Parliament for the County of Lancaster," in *English Historical Documents: 1714–1783*, 624–28.

8. *English Historical Documents: 1714–1783*, 625, 624. In 1759 another petition was received by the House of Commons regarding the quartering of soldiers in public houses; this one actually proposed that the soldiers be put into "Barracks." *English Historical Documents: 1714–1783*, 628.

9. Henry Fielding, *The History of Tom Jones, A Foundling*, ed. Fredson Bowers, introduction and notes Martin Battestin (Middletown, Conn.: Wesleyan University Press, 1975), 366; all subsequent citations are to this edition (hereafter cited as *TJ*).

10. On the subject of quartering, see Walton, *Standing Army*, 712–16; Childs, *Armies and Warfare*, 185–86, 189; and Scouller, *Armies of Queen Anne*, 162–65.

11. It was allowed to expire in 1697 after the Treaty of Ryswick and was only renewed in 1701 at the outset of the Spanish Succession War. Otherwise it was generally passed annually from 1689 to the end of the eighteenth century. Its expiration was the occasion of a pamphlet war in which Defoe and Prior argued for the standing army and Trenchard and others against it.

12. Childs, *The Army of Charles II*, 15–20.

13. *Cymon and Iphigenia*, lines 399–408, *The Poems of John Dryden*, ed. James Kinsley (Oxford: Clarendon Press, 1958), 4:1751.

14. Fortescue, *History of the British Army* 2:571.

15. *Cobbett's Parliamentary History of England* 11:1415, 1432.

16. Ibid., 11:1457

17. Ibid., 11:1465.

18. Ibid., 11:1471.

19. In his final comments, Campbell, an opposition member, expressed a sentiment that must have been shared by both sides in the debate; ibid., 11:1478: "Sir, I am far from intending to oppose this proposal of five pints, though, upon a rigorous examination, it might appear more than the mere wants of nature require; for I cannot but declare that this question has too long engaged the attention of the House, and that the representatives of a mighty nation, beset with enemies, and encumbered with difficulties, seem to forget their importance and their dignity by wrangling from day to day upon a pint of small-beer."

20. Claude C. Sturgill, "The French Army in Roussillon, 1716–1720," *Adapting to Conditions: War and Society in the Eighteenth Century*, 21. Sturgill contends that "the garrisoning of troops such as a battalion of infantry, a squadron of cavalry, or a battalion of artillery in a locale could mean the difference between great prosperity and near poverty for the population."

21. *The Works of the Celebrated Mrs. Centlivre* (London: 1872), 1:60.

22. *Works of Mrs. Centlivre* 1:61.

23. *A*, 49–56.

24. *Boswell on the Grand Tour: Germany and Switzerland*, 11 September 1764, ed. Frederick A. Pottle (1928; reprint, New York: McGraw-Hill, 1953), 91.

25. Derek Jarrett's analysis of the "March to Finchley" and how the public feared the insolence of the army in Hogarth's time contains some valuable insights. See his *England in the Age of Hogarth* (London: Hart-Davis, MacGibbon, 1974), 38–63. Jarrett clearly distinguishes between soldiers who were seen as the instruments of tyranny and sailors who were viewed more positively as the true protectors of Britain and her overseas trade. For a discussion of the dating of the "March to Finchley" and the frontispiece to Fielding's *Jacobite's Journal*, see W. B. Coley, "Hogarth, Fielding and the Dating of the 'March to Finchley'," *Journal of the Warburg and Courtauld Institutes* 30 (1967): 317–26.

26. Robert Etheridge Moore, *Hogarth's Literary Relationships* (New York: Octagon Books, 1969), 138.

27. George II, quoted in Ronald Paulson, *Hogarth: His Life, Art, and Times* (New Haven: Yale University Press, 1971), 2:90.

28. Paulson, *Hogarth* 2:87. Hogarth's views on war and the military certainly changed according to political and national moods. When the Seven Years' War broke out in 1756, he engraved two propaganda prints (Plate I, "France" and Plate II, "England") to elicit support for the British cause by fueling fears about a French invasion.

29. [John Wilkes], *The North Briton*, No. 17 (London: J. Williams, 1763), 1:164. Wilkes (1:155) also criticizes Hogarth's "grotesque manner": "The darling passion of Mr. *Hogarth* is to shew the *faulty* and *dark* side of every object. He never gives us in perfection the *fair face of nature*, but admirably well holds out her deformities to ridicule. The reason is plain. All objects are painted on his *retina* in a grotesque manner, and he has never felt the force of what the French call *la belle nature*."

30. *The Spectator*, No. 152, 2:97.

31. See Samuel Johnson, "On the Bravery of the English Common Soldiers," *Political Writings*, 278–84. This is a more persuasive argument than that offered by a recent historian who attributed Britian's military successes in the eighteenth-century to the "sound knowledge" and "high morale" of her army; see Colonel H. C. B. Rogers, *British Army*, 13.

32. Ronald Paulson, *Popular and Polite Art in the Age of Hogarth and Fielding* (Notre Dame, Ind.: Notre Dame University Press, 1979), 206.

33. *The New Oxford Book of Eighteenth-Century Verse*, ed. Roger Lonsdale (Oxford: Oxford University Press, 1984), 111–12.

34. Ibid., 751–52.

35. Ibid., 785–86.

36. *The Spectator*, No. 2, 1:11.

37. John C. Miller, *Triumph of Freedom: 1775–1783* (Boston: Little, Brown and Company, 1948), 9; this passage is quoted by Eric Robson in, "Purchase and Promotion in the British Army in the Eighteenth Century," *History* 36 (1951): 57. For a general discussion of purchased commissions, see ibid.; Fortescue, *History of the British Army* 1:317–19; Childs, *Armies and Warfare*, 84–86, 89–91, and 90–91; Scouller, *Armies of Queen Anne*, passim; and Alan J. Guy, *Oeconomy and Discipline: Officership and Administration in the British Army, 1714–63* (Manchester: Manchester University Press, 1985), passim.

38. Childs, *Armies and Warfare*, 84. Although Childs's comments seem to pertain to the French army, they may also be applied to the British.

39. See N. A. M. Rodger, *Wooden World*, 113–23.

40. Michael Lewis, *England's Sea-Officers: The Story of the Naval Profession* (London: George Allen & Unwin, 1939), 83–89.

41. Fortescue, *History of the British Army* 1:561, 1:562.

42. Frederick A. Pottle, "Introduction," *Boswell's London Journal: 1762–1763*, ed. Frederick A. Pottle (New York: McGraw-Hill, 1950), 19–21.

43. *The Champion*, in *The Works of Henry Fielding Esq.*, ed. Leslie Stephen (London: Smith, Elder & Co., 1882), 5:209.

44. *Works of Henry Fielding* 5:210.

45. See Brian McCrea, *Henry Fielding and the Politics of Mid-Eighteenth-Century England* (Athens: University of Georgia Press, 1981), 48–49.

46.
> No more you mourn your once loved husband's fate,
> Who bravely perished for a thankless state.
> For rolling years thy piety prevailed;
> At length, quite sunk—thy hope, thy patience failed.
> Distracted now you tread on life's last stage.

(lines 3–7)

New Oxford Book of Eighteenth-Century Verse, 233. Barber closes her poem with a national warning: "Britain, for this impending ruin dread; / Their woes call loud for vengeance on thy head: / Nor wonder, if disasters wait your fleets" (lines 27–29).

47. See M. Dorothy George, *Hogarth to Cruikshank: Social Change in Graphic Satire* (New York: Walker and Company, 1967), 103–4.

48. Robson, "Purchase and Promotion," 58.

49. Fortescue, *History of the British Army* 1:579.

50. Ibid.

51. Defoe, *Colonel Jack*, 105.

52. Ibid., 207, 209.

53. *English Historical Documents: 1714–1783*, 614.

54. Quoted by Robson, "Purchase and Promotion," 71.

55. Quoted by ibid., 71–72.

56. Jane Austen, *Pride and Prejudice*, eds. James Kinsley and Frank W. Bradbrook (Oxford: Oxford University Press, 1970), 25.

57. Mary Wollstonecraft, *A Vindication of the Rights of Women*, ed. Urich H. Hardt (Troy, N.Y.: Whitston, 1982), 63. Hardt notes that Wollstonecraft borrowed "a passion for a scarlet coat" from Swift's poem "The Furniture of a Woman's MIND"; see *Poems* 2:415, line 2.

58. See Battestin, "General Introduction," *Amelia*, xix.

59. See Thomas Cleary's comments on this scene, *Henry Fielding: Political Writer* (Waterloo, Ont.: Wilfred Laurier University Press, 1984), 170–73.

60. Paulson, *Popular and Polite Art*, 196–97.

61. The French army was the largest of its kind in the eighteenth century; for some comparative statistics, see Childs, *Armies and Warfare*, 42.

62. This fact is noted by Morris Golden, "Fielding's Politics," in *Justice Observed*, 48.

63. *The History of the Life of the Late Jonathan Wild the Great*, in *Works of Henry Fielding* 5:5, 5:48, 5:155.

64. *Works of Henry Fielding* 5:103–4.

65. John Gay, *The Beggar's Opera* 2.1.10–11, in *Dramatic Works*, ed. John Fuller (Oxford: Clarendon Press, 1983), 2:23.

66. *Tom Thumb and the Tragedy of Tragedies*, ed. L. J. Morrissey (Berkeley and Los Angeles: University of California Press, 1970), 142.

67. "Of True Greatness," in *Miscellanies by Henry Fielding, Esq.*, ed. Henry Knight Miller (Middletown, Conn.: Wesleyan University Press, 1972), 1:22, lines 77–82.

68. Ibid., 1:232, 1:234.

69. Ibid., 1:235.

Chapter 5. Sterne: Military Veterans and "Humours"

1. Roger Sterne fought under Marlborough and ended his military career as a lieutenant—the highest rank that a commoner without money could expect to attain. On the military environment of Sterne's childhood, see Arthur Cash, *Laurence Sterne: The Early and Middle Years* (London: Methuen, 1975), 1–23, 36–39.

2. Laurence Sterne, *A Sentimental Journey Through France and Italy by Mr. Yorick*, ed. Gardner D. Stout, Jr. (Berkeley and Los Angeles: University of California Press, 1967), 170–71; all subsequent citations are made to this edition (hereafter cited as *SJ*).

3. *New Oxford Book of Eighteenth-Century Verse*, 511. The poem was published with an accompanying print in 1773.

4. Ibid., 786, lines 40–41.

5. See J. Walter Nelson, "War and Peace and the British Poets of Sensibility," *Studies in Eighteenth-Century Culture*, vol. 7, ed., Rosann Runte (Madison: University of Wisconsin Press, 1978), 345–66.

6. *Collected Works of Oliver Goldsmith* 4:293, lines 155–58.

7. *Oxford Book of Eighteenth-Century Verse*, 295.

8. Defoe, *Colonel Jack*, 11. Later, on his tobacco plantation, Jack does read much history, especially military, and he travels to Ghent just to see the fortified city and military preparations, to his "Delight"; see 157, 172, 183–84.

9. *Boswell's London Journal: 1762–1763*, 22 December 1762, 100.

10. William Wordsworth, *The Prelude*, in *Poetical Works*, ed. Thomas Hutchinson, rev. Ernest de Selincourt (1936; reprint, Oxford: Oxford University Press, 1975), 520–21; all subsequent citations are to this edition.

11. *Collected Works of Oliver Goldsmith* 2:465.

12. *Poems and Songs of Robert Burns* 1:197.

13. Nelson, "War and Peace," 357. "Johnny, I Hardly Knew Ye," in *Eighteenth-Century English Literature*, ed. Geoffrey Tillotson, Paul Fussell, Jr., and Marshall Waingrow, with Brewster Rogerson (New York: Harcourt Brace Jovanovich, 1969), 1525.

14. *Collected Works of Oliver Goldsmith* 4:338.

15. *The Tatler*, No. 132, 3:99. On Steele and the military, see Richard H. Dammers, "Soldiers and Philosophers: Captain Steele and Captain Ayloffe," *Eighteenth-Century Life* 3, no. 2 (December 1976): 52–55.

16. *The Spectator*, No. 2, 1:11.

17. Ibid.

18. See Ronald Paulson, *Satire and the English Novel* (New Haven: Yale University Press, 1967), 285.

19. In *The Philosophical Irony of Laurence Sterne* (Gainesville: University Presses of Florida, 1975), 85, Helene Moglen observes, "Although Toby's wholehearted, childish immersion in his hobby has its delightful side, there is a more menacing aspect to it in his dependence for the continuation of his play upon the continuation of actual combat and in his sorrow at the signing of the Peace

of Utrecht." This fact is not emphasized in the most extensive study of the "game" or "play" aspect of Toby's hobbyhorse; see Richard A. Lanham, *"Tristram Shandy": The Games of Pleasure* (Berkeley and Los Angeles: University of California Press, 1973), 37–51, 77–92. Lanham claims (85), "Sterne sees . . . Toby's war as a kind of applied pastorality, using the mechanism of pastoral to discharge quite unpastoral impulses."

20. *The Florida Edition of the Works of Laurence Sterne* ed. Melvyn New, Joan New, Richard A. Davies, and W. D. Day (Gainesville: University Presses of Florida, 1978–84), 2:552; all subsequent citations are made to this edition (hereafter cited as *TS*).

21. Kayser, *Grotesque*, 51.

22. See Bakhtin, *Rabelais*, 36–37, 47; and Bakhtin, *The Dialogic Imagination*, 237, 308–10.

23. Bakhtin, *Rabelais*, 38–9, 90; and Bakhtin, *The Dialogic Imagination*, 237.

24. See Bosmajian, "The Nature of the Grotesque Image in Eighteenth-Century English Literature," which includes an insightful chapter on *Tristram Shandy*: and Lilian R. Furst, "The Dual Face of the Grotesque in Sterne's *Tristram Shandy* and Lenz's *Der Waldbruder*," *Comparative Literature Studies* 13 (1976): 15–21, which concentrates on the narrative disjointedness of the novel. See also Jean Claude Dupas, "*Tristram Shandy*: une rhapsodie grotesque," *Bulletin de la Societé d'études anglo-américaines des XVIIe et XVIIIe Siècles* 6 (June 1978): 61–75. None of these critics is specifically concerned with the novel's military content.

25. Samuel Johnson, "Grotesque," vol. 1 of *A Dictionary of the English Language*, 5th ed. (London: W. & A. Strachan, 1784).

26. Barasch has made the most detailed study to date of how "grotesque" began to be used as an art, and then generic, term from the late seventeenth to the late eighteenth century; see his *The Grotesque: A Study in Meanings*, 56, 103, 144.

27. *TS*, 2:544: "Let me stop and give you a picture of the corporal's apparatus; and of the corporal himself in the height of this attack just as it struck my uncle *Toby*, as he turned towards the sentry box, where the corporal was at work,—for in nature there is not such another,—nor can any combination of all that is grotesque and whimsical in her works produce its equal." Bosmajian refers to this use of "grotesque."

28. Anonymous, *Critical Review* 11 (April 1761), quoted from *Sterne: The Critical Heritage*, ed. Alan B. Howes (London: Routledge & Kegan Paul, 1974), 125. I am indebted to Bosmajian for this source.

29. Patricia Spacks's comments on comedy and point-of-view in *Tristram Shandy* are appropriate in this context; see *Imagining a Self* (Cambridge: Harvard University Press, 1976), 138: "Perhaps it can be argued that comedy distinguishes itself from tragedy entirely by its point-of-view. . . . One stamps his foot at the universe: how grotesque!"

30. Yorick's philosophy of humor, of course, derives from the grotesque gravedigging scene in *Hamlet* 5.1.

31. See Edward Niehus, "Quixotic Figures in the Novels of Sterne," *Essays in Literature* 12, no. 1 (1985): 49: "In sentimentality, as in most things human, Sterne saw elements of both the absurd and the noble, the comic and the serious." Alan B. Howes holds that Sterne combines Rabelaisian and Cervantic humour in his characterization; see "Laurence Sterne, Rabelais, and Cervantes:

The Two Kinds of Laughter in *Tristram Shandy*," *Laurence Sterne: Riddles and Mysteries*, ed. Valerie Grosvenor Myer (London: Vision and Barnes & Noble, 1984), 55.

32. Lanham, "*Tristram Shandy*," 88, draws upon Huizinga's *Homo Ludens* and the game theory of others; he ultimately sees Toby's hobbyhorse as a combination of pastoral and chivalrous play.

33. Peter Stevick, "Miniaturization in Eighteenth-Century English Literature," *University of Toronto Quarterly* 38, no. 2. (1969): 173.

34. Hobbies are supposed to be therapeutic, and Michael Deporte discusses uncle Toby's somewhat mad game on the bowling green in exactly this respect; see his *Nightmares and Hobbyhorses: Swift, Sterne, and Augustan Ideas of Madness* (San Marino, Calif.: Huntington Library, 1974), 114–19.

35. See J. M. Stedmond, "Uncle Toby's 'Campaigns' and Raree-Shows," *Notes and Queries* 201, New Series, no. 3 (1956) 28; and George Speaight's "Reply" in the same issue, 133–34.

36. *The London Stage, 1660–1800, Part 3: 1729–1747*, ed. Arthur H. Scouten (Carbondale: Southern Illinois University Press, 1961), 1059–60.

37. On the history of military miniatures, see Max von Boehn, *Puppets and Automata*, trans. Josephine Nicoll (New York: Dover, 1972), 37–47; and Fraser, *A History of Toys*, 18, 61, 74, 86.

38. Ibid., 86.

39. In Arthur Cash's words, *Laurence Sterne*, 16, "It was indeed a family of soldiers that Laurence grew up in."

40. Bryson, *Word and Image*, 36.

41. Ibid.

42. Kayser, *Grotesque*, 183: "The mechanical object is alienated by being brought to life, the human being by being deprived of it. Among the most persistent motifs of the grotesque we find human bodies reduced to puppets, marionettes, and automata." See also ibid., 198.

43. Exactly how Sterne adapts Locke's philosophy has been the subject of much criticism on *Tristram Shandy*. See Peter Briggs, "Locke's Essay and the Tentativeness of *Tristram Shandy*," *Studies in Philology* 82, no. 4 (1985): 502, 506, wherein Briggs argues, "Sterne quite consistently adopted Lockean notions of the mind's *mechanisms* for understanding, but with equal consistency he reserved for himself the right to interpret the *value* of those mechanisms"; as an example, he cites Locke's negative view of fantasies and concludes, "Sterne agreed with Locke as to what a fantasy was, but he saw in fantasy a real potential for human good; military fantasies cure Uncle Toby's wound when the reasonable measures urged by doctors fail, and imagined battles on the bowling-green add life and color to an otherwise drab and frustrated retirement."

44. Frye, *Anatomy of Criticism*, 168.

45. Deporte, *Nightmares*, 126, argues that the mechanical or "determined" quality about the Shandean world is "one reason why the novel contains so little true satire."

46. Stuart Peterfreund, "Sterne and Late Eighteenth-Century Ideas of History," *Eighteenth-Century Life* 7, no. 1 (1981): 48.

47. Henri Bergson, *Laughter*, trans. Cloudesley Brereton and Fred Rothwell (London: Macmillan, 1911), 69. In this context, it is interesting to note Northrop Frye's claim (*Anatomy of Criticism*, 62) that "cyclical theories of history [are] . . . a typical phenomenon of the ironic mode."

48. *An Essay on Man*, ed. Maynard Mack (London: Methuen, 1950), 1:14, 35; Epistle 1, lines 15–16, 157–60.

49. Especially in the Renaissance; see Alvin Kernan, *The Cankered Muse* (New Haven: Yale University Press, 1959), 93.

50. James Boswell, *A Tour to the Hebrides*, ed. Frederick A. Pottle and Charles H. Bennett (New York: Literary Guild, 1936), 106–7.

51. Sterne probably inherited it from Robert Burton who in the Third Partition of *The Anatomy of Melancholy* argues persuasively that the extreme all-for-love attitude is responsible for more war and madness than anything else.

52. James Aiken Work suggests that this is a reference to the fact that Louis XIV financed many of his "long and expensive campaigns" by obtaining "forced loans from the clergy," but the editors of the Florida edition believe that Sterne may have meant the statement to be literal since church bells were commonly confiscated for their valuable metal (see *TS*, 3:368).

53. Clayborough, *Grotesque*, 72.

54. Bryson, *Word and Image*, 36.

55. H. J. Jackson, "Sterne, Burton, and Ferriar: Allusions to the *Anatomy of Melancholy* in Volumes Five to Nine of *Tristram Shandy*," *Philological Quarterly* 54 (1975): 464.

56. Right Honourable Anthony Earl of Shaftesbury, "An Essay on the Freedom of Wit and Humour," in *Characteristics of Men, Manners, Opinions, Times, etc.*, ed. John M. Robertson (London: Grant Richards, 1900), 1:75–76.

57. See Lila V. Graves, "Locke's Changeling and the Shandy Bull," *Philological Quarterly* 60, no. 2 (1981): 260, 258. Graves believes that Sterne may have been influenced by Locke's views on the "changeling" and "monster."

58. Tanner, "Reason and the Grotesque," 828–31. See "Introduction," p. 19.

Conclusion: The Last Line of Fortification

1. *Boswell on the Grand Tour: Germany and Switzerland*, 13 July 1764, 24.

2. Ibid., 25.

3. "The Vision of Judgment," 5, in *The Poetical Works of Lord Byron* (London: Oxford University Press, 1964), 157–58.

4. Joseph Fawcett, *Civilized War* [originally published as *The Art of War* (1795)], in *Poems* (London: J. Johnson, 1798), 201.

5. *Coleridge: Poetical Works*, ed. Ernest Hartley Coleridge (London: Oxford University Press, 1969), 260.

6. Ibid.

7. Ibid.

8. *The English Dance of Death*, illus. Thomas Rowlandson (London: Methuen, 1903), 230–31. Ronald Paulson associates Rowlandson with the "Grotesque," but he makes no mention of the death figure in the battle-piece; see *Rowlandson: A New Interpretation* (Oxford: Oxford University Press, 1972), 45–66.

9. *New Oxford Book of Eighteenth-Century Verse*, 656. Other poems in this collection that deal with the American War of Independence in a similar way are "Boston in Distress" (1776), 640, and Thomas Penrose's "The Helmets, A Fragment" (1775), 628–29. Penrose's poem recalls the English civil war between Charles I and Parliament and predicts civil disturbances for England as a consequence of disputes with the American colonists.

10. Peckham, "Art and Disorder," 279–80.

11. See Charles Baudelaire, "On the Essence of Laughter," in *The Mirror of Art*, trans. and ed. Jonathan Mayne (London: Phaidon Press, 1955), 133–53.

12. For a discussion of the laughter of the gods in eighteenth-century English Literature, see J. S. Cunningham, "On Earth as it Laughs in Heaven: Mirth and the 'Frigorifick Wisdom'," *Augustan Worlds*, ed. J. C. Hilson, M. M. B. Jones, J. R. Watson (New York: Barnes & Noble, 1978), 131–51.

13. Thomas Carlyle, *Sartor Resartus*, ed. Charles Frederick Harrold (New York: Odyssey Press, 1937), 173–74.

14. Kurt Vonnegut Jr., *Slaughterhouse–Five* (1968; reprint, New York: Dell, 1977). The line first appears on page 2 and is repeated throughout the novel.

15. Joseph Campbell and Henry Morton Robinson, *A Skeleton Key to "Finnegans Wake"* (1944; reprint, New York: Viking Press, 1969), 11, 27.

16. *Boswell on the Grand Tour: Germany and Switzerland,* 9 October 1764, 133.

17. *The Complete Letters of Lady Mary Wortley Montagu,* ed. Robert Halsband (Oxford: Clarendon Press, 1965), 1:284.

18. Wright, *The Study of War* 1:644–46. The tables of war statistics (casualites, etc.), which cover these and other pages of Wright's appendices, may well produce a grotesque impression on the reader by virtue of their colossal inadequacy to account for human suffering with numerical exhaustion.

19. *Miniature Wargames* (ISSN 0266-3228), ed. Iain Dickie, is published by A. E. Morgan in Epsom, Surrey.

20. Konrad Lorenz, *On Aggression,* trans. Marjorie Kerr Wilson (New York: Harcourt, Brace & World, 1966), 293.

21. Franco Fornari, *The Psychoanalysis of War,* trans. Alenka Pfeifer (Bloomington: Indiana University Press, 1975), 167.

Bibliography

General Military and Historical

Barnett, Correlli. *Marlborough*. London: Eyre Methuen, 1974.

Carlyle, Thomas. *Frederick the Great*. Vol. 6. London: Chapman & Hall, 1888.

Chandler, David. *The Art of Warfare in the Age of Marlborough*. London: Hippocrene, 1976.

Childs, John. *The Army of Charles II*. London: Routledge and Kegan Paul, 1976.

———. *The Army, James II and the Glorious Revolution*. Manchester: Manchester University Press, 1980.

———. *Armies and Warfare in Europe: 1648–1789*. New York: Holmes & Meier, 1982.

———. *The British Army of William III*. Manchester: Manchester University Press, 1987.

Clarendon, Edward Hyde, earl of. *The History of the Rebellion and Civil Wars in England*. Edited by W. Dunn Macray. 6 vols. Oxford: Clarendon Press, 1888.

Clark, Sir George. *War and Society in the Seventeenth Century*. Cambridge: Cambridge University Press, 1958.

Cobbet, W. *Parliamentary History of England*. Vol. 11. London: T. C. Hansard, 1812.

[D'Assigny, M.] *A Collection of the Brave Exploits and Subtil Stratagems of Several Famous Generals Since the Roman Empire*. London: S. Heyrick, 1686.

English Historical Documents: 1714–1783. Edited by D. B. Horn and Mary Ransome. London: Eyre & Spottiswoode, 1969.

Flavius Vegetius Renatus. *De Re Militari*. Translated by Lieutenant John Clarke. Harrisburg, Pa.: Stackpole Books, 1944.

Foot, Michael. *The Pen and the Sword*. London: Macgibbon & Kee, 1957.

Fortescue, J. W. *A History of the British Army*. Vols. 1–3. London: Macmillan, 1910.

Gibbon, Edward. *The Decline and Fall of the Roman Empire*. Edited by J. B. Bury. Vol. 1. London: Methuen, 1909.

Gordon, Robert C. "Jonathan Swift and the Modern Art of War." *Bulletin of Research in the Humanities* 83 (1980): 187–202.

Grotius, Hugo. *The Law of War and Peace*. [De Jure Belli.] Translated by Francis W. Kelsey. Introduced by James Brown Scott. 1925. Reprint. Carnegie Endowment for International Peace. New York: Bobbs-Merrill, 1962.

Guerlac, Henry. "Vauban: The Impact of Science on War." In *Makers of Modern Military Strategy: Military Thought from Machiavelli to Hitler*, edited by Edward Meade Earle, 26–48. Princeton: Princeton University Press, 1971.

Guy, Alan J. *Oeconomy and Discipline: Officership and Administration in the British Army, 1714–63.* Manchester: Manchester University Press, 1985.

Hale, J. R. *Renaissance War Studies.* London: Hambledon, 1983.

Herodotus. 4 vols. Translated by A. D. Godley. Loeb Classical Library. 1921.

Houlding, J. A. *Fit for Service, The Training of the British Army, 1715–1795.* Oxford: Clarendon Press, 1981.

Howard, Michael. *War in European History.* London: Oxford University Press, 1976.

Hutchinson, J. R. *The Press-Gang: Afloat and Ashore.* London: Eveleigh Nash, 1913.

Lewis, Michael. *England's Sea-Officers: The Story of the Naval Profession.* London: George Allen & Unwin, 1939.

McNeill, John R. "The Ecological Basis of Warfare in the Caribbean: 1700–1804." In *Adapting to Conditions: War and Society in the Eighteenth Century,* edited by Maarten Ultee, 26–55. Tuscaloosa, Ala.: University of Alabama Press, 1986.

A Military Dictionary. Explaining All difficult Terms in Martial Discipline, Fortification, and Gunnery. London: J. Nutt, 1702.

Miller, John C. *Triumph of Freedom: 1775–1783.* Boston: Little, Brown and Company, 1948.

Robson, Eric. "Purchase and Promotion in the British Army in the Eighteenth Century." *History* 36 (1951): 57–72.

Rodger, N. A. M. *The Wooden World: An Anatomy of the Georgian Navy.* London: Collins, 1986.

Rogers, Colonel H. C. B. *The British Army of the Eighteenth Century.* London: George Allen & Unwin, 1977.

Sallust: The War with Catiline. Translated by J. C. Rolfe. Loeb Classical Library. 1931.

Schwoerer, Lois G. *No Standing Armies!* Baltimore: Johns Hopkins University Press, 1974.

Scouller, R. E. *The Armies of Queen Anne.* Oxford: Oxford University Press, 1966.

Skrine, Francis Henry. *Fontenoy and Great Britain's Share in the War of the Austrian Succession: 1741–48.* London: Blackwood, 1906.

Smollett, Tobias. *The History of England.* 5 vols. London: D. S. Maurice, 1823.

Sturgill, Claude C. "The French Army in Roussillon, 1716–1720." In *Adapting to Conditions: War and Society in the Eighteenth Century,* edited by Maarten Ultee, 16–25. Tuscaloosa, Ala.: University of Alabama Press, 1986.

Walton, Clifford. *A History of the British Standing Army: 1660–1700.* London: Harrison and Sons, 1894.

Western, J. R. *The English Militia in the Eighteenth Century: The Story of a Political Issue, 1660–1802.* London: Routledge & Kegan Paul, 1965.

Whitworth, Rex. *Field Marshal Lord Ligonier: A Story of the British Army, 1702–1770.* Oxford: Clarendon Press, 1958.

Wright, Quincy, *A Study of War.* 2 vols. Chicago: University of Chicago Press, 1942.

General Literary, Philosophical, and Theoretical

Adams, Robert P. *The Better Part of Valor*. Seattle: University of Washington Press, 1962.

Addison, Joseph. "The Campaign." In *The Miscellaneous Works*. Edited by G. C. Guthkelch, vol. 1. 1914. Reprint. London: G. Bell and Sons, 1978.

———. *The Spectator*. Edited by Donald F. Bond. 5 vols. Oxford: Clarendon Press, 1965.

Arbuthnot, John. *The History of John Bull*. Edited by Alan W. Bower and Robert A. Erickson. Oxford: Clarendon Press, 1976.

Aubrey, James R. "Timon's Villa: Pope's Composite Picture." *Studies in Philology* 80, no. 3 (1983): 325–48.

Austen, Jane. *Pride and Prejudice*. Edited by James Kinsley and Frank W. Bradbrook. Oxford: Oxford University Press, 1970.

Bacon, Francis. "Of the True Greatnesse of Kingdomes and Estates." In *The Essayes or Counsels, Civill and Morall*, edited by Michael Kiernan, 89–99. Cambridge: Harvard University Press, 1985.

Bakhtin, Mikhail. *The Dialogic Imagination*. Translated by Caryl Emerson and Michael Holquist; edited by Michael Holquist. Austin: University of Texas Press, 1981.

———. *Rabelais and His World*. Translated by Helene Iswolsky. Cambridge: MIT Press, 1968.

Barasch, Frances K. *The Grotesque: A Study in Meanings*. The Hague: Mouton, 1971.

[Barnett, Stephen.] *War, an Epic-Satyr*. London: 1747.

Basney, Lionel. "Samuel Johnson and the Psychology of War." *Midwest Quarterly* 16, no. 1 (1974): 12–24.

Baudelaire, Charles. "On the Essence of Laughter." In *The Mirror of Art*. Translated and edited by Jonathan Mayne, 133–53. London: Phaidon Press, 1955.

Bergson, Henri. *Laughter*. Translated by Cloudesley Brereton and Fred Rothwell. London: Macmillan, 1911.

Beusse, Jeffrey. "An Investigation of the Value of Genre Analysis," *Interpretations: Studies in Language and Literature* 7 (1975): 44–50.

Bjornson, Richard. *The Picaresque Hero in European Fiction*. Madison: University of Wisconsin Press, 1977.

Boehn, Max von. *Puppets and Automata*. Translated by Josephine Nicoll. New York: Dover, 1972.

Bosmajian, Hamida. "The Nature and Function of the Grotesque Image in Eighteenth-Century English Literature." Ph.D. diss., University of Connecticut, 1968.

Boswell, James. *Boswell on the Grand Tour: Germany and Switzerland*. Edited by Frederick A. Pottle. 1928. Reprint. New York: McGraw-Hill, 1953.

———. *Boswell's Life of Johnson*. Edited by George Birkbeck Hill, revised and enlarged edition by L. F. Powell. 6 vols. Oxford: Clarendon Press, 1971.

———. *Boswell's London Journal: 1762–1763*. Edited by Frederick A. Pottle. New York: McGraw-Hill, 1950.

————. *A Tour to the Hebrides.* Edited by Frederick A. Pottle and Charles H. Bennett. New York: Literary Guild, 1936.

Boucé, Paul-Gabriel. *The Novels of Tobias Smollett.* Translated by Antonia White. London: Longman, 1976.

————. "Smollett's Pseudo-picaresque: A Response to Rousseau's Smollett and the Picaresque." *Studies in Burke and His Time* 14, no. 1 (1972): 73–79.

Briggs, Peter. "Locke's Essay and the Tentativeness of *Tristram Shandy.*" *Studies in Philology* 82, no. 4 (1985): 493–520.

Brown, Tom. *Amusements Serious and Comical and Other Works.* Edited by Arthur L. Haywood. New York: Dodd, Mead and Company, 1927.

Brownell, Morris R. *Alexander Pope & the Arts of Georgian England.* Oxford: Clarendon Press, 1978.

Bryson, Norman. *Word and Image: French Painting of the Ancien Régime.* Cambridge: Cambridge University Press, 1981.

Buckingham, George Villiers, duke of. *The Rehearsal.* Edited by D. E. L. Crane. Durham: University of Durham Press, 1976.

Burke, Edmund. *A Philosophical Enquiry into the Origin of Our Ideas of the Sublime and Beautiful.* Edited by J. T. Boulton. London: Routledge and Kegan Paul, 1958.

Burns, Robert. *The Poems and Songs.* Edited by James Kinsley. 3 vols. Oxford: Clarendon Press, 1968.

Burton, Robert. *The Anatomy of Melancholy.* Edited by Holbrook Jackson. 3 vols. 1932. Reprint. London: Everyman, 1968.

Butler, Samuel. *Hudibras.* Edited by John Wilders. London: Oxford University Press, 1967.

————. *Prose Observations.* Edited by Hugh De Quehen. Oxford: Clarendon Press, 1979.

Buxton, John. *Sir Philip Sidney and the English Renaissance.* London: Macmillan, 1964.

Byron, Lord [George Gordon]. *The Poetical Works.* London: Oxford University Press, 1964.

Caillois, Roger. *Man, Play, and Games.* Translated by Meyer Barash. New York: The Free Press of Glencoe, 1961.

Campbell, Joseph and Henry Morton Robinson. *A Skeleton Key to "Finnegans Wake."* 1944. Reprint. New York: The Viking Press, 1969.

Carlyle, Thomas. *Sartor Resartus.* Edited by Charles Frederick Harrold. New York: Odyssey Press, 1937.

Cash, Arthur. *Laurence Sterne: The Early and Middle Years.* London: Methuen, 1975.

Centlivre, Susana. *The Beau's Duel: Or A Soldier for the Ladies.* In *The Works of the Celebrated Mrs. Centlivre.* Vol. 1. London: 1872.

Clayborough, Arthur. *The Grotesque in English Literature.* Oxford: Clarendon Press, 1965.

Cleary, Thomas. *Henry Fielding: Political Writer.* Waterloo, Ont.: Wilfred Laurier University Press, 1984.

Coley, W. B. "Hogarth, Fielding and the Dating of the 'March to Finchley'." *Journal of the Warburg and Courtauld Institutes* 30 (1967): 317–26.

Coleridge, Samuel Taylor. *Poetical Works*. Edited by Ernest Hartley Coleridge. London: Oxford University Press, 1969.

Connell, Dorothy. *Sir Philip Sidney: The Maker's Mind*. Oxford: Clarendon Press, 1977.

Cox, Richard H. *Locke on War and Peace*. Oxford: Clarendon Press, 1960.

Croft-Murray, Edward. "Louis Laguerre." *Decorative Painting in England: 1537–1837*. London: Country Life, 1962.

Cunningham, J. S. "On Earth as it Laughs in Heaven: Mirth and the 'Frigorifick Wisdom.'" In *Augustan Worlds*, edited by J. C. Hilson, M. M. B. Jones, J. R. Watson, 131–51. New York: Barnes & Noble, 1978.

D'Avenant, Sir William. *The Dramatic Works*. Vol. 3. London: H. Sotheran, 1873.

Defoe, Daniel. "An Argument Shewing, that a Standing Army, with Consent of Parliament, is not Inconsistent with a Free Government" (1698). In *Daniel Defoe*, edited by James Boulton, 35–50. New York: Schocken Books, 1965.

———. *Colonel Jack*. Edited by Samuel Holt Monk. London: Oxford University Press, 1965.

[Defoe, Daniel.] *The Life and Adventures of Mrs. Christian Davies, Commonly Called Mother Ross*. London: Peter Davies, 1928.

DeJean, Joan. *Literary Fortifications: Rousseau, Laclos, Sade*. Princeton: Princeton University Press, 1984.

Delmé, Jean. *A Spiritual Warning for Times of War*. London: Brundenell, 1701.

Deporte, Michael. *Nightmares and Hobbyhorses: Swift, Sterne, and Augustan Ideas of Madness*. San Marino, Calif.: Huntington Library, 1974.

Douglas, Wayne Joseph. "Smollett and the Sordid Knaves: Political Satire in *The Adventures of an Atom*." Ph.D. diss., University of Florida, 1976.

Dryden, John. *Amphitryon*. In *The Works of John Dryden*, edited by Earl Miner, George R. Guffey, Franklin B. Zimmerman, vol. 15, 221–318, 460–95, 537–49. Berkeley and Los Angeles: University of California Press, 1976.

———. "A Discourse Concerning the Original and Progress of Satire." In *Essays of John Dryden*, edited by W. P. Kerr, vol. 2, 15–114. New York: Russell & Russell, 1961.

———. *The Poems*. Edited by James Kinsley. Vol. 4. Oxford: Clarendon Press, 1958.

———. *Troilus and Cressida, or Truth Found too Late: A Tragedy*. In *The Works of John Dryden*, edited by Maximillian E. Novak, George R. Guffey, Alan Roper, vol. 13, 217–355, 497–565. Berkeley and Los Angeles: University of California Press, 1984.

Dupas, Jean Claude. "*Tristram Shandy*: une rhapsodie grotesque." *Bulletin de la Societé d'études anglo-américaines des XVIIe et XVIIIe Siècles* 6 (June 1978): 61–75.

D'Urfey, Thomas. *The Campaigners: or, The Pleasant Adventures at Brussels*. London: A. Baldwin, 1698.

D'Urfey, Thomas, comp. *Wit and Mirth: Or Pills to Purge Melancholy*. 6 vols. New York: Folklore Library Publishers, 1959.

Ehrenpreis, Irvin. *The Personality of Jonathan Swift*. Cambridge: Harvard University Press, 1958.

———. *Swift: The Man, His Works, and the Age*. 3 vols. London: Methuen, 1962, 1967, 1984.

Elliott, Robert. *The Power of Satire*. Princeton: University of Princeton Press, 1960.

Erasmus. *The Colloquies of Erasmus*. Translated by R. Thompson. Chicago: Chicago University Press, 1965.

———. *Encomium Moriae*. In *Opera Omnia*, vol. 4. Hildesheim: Georg Olms Verlagsbuchhandlung, 1961.

Evett, David. "Mammon's Grotto: Sixteenth-Century Visual Grotesquerie and Some Features of Spenser's *Faerie Queene*." *English Literary Renaissance* 12, no. 2 (1982): 180–209.

Fabricant, Carole. *Swift's Landscape*. Baltimore: Johns Hopkins University Press, 1982.

Farnham, Willard. *The Shakespearean Grotesque: Its Genesis and Transformations*. Oxford: Clarendon Press, 1971.

Farquhar, George. *The Beaux' Stratagem*. Edited by Charles N. Fifer. Lincoln: University of Nebraska Press, 1977.

———. *The Recruiting Officer*. Edited by Michael Shugrue. Lincoln: University of Nebraska Press, 1965.

Fawcett, Joseph. *Civilized War*. [Originally published as *The Art of War*, 1795.] *Poems*, 185–242. London: J. Johnson, 1798.

Fielding, Henry. *Amelia*. Edited by Martin Battestin. Introduction and notes by Fredson Bowers. Middletown, Conn.: Wesleyan University Press, 1984.

———. *The Champion*. In *The Works of Henry Fielding Esq.*, edited by Leslie Stephen, vol. 5. London: Smith, Elder & C., 1882.

———. *The History of the Life of the Late Jonathan Wild the Great*. In *The Works of Henry Fielding, Esq.*, edited by Leslie Stephen, vol. 5. London: Smith, Elder & Co., 1882.

———. *The History of Tom Jones, A Foundling*. Edited by Fredson Bowers. Introduction and notes by Martin Battestin. Middletown, Conn.: Wesleyan University Press, 1975.

———. *The Jacobite's Journal and Related Writings*. Edited by W. B. Coley. Middletown, Conn.: Wesleyan University Press, 1974.

———. *Joseph Andrews*. Edited by Martin Battestin. Introduction by Fredson Bowers. Middletown, Conn.: Wesleyan University Press, 1967.

———. *Tom Thumb and the Tragedy of Tragedies*. Edited by L. J. Morrissey. Berkeley and Los Angeles: University of California Press, 1970.

———. *Miscellanies*. Edited by Henry Knight Miller. Vol. 1. Middletown, Conn.: Wesleyan University Press, 1972.

Fink, Z. S. "Political Theory in *Gulliver's Travels*." *English Literary History* 14 (1947): 151–61.

Fornari, Franco. *The Psychoanalysis of War*. Translated by Alenka Pfeifer. Bloomington: Indiana University Press, 1975.

Fowler, Alastair. *Kinds of Literature: An Introduction to the Theory of Genres and Modes*. Cambridge: Harvard University Press, 1982.

Fraser, Antonia. *A History of Toys*. London: Spring Books, 1972.

Fredman, Alice Green. "The Picaresque in Decline: Smollett's First Novel." In *English Writers of the Eighteenth Century*, edited by John H. Middendorf, 189–207. New York: Columbia University Press, 1971.

Freeman, James A. *Milton and the Martial Muse: "Paradise Lost" and European Traditions of War*. Princeton: Princeton University Press, 1980.

Frye, Northrop. *Anatomy of Criticism*. Princeton: University of Princeton Press, 1957.

―――. "Norms, Moral or Other, in Satire: A Symposium." *Satire Newsletter* 2 (Fall 1964): 9.

Furst, Lilian R. "The Dual Face of the Grotesque in Sterne's *Tristram Shandy* and Lenz's *Der Waldbruder*." *Comparative Literature Studies* 13 (1976): 15–21.

Gay, John. *The Beggar's Opera*. In vol. 2 of *Dramatic Works*. Edited by John Fuller, 2 vols. Oxford: Clarendon Press, 1983.

George, M. Dorothy. *English Political Caricature to 1792*. Oxford: Clarendon Press, 1959.

―――. *Hogarth to Cruikshank: Social Change in Graphic Satire*. New York: Walker and Company, 1967.

Gleeson, Patrick. "*Gulliver's Travels* as a Version of the Grotesque." Ph.D. diss., University of Washington, 1964.

Golden, Morris. "Fielding's Politics." In *Henry Fielding: Justice Observed*, edited by K. D. Simpson, 34–55. London: Vision and Barnes & Noble, 1985.

Goldsmith, Oliver. *Collected Works*. Edited by Arthur Friedman. 5 vols. Oxford: Clarendon Press, 1966.

Graves, Lila V. "Locke's Changeling and the Shandy Bull." *Philological Quarterly* 60, no. 2 (1981): 257–64.

Green, David. *Blenheim Palace*. London: Country Life, 1951.

Greene, Donald J. "Samuel Johnson and the Great War for Empire." In *English Writers of the Eighteenth Century*, edited by John H. Middendorf, 37–65. New York: Columbia University Press, 1971.

Greene, Graeme. *The Lawless Roads*. London: Heinemann, 1955.

Grimmelshausen, Hans Jacob Christoffel von. *Simplicissimus, The Vagabond*. Translated by A. T. S. Goodrick. Introduction by William Rose. London: George Routledge, 1912.

Hagstrum, Jean H. *The Sister Arts: The Tradition of Literary Pictorialism and English Poetry from Dryden to Gray*. Chicago: University of Chicago Press, 1958.

Hansford, J. H. "Milton and the Art of War." *Studies in Philology* 18 (1921): 232–66.

Henning, Sylvie Debevec. "La Forme IN-Formante: A Reconsideration of the Grotesque." *Mosaic* 14, no. 4 (1981): 107–21.

Herrick, Marvin. *Comic Theory in the Sixteenth Century*. Urbana: University of Illinois Press, 1964.

Hesiod: The Homeric Hymns and Homerica. Translated by Hugh G. Evelyn-White. Loeb Classical Library. 1936. Reprint. 1959.

Hobbes, Thomas. *Leviathan*. Edited by Michael Oakeshott. Oxford: Basil Blackwell, 1946.

Homer: The Iliad. 2 vols. Translated by A. T. Murray. Loeb Classical Library. 1924, 1925.

Hopkins, Robert. "The Function of the Grotesque in *Humphry Clinker.*" *Huntington Library Quarterly* 32 (February 1969): 163–77.

Howes, Alan B. "Laurence Sterne, Rabelais, and Cervantes: The Two Kinds of Laughter in *Tristram Shandy.*" *Laurence Sterne: Riddles and Mysteries*, edited by Valerie Grosvenor Myer, 39–56. London: Vision and Barnes & Noble, 1984.

Howes, Alan B., Ed. *Sterne: The Critical Heritage.* London: Routledge & Kegan Paul, 1974.

Huizinga, J. *Homo Ludens: The Play-Element in Culture.* Boston: Becan Press, 1950.

Hytier, Andrienne D. "The Battle in Eighteenth-Century French Fiction." *Eighteenth-Century Life* 8, no. 1 (1982): 1–13.

Isler, Alan D. "Sidney, Shakespeare, and the 'Slain-Notslain'." *University of Toronto Quarterly* 37, no. 2 (1968): 175–85.

Jackson, H. J. "Sterne, Burton, and Ferriar: Allusions to the *Anatomy of Melancholy* in Volumes Five to Nine of *Tristram Shandy.*" *Philological Quarterly* 54 (1975): 457–70.

Jackson-Stops, Gervase. *The English Country House: A Grand Tour.* Boston: Little, Brown and Company, 1985.

Jarrett, Derek. *England in the Age of Hogarth.* London: Hart-Davis, MacGibbon, 1974.

Jennings, Lee Byron. *The Ludicrous Demon.* Berkeley and Los Angeles: University of California Press, 1963.

"Johnny, I Hardly Knew Ye." In *Eighteenth-Century English Literature.* Edited by Geoffrey Tillotson, Paul Fussell, Jr., and Marshall Waingrow, with Brewster Rogerson, p. 1525. New York: Harcourt Brace Jovanovich, 1969.

Johnson, J. W. *The Formations of English Neo-Classical Thought.* Princeton: Princeton University Press, 1967.

———. "Swift's Historical Outlook." *Journal of British Studies* 4, no. 2 (1965): 52–77.

Johnson, Samuel. *A Dictionary of the English Language.* 5th Ed. 2 vols. London: W. & A. Strachan, 1784.

———. *The Idler and Adventurer.* Edited by W. J. Bate, John M. Bullitt, L. F. Powell. New Haven: Yale University Press, 1963.

———. *Poems.* Edited by E. L. McAdam with George Milne. New Haven: Yale University Press, 1964.

———. *Political Writings.* Edited by Donald Greene. New Haven: Yale University Press, 1977.

Jones, Myrddin. "A Living Treasury of Knowledge and Wisdom: Some Comments on Swift's Attitude to the Writing of History." *Durham University Journal* 36 (1974): 180–88.

Jorgensen, Paul A. *Shakespeare's Military World.* Berkeley and Los Angeles: University of California Press, 1956.

Kayser, Wolfgang. *The Grotesque in Art and Literature.* Translated by Ulrich Weisstein. Bloomington: Indiana University Press, 1963.

Kearful, Frank J. "Spanish Rogues and English Foundlings: On the Disintegration of Picaresque." *Genre* 4, no. 4 (1971): 376–91.

Kernan, Alvin. *The Cankered Muse*. New Haven: Yale University Press, 1959.

Knapp, Lewis M. "The Naval Scenes in *Roderick Random*." *PMLA* 49 (1934): 593–98.

Landa, Louis A. "'A Modest Proposal' and Populousness." In *Eighteenth-Century English Literature: Modern Essays in Criticism*, edited by James L. Clifford, 102–111. London: Oxford University Press, 1959.

Lanham, Richard A. "*Tristram Shandy": The Games of Pleasure*. Berkeley and Los Angeles: University of California Press, 1973.

Lieb, Michael. *The Dialectics of Creation: Patterns of Birth and Regeneration in "Paradise Lost"*. Amherst: University of Massachusetts Press, 1970.

[Lipsius, Justus.] *War and Peace Reconciled*. Translated by N. Wanley. London: 1672.

Lock, F. P. *The Politics of "Gulliver's Travels."* Oxford: Clarendon Press, 1980.

———. *Swift's Tory Politics*. London: Duckworth, 1983.

London Magazine. London, 1743.

Lonsdale, Roger, ed. *The New Oxford Book of Eighteenth-Century Verse*. Oxford: Oxford University Press, 1984.

Lorenz, Konrad. *On Aggression*. Translated by Marjorie Kerr Wilson. New York: Harcourt, Brace & World, 1966.

Low, Donald. "Mr. Fielding of Bow Street." In *Henry Fielding: Justice Observed*, edited by K. D. Simpson, 13–33. London: Vision and Barnes & Noble, 1985.

Lucan: The Civil War. Translated by J. D. Duff. Loeb Classical Library. 1928.

Lucian's Dialogues. Translated by Howard Williams. Bohn's Classical Library. London: George Bell and Sons, 1888.

Lynn, Joanne Lewis. "Configurations of the Comic Grotesque in the Novels of Tobias Smollett." Ph.D. diss., University of California, Irvine, 1974.

McCrea, Brian. *Henry Fielding and the Politics of Mid-Eighteenth-Century England*. Athens: University of Georgia Press, 1981.

Mandeville, Bernard. *The Fable of the Bees*. Edited by F. B. Kaye. 2 vols. 1924. Reprint. Oxford: Clarendon Press, 1966.

Marlowe, Christopher. *Tamburlaine the Great I & II*. Edited by Una Ellis-Fermor. Rev. Ed. London: Methuen, 1951.

Martz, Louis L. *The Later Career of Tobias Smollett*. Hamden, Conn.: Archon Books, 1967.

———. "Smollett and the Expedition to Carthagena." *PMLA* 56 (1941): 428–46.

Marvell, Andrew. *Complete Poetry*. Edited by George de F. Lord. New York: Modern Library, 1968.

Marvell, A., Jr. "Satirical and Panegyrical Instructions to Mr. William Hogarth, Painter, on Admiral Vernon's Taking Porto Bello With Six Ships of War Only." London: H. Goreham, 1740.

Meyer, Henry. *Voltaire on War and Peace*. Banbury: The Voltaire Foundation, 1976.

Mezciems, Jenny. "Swift's Praise of Gulliver: Some Renaissance Background to the *Travels*." In *The Character of Swift's Satire: A Revised Focus*, edited by Claude Rawson, 245–81. Newark: University of Delaware Press, 1983.

Milton, John. *The Complete Poetical Works*. Edited by Douglas Bush. Boston: Houghton Mifflin, 1965.

Moglen, Helene. *The Philosophical Irony of Laurence Sterne*. Gainesville: University Presses of Florida, 1975.

Montagu, Lady Mary Wortley. *The Complete Letters*. Edited by Robert Halsband. Vol. 1. Oxford: Clarendon Press, 1965.

Moore, Robert Etheridge. *Hogarth's Literary Relationships*. New York: Octagon Books, 1969.

Nashe, Thomas. *The Unfortunate Traveller*. In *The Works*. Edited by Ronald B. McKerrow. Revised by F. P. Wilson. Vols. 2, 4. Oxford: Basil Blackwell, 1958.

Nelson, J. Walter. "War and Peace and the British Poets of Sensibility." *Studies in Eighteenth-Century Culture*, vol. 7, edited by Rosann Runte, 345–66. Madison: University of Wisconsin Press, 1978.

Niehus, Edward. "Quixotic Figures in the Novels of Sterne." *Essays in Literature* 12, no. 1 (1985): 41–60.

Oakleaf, David. "*Trompe l'Oeil*: Gulliver and the Distortions of the Observing Eye." *University of Toronto Quarterly* 53 (Winter 1983/84): 166–80.

O'Connor, John J. "Physical Deformity and Chivalric Laughter in Renaissance England." In *Comedy: New Perspectives*, edited by Maurice Charney. *New York Literary Forum* 1 (Spring 1978): 59–71.

Otway, Thomas. *The Souldiers Fortune*. In *The Works of Thomas Otway*, edited by J. C. Ghosh, vol. 2. Oxford: Clarendon Press, 1932.

Ovid. *Being Arthur Golding's Translation of "The Metamorphoses."* Edited by W. H. D. Rouse. New York: Norton, 1966.

———. "Book 12" of *The Metamorphoses*. In *Ovid: Metamorphoses*, vol. 1, translated by Frank Justus Miller. Loeb Classical Library. 1916. Reprint. 1958.

Parker, Alexander A. *Literature and the Delinquent: The Picaresque Novel in Spain and Europe: 1599–1753*. Edinburgh: Edinburgh University Press, 1967.

Parker, Samuel. "Homer in a Nutshell." London: 1700.

Paulson, Ronald. *Hogarth: His Life, Art, and Times*. 2 vols. New Haven: Yale University Press, 1971.

———. *Popular and Polite Art in the Age of Hogarth and Fielding*. Notre Dame, Ind.: Notre Dame University Press, 1979.

———. *Rowlandson: A New Interpretation*. Oxford: Oxford University Press, 1972.

———. *Satire and the English Novel*. New Haven: Yale University Press, 1967.

Peckham, Morse. "Art and Disorder." In *The Triumph of Romanticism: Collected Essays*, 255–80. Columbia: University of South Carolina Press, 1970.

Pepys, Samuel. *The Diary*. Edited by Robert Latham and William Matthews. 11 vols. London: Bell, 1972.

Peterfreund, Stuart. "Sterne and Late Eighteenth-Century Ideas of History." *Eighteenth-Century Life* 7, no. 1 (1981): 25–53.

Philips, John. "Blenheim." In *The Whole Works*, 29–60. London: J. Tonson, 1720.

Pinkus, Philip. "Swift and the Ancients-Moderns Controversy." *University of Toronto Quarterly* 29, no. 1 (1959): 46–58.

Plato. *The Republic*. 2 vols. Translated by Paul Shorey. London: Heinemann, 1930.

Pope, Alexander. *The Art of Sinking in Poetry*. Edited by Edna Leake Steeves. New York: King's Crown Press, 1952.

———. *The Correspondence*. Edited by George Sherburn. 5 vols. Oxford: Clarendon Press, 1956.

———. *An Essay on Man*. Edited by Maynard Mack. 2 vols. London: Methuen, 1950.

———. *The Iliad of Homer: Books I–IX*. Edited by Maynard Mack. London: Methuen, 1967.

———. *The Iliad of Homer: Books X–XXIV*. Edited by Maynard Mack. London: Methuen, 1967.

———. *Memoirs of the Extraordinary Life, Works, and Discoveries of Martinus Scriblerus*. Written in collaboration by members of the Scriblerus Club. Edited by Charles Kerby-Miller. New York: Russell & Russell, 1966.

———. *Minor Poems*. Edited by Norman Ault and John Butt. London: Methuen; New Haven: Yale University Press, 1954.

———. *Pastoral Poetry and An Essay on Criticism*. Edited by E. Aura and Aubrey Williams. London: Methuen, 1961.

Prior, Matthew. *Literary Works*. Edited by H. Bunker Wright and Monroe K. Spears. 2 vols. Oxford: Clarendon Press, 1959.

Rawson, Claude J. *Gulliver and the Gentle Reader: Studies in Swift and Our Time*. London: Routledge & Kegan Paul, 1973.

"Reflections on the Poems Made upon the Siege and Taking of Namur, &c." London: M. Whillock, 1696.

Rhodes, Neil. *Elizabethan Grotesque*. London: Routledge & Kegan Paul, 1980.

The Riverside Shakespeare. Edited by G. Blakemore Evans. Boston: Houghton Mifflin, 1974.

Rochester, John Wilmot, earl of. *The Complete Poems*. Edited by David M. Vieth. New Haven: Yale University Press, 1968.

Ross, Angus. "The 'Show of Violence' in Smollett's Novels." In vol. 2 of *The Yearbook of English Studies*, edited by T. J. B. Spencer and R. L. Smallwood, 118–29. London: Modern Humanities Research Association, 1972.

Rousseau, G. S. "Smollett and the Picaresque: Some Questions about a Label." *Studies in Burke and His Times* 12, no. 3 (1971): 1886–1904.

Rowlandson, Thomas, illus. *The English Dance of Death*. London: Methuen, 1903.

Ruskin, John. "Grotesque Renaissance." In vol. 11 of *The Complete Works*, edited by E. T. Cook and Alexander Wedderburn, 151–195. London: George Allen, 1904.

St. Augustine: *The City of God*. Vol. 1 (Bks. 1–3). Translated by George E. McCracken. Loeb Classical Library. 1957.

Schiller, Frederich. *Naive and Sentimental Poetry and On the Sublime*. Translated by Julis A. Elias. New York: F. Ungar, 1967.

Seneca. "*De Beneficiis*" 7. In vol. 3 of *Seneca: Moral Essays*, 460–63. Translated by John W. Basore. Loeb Classical Library. 1928.

————. "On the Value of Advice" 94. In vol. 3 of *Seneca: Epistulae Morales*, 50–53. Translated by Richard M. Gummere. Loeb Classical Library. 1917.

[Shadwell, Charles.] *The Fair Quaker of Deal, or, The Humours of the Navy.* London: James Knapton, 1710.

[Shadwell, Charles.] *The Humours of the Army.* London: James Knapton, 1713.

Shadwell, Thomas. *The Volunteers.* In vol. 5 of *The Complete Works*, edited by Montague Summers, 151–224. London: Fortune Press, 1927.

Shaftesbury, Right Honourable Anthony, earl of. "An Essay on the Freedom of Wit and Humour." In vol. 1 of *Characteristics of Men, Manners, Opinions, Times, etc.* Edited by John M. Robertson. London: Grant Richards, 1900.

Sidney, Sir Philip. *The Complete Prose Works.* Edited by Albert Feuillerat. 4 vols. 1912. Reprint. Cambridge: Cambridge University Press, 1963.

————. *The Countess of Pembroke's Arcadia (The Old Arcadia).* Edited by Jean Robertson. Oxford: Clarendon Press, 1973.

Sieber, Harry. *The Picaresque.* Critical Idiom #33. London: Methuen, 1977.

Smollett, Tobias. *The Adventures of Peregrine Pickle.* Edited by James L. Clifford. Revised Paul-Gabriel Boucé. Oxford: Oxford University Press, 1983.

————. *The Adventures of Roderick Random.* Edited by Paul-Gabriel Boucé. Oxford: Oxford University Press, 1979.

————. *The Complete Works.* Edited by Thomas Roscoe. London: George Bell, 1887.

————. *The Expedition of Humphry Clinker.* Edited by Lewis M. Knapp. London: Oxford University Press, 1966.

————. *Ferdinand Count Fathom.* Edited by Damian Grant London: Oxford University Press, 1971.

————. *The Life and Adventures of Sir Launcelot Greaves.* Edited by David Evans. London: Oxford University Press, 1973.

————. *The Reprisal: or, the Tars of Old England. Plays and Poems.* London: T. Evans and R. Baldwin, 1777.

————. *Travels Through France and Italy.* Ed. Frank Felsenstein. Oxford: Oxford University Press, 1981.

Smollett, Tobias, trans. *Gil Blas.* New York: Thomas Y. Crowell, n.d.

Spacks, Patirica. *Imagining a Self.* Cambridge: Harvard University Press, 1976.

Speaight, George. "Reply to J. M. Stedmond [see below]." *Notes and Queries* 201, New Series, no. 3 (1956): 133–34.

Speck, W. A. "Swift and the Historian." In *Proceedings of the First Münster Symposium on Jonathan Swift*, edited by Hermann J. Real and Heinz J. Vienken, 257–68. Munich: Wilhelm Fink Verlag, 1985.

Stedmond, J. M. "Uncle Toby's 'Campaigns' and Raree-Shows." *Notes and Queries* 201, New Series, no. 3 (1956): 28.

Steele, Peter. *Jonathan Swift: Preacher and Jester.* Oxford: Clarendon Press, 1978.

Steele, Sir Richard. *The Tatler.* Edited Donald E. Bond. 3 vols. Oxford: Clarendon Press, 1987.

Steig, Michael. "Defining the Grotesque: An Attempt at Synthesis," *Journal of Aesthetics and Art Criticism* 29, no. 2 (1970): 253–59.

Sterne, Laurence. *The Florida Edition of the Works*. Vols. 1–3. Edited by Melvyn New, Joan New, Richard A. Davies, and W. D. Day. Gainesville: University Presses of Florida, 1978–84.

———. *The Life and Opinions of Tristram Shandy, Gentleman*. Edited by James Aiken Work. New York: The Odyssey Press, 1940.

———. *A Sentimental Journey Through France and Italy by Mr. Yorick*. Edited by Gardner D. Stout, Jr. Berkeley and Los Angeles: University of California Press, 1967.

Stevick, Philip. "Miniaturization in Eighteenth-Century English Literature." *University of Toronto Quarterly* 38, no. 2 (1969): 159–73.

———. "Smollett's Picaresque Games." In *Tobias Smollett: Bicentennial Essays Presented to Lewis M. Knapp*, edited by G. S. Rousseau and P.-G. Boucé, 111–130. New York: Oxford University Press, 1971.

Summers, Montague. "Introduction." *The Rehearsal*. Stratford-Upon-Avon: Shakespeare Head Press, 1914.

Swift, Jonathan. *The Correspondence*. Edited by Harold Williams. 5 vols. Oxford: Clarendon Press, 1963.

———. *Gulliver's Travels and Other Writings*. Edited by Miriam Starkman. New York: Bantam, 1962.

———. *The Poems*. Edited by Harold Williams. 2d Ed. 3 vols. Oxford: Clarendon Press, 1958.

———. *The Prose Works*. Edited by Herbert Davis. 14 vols. Oxford: Basil Blackwell, 1939–68.

———. *A Tale of A Tub &c.*. Edited by A. C. Guthkelch and D. Nichol Smith. 2d Ed. London: Oxford University Press, 1958..

Tanner, Tony. "Reason and the Grotesque: Pope's *Dunciad*." In *Essential Articles for the Study of Alexander Pope*, edited by Maynard Mack, rev. ed., 825–44. Hamden, Conn.: Archon, 1968.

Temple, Sir William. *The Works*. 2 vols. London: 1720.

Trompf, G. W. *The Idea of Recurrence in Western Thought: From Antiquity to the Reformation*. Berkeley and Los Angeles: University of California Press, 1979.

Uccello, Paolo. *The Complete Works*. Compiled by John Pope-Hennessy. London: Phaidon Press, 1950.

Vanbrugh, Sir John. *The Complete Works*. Edited by Geoffrey Webb. 4 vols. London: Nonesuch Press, 1928.

Veits, M. D., Henry. "Smollett, the 'War of Jenkins's Ear' And 'An Account of the Expedition to Cartagena,' 1743." *Bulletin of the Medical Library Association* 28, Series 1 (1940): 178–81.

Virgil. 2 vols. Translated by H. Rushton Fairclough. Loeb Classical Library. 1935 and 1934.

Voltaire. "Guerre." *Dictionnaire Philosophique*. In vol. 19 of OEuvres Complètes de Voltaire, 318–22. Paris: Garnier Frères, 1879.

———. *Candide, ou l'optimisme*. Edited by René Pomeau. OEuvres Complètes de Voltaire. Vol. 48. Oxford, Taylor Institution: The Voltaire Foundation, 1980.

Vonnegut Jr., Kurt. *Slaughterhouse-Five*. 1968. Reprint. New York: Dell, 1977.

Wace, Alan. *The Marlborough Tapestries at Blenheim Palace.* London: Phaidon, 1968.

[Wilkes, John.] *The North Briton,* No. 17. In vol. 1 of *The North Briton,* 154–65. London: J. Williams, 1763.

Wilkinson, L. P. *Ovid Recalled.* Cambridge: Cambridge University Press, 1955.

Winn, James A. "Milton on Heroic Warfare." Yale Review 66 (1976): 70–86.

Wollstonecraft, Mary. *A Vindication of the Rights of Women.* Edited by Urich H. Hardt. Troy N.Y.: Whitston, 1982.

Wordsworth, William. *The Prelude.* In *Poetical Works.* Edited by Thomas Hutchinson. Revised by Ernest de Selincourt. 1936. Reprint. Oxford: Oxford University Press, 1975.

Wright, Thomas. *A History of Caricature and Grotesque in Literature and Art.* London: Virtue Brothers & Co., 1865.

Index

For references to individual works, see under author.